sono

PLAYA DEL CARMEN, TULUM & THE RIVIERA MAYA

EXPLORER'S GUIDE

PLAYA DEL CARMEN, TULUM & THE RIVIERA MAYA

FIFTH EDITION

JOSHUA EDEN HINSDALE

With contributions by Andrea Loera Hinsdale

THE COUNTRYMAN PRESS
A division of W. W. Norton & Company
Independent Publishers Since 1923

For information about permission to reproduce selections from this book, write to Permissions,
The Countryman Press, 500 Fifth Avenue, New York, NY 10110

For information about special discounts for bulk purchases, please contact
W. W. Norton Special Sales at specialsales@wwnorton.com or 800-233-4830

Manufacturing by Versa Press
Book design by Chris Welch
Production manager: Lauren Abbate

The Countryman Press
www.countrymanpress.com

A division of W. W. Norton & Company, Inc.
500 Fifth Avenue, New York, NY 10110
www.wwnorton.com

978-1-68268-217-3 (pbk.)

10 9 8 7 6 5 4 3 2 1

This book is dedicated to my ever-supportive parents,
my beautiful wife Andrea, and our young children Maya and Finn,
who have developed a love for the beach, a passion for exploration,
and an openness to learn from the people they meet around the world.

EXPLORE WITH US!

WHAT'S WHERE In the beginning of the book you'll find an alphabetical listing of highlights, important information, and other details that you may need to reference quickly as you navigate the book, the Riviera Maya, and its culture.

GEOGRAPHIC ORIENTATION The cities and towns of the Yucatán Peninsula and the Riviera Maya reported on in this book commence with Playa del Carmen (frequently referred to as "Playa" throughout the book), the conceptual and physical center of the Riviera Maya. Subsequent chapters cover the Riviera Maya to the south and to the north of Playa, followed by other nearby destinations not technically a part of the Riviera Maya, including Cancún, Cozumel, and the Costa Maya.

Many locations are found along Highway 307, which runs parallel to the coastline and traverses the region north to south from Cancún to Tulum and beyond. Whenever possible, addresses are given using Highway 307 as a primary reference point, which should be especially useful for self-guided travelers who choose to explore the region on their own.

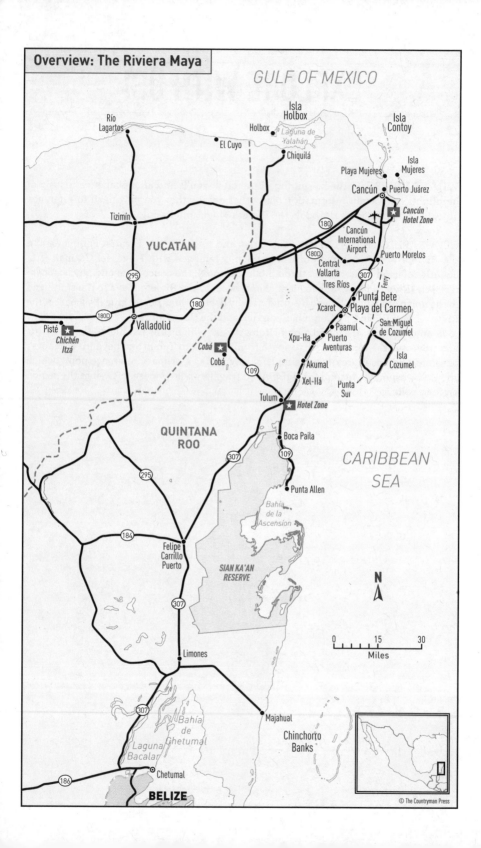

Overview: The Riviera Maya

GULF OF MEXICO

CARIBBEAN SEA

Isla Holbox

Isla Contoy

Río Lagartos

Holbox

El Cuyo

Chiquilá

Isla Mujeres

Playa Mujeres

Cancún

Puerto Juárez

Cancún Hotel Zone

Tizimín

YUCATÁN

295

180

Cancún International Airport

180D

Puerto Morelos

Central Vallarta

307

Ferry

Tres Ríos

Punta Bete

180

Xcaret

Playa del Carmen

180D

Valladolid

Paamul

San Miguel de Cozumel

Pisté

Chichén Itzá

Xpu-Ha

Puerto Aventuras

Cobá

Cobá

Akumal

Isla Cozumel

109

Xel-Ilá

Punta Sur

Tulum

Hotel Zone

QUINTANA ROO

Boca Paila

307

109

Punta Allen

295

Bahía de la Ascensión

SIAN KA'AN RESERVE

184

Felipe Carrillo Puerto

307

Miles
0   15   30

N

Limones

307

Majahual

Chinchorro Banks

Bahía de Chetumal

Laguna Bacalar

Chetumal

186

BELIZE

© The Countryman Press

CONTENTS

MAPS

ACKNOWLEDGMENTS

I am forever grateful to my friends and family as well as to the many strangers who have directly or indirectly assisted me with this project:

My mother introduced me to *Jonathan Livingston Seagull*, Willie Nelson, and the beach, and she also instilled in me a sense of wonder and delight. She encouraged me to explore the world, took motorcycle riding lessons with me when I was fifteen, cried when I left for college, and always made coming home a warm and wonderful experience.

My father taught me to water-ski, play baseball, and valuable lessons about the stock market. He took me fishing, learned scuba so we could dive together, validated my wanderlust, and always led by example. He taught me that you can have an exciting life and still be responsible.

I met Andrea in Austin, Texas, and took her to Playa del Carmen, hoping she'd fall in love with me (lucky for me, it worked). She travels with me when she can and understands that I still need to go when she can't. I carry her in my heart wherever I am. And when I return, she reminds me why there's no place like home. She is the most patient, supportive, and beautiful person I have ever known.

Thanks also to my first dive buddies—Eric "Rico" Andrews, Keri Kennerly, Chris Glisan, Ellen Lock, and Amanda Miller—as well as to Willie Nelson, John D. MacDonald, Adam Duritz, and Jimmy Buffett for their inspiration, and to everyone I've ever been to Mexico with or met while there. Special thanks to Chip Rankin for his destination insight and market intelligence.

I am thankful for the kindness and assistance of the hundreds of hoteliers, restaurant owners, tour operators, bartenders, taxi drivers, and others I met and from whom I learned during my research. Thanks to the hotel associations, tourism boards, and other official organizations that offered information and support. And thanks to the people of the Riviera Maya, who smiled at me as I walked the beaches and streets of their hometowns.

FOREWORD

When I was asked to write a foreword to this guidebook, I thought about how I could spend 10 years traveling through Mexico, and each day would still bring a fresh sense of discovery, new faces, and plenty of surprises. I have been visiting Mexico for more than 30 years and love it so much that I make my home in Los Cabos, where I run the Cabo Wabo Cantina, hang out, drink tequila, and jam with friends. Whether I'm down there or across the country in Playa del Carmen and the Riviera Maya, it's always great to be in Mexico.

Many tourists have discovered the charms of Mexico over the past three decades, but I find that some things never change. I continue to find adventure around every corner and still get a thrill when I'm the only gringo in a backstreet cantina. Often a sunrise means my day is ending, rather than beginning. For me, Mexico remains a magical and mystical place. There is a sense of timelessness and deep-rooted folklore everywhere you go.

Most of all, I love the white-sand beaches, the music, the food, the fiestas, and enjoying time with family and friends. It's a place where the warmth of the sun is equaled by the warmth of the people. Mexico inspires me. It might mean a new song, a new idea, or a renewed outlook. Whatever it does to you, Mexico will remind you to enjoy life.

See you on the beach!

—Sammy Hagar
The Red Rocker, former lead singer of Van Halen

THE HAMMOCKS AT XEL-HA ARE THE PERFECT PLACE FOR A NAP PHILIP GAMON

INTRODUCTION

My parents first traveled to the Riviera Maya in 1980, when it was known only by the not-so-catchy designation "area south of Cancún." They went to Xcaret when the entry fee cost twenty-five cents and the road had yet to be paved. They went to Xel-Ha and Garrafon, in Isla Mujeres, where they marveled at the tropical fish and deserted beaches. They ate lobster on the beach in Cancún and snorkeled the virgin reefs of Cozumel. When they came home, they showed me their pictures and talked of their adventures, and I knew I'd go there one day too.

GUESTS AT MAYAKOBA CAN EXPLORE THE RESERVE'S CANALS ON A BOAT TOUR, HIGHLIGHTING THE LOCAL FLORA AND FAUNA MAYAKOBA

My first Caribbean experience was in Belize, when I was sixteen. I went diving off Turneffe Island and was enchanted by the color of the water, the number of fish, and the relaxing island lifestyle. A year later, I went on a dive trip to Cozumel with a group of friends from school. I loved the food, the freedom, and the excitement. We took the ferry to the then-tiny town of Playa del Carmen, where we could hardly find a place that was open to eat lunch.

For each of the next 10 years, I went to Mexico every chance I could get. Eventually I was leading group trips, selling travel packages, and making friends around the country. In college, I also spent a year at the University of Costa Rica, studying Spanish and traveling around every weekend. After graduating from the University of Texas, I took a job with a Mexico-based tourism developer with the exciting task of contributing to the early stages of the creation of Playacar.

At that point, I moved to Cozumel, worked in a hotel, and traveled the region extensively. I later moved to Cancún, reported for the *Cancún News* (the English daily newspaper, now defunct), and made frequent trips to Playa del Carmen. In 1993, I visited Xpu-Ha for a photo shoot at one of the first all-inclusive hotels in the region. I could never have imagined back then the development that would soon follow up and down the coast.

When I met the woman who would later become my wife, the first trip we took together was to Playa del Carmen, where I hoped she'd fall in love with me. We stayed at a tiny pension along Quinta Avenida when it was still a dusty cobblestone street with just a handful of restaurants, shops, and bars. Lucky for me, the ploy worked, and later we named our first daughter Maya, after the region that we all enjoy together now.

Over the years, I have stayed active in the Riviera Maya community, splitting my frequent trips among Cancún, Cozumel, and Playa. As many others have, I've watched the area boom and grow, amazed with each trip at the new hotels, restaurants, and other attractions.

The region continues to draw me, almost magically, to its sandy beaches, taco bars, secret fishing holes, and buzzing nightspots. The Riviera Maya is alive within my soul and has become an important part of who I am. I love being there, I love talking about it—and I love sharing this special place with other travelers.

WHAT'S WHERE IN PLAYA DEL CARMEN, TULUM & THE RIVIERA MAYA

Travel should be easy, it should be carefree, and it should be comfortable. Unfortunately, that's not always the case. Getting around, having the proper paperwork, and making sense of unfamiliar rules and regulations can cause a fair amount of stress during any vacation, and travel to the Riviera Maya is no different.

A popular adage that scuba divers like to repeat is, "Plan your dive and dive your plan." This wisdom should be applied to vacation travel as well. Taking some time before your trip to learn a bit about the region where you'll be traveling and to create a plan for how you're going to get around is essential to enjoying your vacation to the fullest.

Arrival & Transportation

Most international visitors get to Playa del Carmen and the Riviera Maya by flying into the **Cancún International Airport** (CUN, www.cancun-airport.com), forty-five miles north of Playa and 10 miles south of the resort city of Cancún.

Inaugurated in 1974, the airport has had regular renovations, leaving it in excellent condition. There are three terminals, and most international visitors

ONCE OUTSIDE THE DOORS OF THE CANCUN AIRPORT, YOU'RE OFFICIALLY IN THE TROPICS—AND THAT MUCH CLOSER TO THE BEACH   CHIP RANKIN

will arrive and depart through Terminal 2 or 3, which, according to the official airport website, served more than 20 million passengers in 2016. The terminals are quite modern and efficient, with Starbucks, Margaritaville Café, and other familiar conveniences. International flights also arrive at the smaller **Cozumel International Airport** (CZM), and transportation to the mainland is available via ferry. Charter and regional flights are also available at small airports in **Playa del Carmen** and on **Isla Mujeres** and **Isla Holbox**.

If your transportation's not pre-arranged through your vacation package or hotel, you can find several options for getting where you need to go. You can also conveniently and securely book a shuttle from the airport to your hotel on the airport's official website. Uber is now available as well in the Riviera Maya, but it is neither officially recommended nor legal. Skip it, and book local transportation instead.

CAR RENTAL If you plan to do much local exploring and prefer a self-guided trip over planned excursions, renting a car may be your best option. And since the price of car rental for a day is about the same as taking a taxi from the Cancún airport to Playa del Carmen, it

usually makes sense to pick up the car at the airport and drop it off on your way back. Alternatively, you can choose to get your car once you're at your hotel or drop it off early at one of your rental agency's offices in the Mayan Riviera.

When renting a car in Mexico, it's important to investigate your insurance options. You're required to carry at least liability, and it will be clearly marked on your rental contract. Collision and comprehensive add-ons are available and can add fifty to one hundred percent to the car rental price. Verify in advance whether your existing car insurance or even credit card contract provides for rental car coverage, and ensure that the coverage extends to vehicles rented in Mexico. Many plans don't.

CITY BUSES Public bus service ($10) runs between the Cancún airport and the main Playa del Carmen bus terminal (Quinta and Juárez), a short walk or taxi ride to most Playa hotels. Purchase tickets just after you clear customs and immigration and before you leave the airport. Once you have your ticket, you'll be directed to the departure location. Any airport employee can point the way, but make sure you're getting on the right bus, and don't be talked into paying additional fares for different services.

CUSTOMS & IMMIGRATION All visitors must have a valid passport book to enter Mexico. Before your arrival on an international flight, you'll be required to fill out a tourist card (good for up to 90 days) and customs form. Usually handed out on the plane, they're also available at the airport.

As you deplane, stay with your group as you're funneled to Immigration. The wait can range from a few minutes to nearly an hour, depending on flight schedules. Have your passport and forms ready, and then remember to save your copy of the tourist card, which the agent will return to you with your passport. You must have it when you depart. If lost,

GO HOG WILD IN THE RIVIERA MAYA

For some travelers, taking a guided trip in a tour bus or even setting out on their own in a rental car is just too tame. For these intrepid travelers, renting a Harley Davidson may be the best way to visit the ruins, discover hidden beaches, and make a style statement, all while getting a tan. Harley Adventures (www .harleyadventures.com) offers 883 Sportsters, 1200 Customs, and Softail Fat Boys for around $95, $145, and $195 per day.

Riders are encouraged to exercise extreme caution while riding along busy sections of Highway 307 and any unpaved roads they encounter.

A *COLECTIVO* CHARGES PER PERSON AND MAKES MULTIPLE STOPS

there's a $40 fee, and you can expect a bit of an interrogation at the airport when you leave. After you claim any bags, you'll proceed to the customs checkpoint. Hand your customs form to the agent standing next to the vertical traffic light mounted on a pole about chest-high. You'll be asked to push the button. Green means "go," and red means your baggage will be opened and inspected.

PLAYA COMMUTER FLIGHTS Mostly used by private aircraft, the small

A SINGLE TAXI AWAITS ARRIVALS AT THE CANCUN AIRPORT IN 1970 CANCUN HISTORY CENTER

airfield in downtown Playa del Carmen, a few blocks behind the Playacar Palace hotel, also has charter flights available through **AeroSaab** (www.aerosaab.com) to Cancún, Cozumel, Merida, Isla Holbox, and nearby destinations.

SHUTTLE BUSES Shuttle buses, called *colectivos*, are available for transportation to Playa del Carmen. You'll generally ride with other travelers, stopping at other hotels along the way, but it's a good way to save a few pesos. Fares to Playa del Carmen are around $20 per person.

TAXIS Taxi service from the airport is heavily regulated; only specially licensed cabs are allowed to pick up passengers. As a result, fares from the airport are higher than those for return trips to the airport. The official fare at publication date from the airport to the Cancún hotel zone was $50, and a trip to Playa del Carmen will run you around $90 to $100 per vehicle.

A return trip from Playa should be about $60, but ask your driver for a price before you get into the cab. Your best bet is to hire a Super Shuttle private taxi with plenty of room, cold air conditioning, and a cold beer purchased at the airport ($70 to Playa del Carmen).

THE COZUMEL FERRY If you hit the schedule just right, getting to Playa del Carmen from Cozumel can take even less time than arriving through Cancún. The Cozumel International Airport (CZM) is smaller than Cancún's, with only two runways and a small terminal. As your plane slows to a stop on the runway, you'll think the wingtips are about to snip the treetops off the palm trees that line the strip, but it's a safe and modern facility, even if it lacks the pretensions of the more recently renovated Cancún airport.

As in Cancún, taxi service at the Cozumel airport is regulated, and taxi fare or shuttle service must be paid for at a kiosk in the airport. Visitors with little luggage looking to save a few bucks can walk off the airport grounds and hail a taxi on the street for about $14. Either way, the ride is only 10 minutes and will take you through a quick tour of the town of San Miguel before letting you out at the base of the ferry landing, or *muelle* in Spanish.

As of press time, there are three ferry companies crossing from Playa to Cozumel: **Ultramar** (www.ultramarferry.com), **México Waterjets** (www.mexicowaterjets.com), and **Barcos Caribe** (www.barcos caribe.com). Each company claims to have the newest and fastest boats, but opt for the ride with the nearest departure time. Schedules are clearly posted for each ferry at their respective kiosks near the pier. Seating more than 200, ferries have air conditioning, snack bars, restrooms, and both indoor and outdoor seating. The ride takes from 30 to 45 minutes, depending on the boat and the water conditions. On windy days, the ride can be a little rough, so it's recommended that you use the restroom prior to boarding or before departure, in case it's too rocky to safely move around. Fares range from around $7–$10 each way, and ferries depart every hour on the hour from approximately 6 AM–11 PM. You're best off purchasing a one-way ticket to allow for a more flexible departure time from Cozumel, especially since

THE FERRY BOAT TO COZUMEL TAKES LESS THAN 30 MINUTES

VACATION PACKING TIPS

Swimsuit: Check. Underwear. Check. Clothes. Check. Toiletries. Check. You may have your basic packing list mastered by now, but there are a few things you might not remember to shove into your suitcase.

TO PACK

- **Bug repellent:** You can buy it there if you forget, but the brand you're used to is likely cheaper at home.
- **Waterproof phone case:** *Cenote* and beach photos are best with some backup protection.
- **Mesh water shoes:** Kids will especially appreciate better footing on those slippery rocks.
- **Reef-safe sunscreen:** A must if you plan on any snorkeling trips.
- **Day pack or backpack:** Ideal for packing hats, snacks, water, and anything extra for day trips.
- **First aid kit:** Boo-boos happen. Be prepared.
- **Bluetooth speaker:** If you have some chill time in your room, it's nice to listen to some tunes.

LEAVE AT HOME

- **Expensive jewelry and electronics:** Hopefully you won't have to bring your laptop on vacation.
- **Large amounts of cash:** Obviously.
- **Beach towels:** Bring your favorite beach bag, but hotels will have towels to use by the pool.
- **Snorkel & mask:** If space is an issue, you can stop by the Walmart for some snorkel gear, or ask the front desk. Most all-inclusive hotels will have equipment to borrow.

round-trip tickets are non-transferrable between ferry companies.

Upon arriving in Playa, you'll walk down a metal ramp onto the wide concrete pier. If you've checked bags, they'll be delivered to you on the dock, near the ferry's bow. Tricycle taxis are available to help carry you and/or your bags to the street to catch a proper taxi or all the way to your hotel, if you're staying in the immediate downtown area.

General Information

Geographically speaking, "Yucatán" can refer to the overall peninsula or to the easternmost quadrant of Mexico that juts into the Caribbean Sea, to the jungle that engulfs much of that area, or to the Mexican state that borders Quintana Roo to the northwest. The word can also be used to denote traditional cultural and/or geographical features long associated with this lush and storied region of Mexico.

Named for a key figure in the Mexican War for Independence, Andrés Quintana Roo, who hailed from the Yucatán Peninsula, the Mexican state of Quintana Roo was officially formed in 1974. It contains the entirety of the country's Caribbean coastline, including Cancún, Cozumel, the Riviera Maya, and the Costa Maya. Stretching from Puerto Morelos to Tulum and encompassing Playa del Carmen, the Riviera Maya has surpassed Cancún itself in its number of hotel rooms and visitors. However, unlike Cancún's high-rises, the area's beloved low-rise development is spread out over a much greater and typically quieter area. English-speakers often refer to it as the Mayan Riviera, but this book has opted to use the local vernacular.

BANKING Before heading to Mexico, be sure to notify your bank of international travel, so that your credit card will not be deactivated for suspicious activity. Skip the traveler's checks and exchanging any money before you get to Mexico. Once there, look for a money exchange or Casa de Cambio (most will require you to have your passport as identification) to trade dollars for pesos at a better rate than at home. If using an ATM, remember to walk the extra few blocks for a bank branch ATM like Scotia Bank or Bancomer Bank to avoid security issues with your debit card.

CHILDREN You don't have to leave the kids at home to have a fun vacation in the Riviera Maya. Many resorts have special facilities for kids, including playgrounds, kid-friendly meals, activities programs, and complimentary child care. In-room babysitting can be arranged through hotel concierges, who maintain a list of recommended caretakers. Smaller hotels can often arrange for a housekeeper to look after the kids

while parents enjoy a tour, though the region's nature parks, theme parks, and zoos also provide exciting day-trip opportunities for the whole family. At the beach, kids enjoy collecting shells, watching the pelicans dive for fish, and building sand castles. In most areas, there is little wave action, so introducing little ones to the ocean is a breeze.

CONSULATE OFFICES **The United States** (www.usembassy.gov), **Canada** (www .canadainternational.gc.ca), and **United Kingdom** (www.ukinmexico.fco .gov.uk) all have consular offices in the region. All three have offices in Cancún, and both the US and Canada maintain offices in Playa del Carmen. There is also a US office in Cozumel.

CURRENCY The official currency of Mexico is the peso. Although its value

THIS PLAYGROUND IS IN THE MIDDLE OF THE TOWN SQUARE IN PLAYA DEL CARMEN

KEEPING YOU ON TRACK

Exploring is fun, but so is knowing where you are. The creators of the CancunMap series, Iowa couple Laura (a.k.a. "MapChick") and Perry McFarlin have explored the region for more than 30 years and likely know more about its back roads, secret beaches, and hidden attractions than any other non-locals on Earth. They tag the area's top resorts, restaurants, beaches, and other highlights, but their true love is uncovering lesser-known attractions and off-the-beaten-path adventures. Maps contain the couple's unique take on the area and their personal recommendations and advice. Their exhaustively researched and individually produced maps cover Cancún, Cozumel, Isla Mujeres, Playa del Carmen, Mayan landmarks, and the Riviera Maya, and sell for $15 each (www.cancunmap.com).

through customs or say *adiós* to your new bottle of tequila.

ELECTRICITY Electrical power is the same as it is in the States: 110 volts AC. Outlets are the same size, and most US plugs will work without any problem. Some hotels do not offer polarized plugs (where one prong is slightly larger than the other), so if your important electronic gadget has a polarized plug, grab an adapter at your local hardware or discount store. Adapters are very inexpensive and could save the day if you have an uncooperative outlet at your hotel.

GAS STATIONS Owned by the government's oil distribution company Pemex, the gas stations along Highway 307 from Cancún to Tulum are all full-service and plentiful. Travelers heading south of Tulum or west across the peninsula

fluctuates daily against the US dollar, there is rarely a notable difference in the rate during a visitor's trip. In tourist areas, prices are sometimes listed in American dollars, and since both currencies use the dollar sign ($), that sometimes breeds confusion. This book uses the dollar sign ($) to signify US dollars and the word *pesos* when referring to Mexican pesos.

DUTY-FREE The notion of duty-free sales of alcohol, tobacco, and other taxable goods sometimes seems like a hold-over from travel's more exotic heyday. But large shops selling duty-free goods can be found at the Cancún and Cozumel airports, and many travelers continue to buy their allotment to take home. However, if you're to traveling back to the US and have to transfer to a connecting flight, remember that TSA officials will not allow you to bring a liquor bottle in your carry-on baggage when you enter the terminal for your domestic flight. So be prepared to transfer your purchase to your checked luggage after you pass

LOCAL TROPICAL FRUITS LIKE MANGO, PAPAYA, RAMBUTAN, PRICKLY PEAR, AND COCONUT ARE A BREAKFAST STAPLE CHIP RANKIN

WORDS AND PHRASES

ENGLISH	SPANISH
Another one	Otra
ATM	Cajero automático
Bathroom	Baño
Beach	Playa
Beef	Carne de rés
Beer	Cerveza
Big	Grande
Boat	Lancha
Bottled water	Agua en botella
Breakfast	Desayuno
Bus	Autobús
Car rental	Renta de autos
Check/bill	La cuenta
Chicken	Pollo
Coffee with milk	Café con leche
Dinner	Cena
Downtown	El centro
Drunk	Borracho
Eat	Comer
Fishing	La pesca
Goodbye	Adiós, hasta luego
Good morning	Buenos días
Good night	Buenas noches
Happy	Felíz
Hello	Hola
How much	Cuánto
Ice	Hielo
I want	Yo deseo
Lime	Limón
Lobster	Langosta
Luggage	Equipaje
Lunch	Comida
Money	Dinero
Money exchange	Cámbio de dinero
More	Más
My name is	Me llamo
Nice to meet you	Mucho gusto
Orange juice	Jugo de naranja
Please	Por favór
Post office	El correo
Rain	Llúvia
Scuba diving	Buceo
Shrimp	Camarón
Shuttle bus	Colectivo
Sick	Enfermo
Silly tourist	Turista loca
Small	Pequeña
Sunscreen	Bronceadora
Swim	Nadar
Swimsuit	Traje de baño
Tax	Impuestos
Thank you	Graciás
Tip	Propina
Towel	Toalla
Waiter	Mesero
Walk	Caminar
Why	Porqué
You're welcome	De nada

Try a Little Mayan

Hello, what's up?	Ba'ax ka wa'alik?
What's going on?	Bix a bel?
I'm fine.	Ma'alob.
See you later.	Taak tu lakin.
I'm just looking.	Chen tin wilik.
How much is it?	Bahúux leti'?
Tastes good.	Ki.'
Hot pepper	Lik
Juice	K'aab
Where	Tu'ux
Plaza	K'iiwik
Thank you	Dios bo'otik
You're welcome	Mixba'al

should plan to fill up at every stop. Prices run a little higher than in most US cities.

HIGH SEASON As in much of Mexico and the Caribbean, the peak season lasts from early February until early May. The two weeks over Christmas and New Year's are also very busy, and most hotels charge their highest rates of the year during that time.

HONEYMOONS From intimate boutique hotels, quiet beaches, and relaxing spa treatments to bustling restaurant scenes, plush resorts, and adventurous excursions, the Riviera Maya offers honeymoon options to suit almost every couple. Many venues offer wedding planning services and often feature additional special packages for the newly married. But don't be afraid to custom design a unique honeymoon to fit your unique tastes, style, and budget.

IPHONE OR ANDROID Using your cell phone in Mexico is easy (and inexpensive) if you remember a few things. First, go to your settings and switch on "airplane mode" to avoid any international data charges, and then make sure your Wi-Fi is on. Your hotel and many restaurants, coffee shops, and cafés will have free Wi-Fi available to check in with work and family. If you need to chat or text, try an app like Facetime, Skype, or WhatsApp.

SEMANA SANTA "Holy Week" in English, this usually refers to the week prior to the Easter holiday but often also includes the week following it. Children in Mexico get two weeks off over Easter, during which time families typically travel to the coasts. Hotels and resorts frequently fill up completely. When Semana Santa overlaps with the US spring break season, expect rooms to be particularly hard to find.

SPANISH Mexico's official language remains dominant in the Riviera Maya, even among Mayans. However, many Mayan words continue to be used and augment the local lexicon. Tourists can probably get by on English alone in Playa, Cancún, Isla Mujeres, and much of the Riviera Maya, but they may still want to consider enrolling in a local Spanish language school or program. Consider **Don Quijote** (www.donquijote.org), **Solexico Spanish School** (www.solexico .com), or **International House** (www .ihrivieramaya.com), which also offers cooking classes, Latin dancing, and scuba instruction.

SPRING BREAK From late February through early April, with a sharp spike in mid-March, American college students visit Mexico in full force. Although they're typically focused on Cancún,

IT'S HARD TO IMAGINE EVER HAVING A BAD DAY AT THE BEACH LOCOGRINGO.COM

YO AMO TACOS IS THE PERFECT PLACE TO SIT BACK WITH A DRINK AND WATCH PLAYA'S EVENING PARADE OF PASSERSBY CHIP RANKIN

there's some spillover to Playa, Cozumel, and other Riviera Maya destinations.

STAYING SAFE Bad things happen, even in paradise, so it's good to know where you can turn. For emergency police, fire, or ambulance assistance, call 066 (the equivalent of 911 in the US) from any phone at no cost. Before traveling to Mexico, be sure to check with your health insurance provider to understand the limits of your health insurance while outside of the States. If you're not fully covered for the duration of your trip, consider purchasing an additional travel health insurance policy to cover emergency medical treatment.

Playa del Carmen is far from the sleepy fishing village where once upon a time everybody knew each other and nobody locked their doors. No longer immune to Mexico's drug-related crime, a shooting at an electronic music festival in January of 2017 left five club-goers dead and more injured. Despite this tragic and terrifying event, expect a region that thrives on tourism to be committed to the safety of its visitors. As the afternoon turns into evening, most streets along Quinta will have

machine-gun-toting police observing the crowds. It's surprisingly not frightening and is designed to keep tourists safe. Don't explore dark, remote streets at night; instead, stay in crowded areas and remain aware of your surroundings.

Petty theft is the main problem from day to day, and tourists are advised to watch their belongings, lock their hotel rooms, and not leave valuables unattended on the beach or elsewhere. Leave your jewels at home, and—like anywhere else—don't flash large amounts of cash or leave drinks unattended at busy nightclubs and bars. Use the hotel safe whenever possible, and don't leave valuables in plain view in your hotel room or rental car. Men should carry their wallets in their front pockets on crowded streets, and women should ensure their bags are fully closed and not swinging freely.

If you go looking for trouble, you'll have a better chance of finding it. Visitors are strongly advised to keep their noses clean and stay well away from any obvious trouble or precarious situations. Don't travel into destitute neighborhoods, especially at night. Don't associate with questionable individuals, and ignore anyone offering drugs.

BEST APPS FOR TRAVELERS

Whether you're looking for free Wi-Fi or to set yourself up with an international cell phone plan, there are a few essential apps for traveling in our modern age.

Google Translate: Download Google's Spanish language pack before your trip and translate on the go without hunting for a Wi-Fi connection. Use the camera translation tool to quickly see what you're ordering on a menu.

WhatsApp: Whether you have an iPhone, Android, or laptop, this free app just needs a Wi-Fi connection to make secure video calls that won't use up your minutes or add any surprise charges. You can also send photos and videos over the app in addition to text messages.

Café Wifi: Use this free app to locate fast and free Wi-Fi connections wherever you are. Ideal for those days when you don't want a little bit of work to ruin your vacation.

XE Currency: Calculate up-to-the-minute exchange rates with this free app.

TIME ZONE In 2015, the state of Quintana Roo opted to no longer observe daylight savings time in order to provide tourists with extended evenings. Simultaneously, the decision was also made to switch from Central Standard Time (CST) to Eastern Standard Time (EST).

TIPS & GRATUITIES Unless your tab specifically lists *servicio* after the tax or you're within the walls of an all-inclusive resort, tips are expected to be given to waiters (ten to fifteen percent), massage therapists, tour guides, dive guides, and similar service providers.

TRAVEL WARNING In August of 2017, the **US Department of State** (travel.state.gov) extended their Mexico travel warning to include the state of Quintana Roo, home to Playa, Cancún, Isla Holbox, and the Riviera Maya. The transcript of the travel warning is as follows: "US citizens

FRESHWATER CANALS WIND THROUGHOUT FAIRMONT MAYAKOBA AND NEIGHBORING RESORTS   MAYAKOBA

WEATHER

Month	High Temp.	Low Temp.	Ocean Temp.	Rainfall
January	80°F	66°F	75°F	3.75 inches
February	81°F	67°F	76°F	2.25 inches
March	83°F	70°F	77°F	1.75 inches
April	84°F	72°F	78°F	1.75 inches
May	87°F	76°F	80°F	4.75 inches
June	88°F	77°F	83°F	7.75 inches
July	89°F	77°F	85°F	4.25 inches
August	89°F	76°F	85°F	4.25 inches
September	88°F	75°F	84°F	9.00 inches
October	86°F	73°F	82°F	8.50 inches
November	83°F	71°F	81°F	3.75 inches
December	81°F	68°F	79°F	4.25 inches

should be aware that according to Government of Mexico statistics, the state of Quintana Roo experienced an increase in homicide rates compared to 2016. While most of these homicides appeared to be targeted criminal organization assassinations, turf battles between criminal groups have resulted in violent crime in areas frequented by US citizens. Shooting incidents, in which innocent bystanders have been injured or killed, have occurred." If you remain vigilant and stick to popular tourist areas, especially at night, you should be fine. Violence is a part of our modern world, but craving amazing adventures at home and in other countries is why you're reading this book in the first place. So, be safe, but also have fun!

WHAT TO BRING The Riviera Maya isn't considered a remote location. You're usually never more than 30 to 45 minutes from a grocery store, pharmacy, clothing boutique, electronics store, hair salon, or even a hardware store, and modern supplies are readily available.

Packing for a trip to Playa and its environs is all about comfort and bringing what you want to have with you to make your trip perfect. Unless you're planning on a serious camping trip to Sian Ka'an or a long-distance jungle hike, you should consider your packing to be an exercise in preparing for a luxurious getaway. What you need to bring is largely determined by where you're staying and what you plan on doing.

Nature & Outdoors

BEACHES White sandy beaches reign supreme in the Riviera Maya. However, visitors will encounter the occasional rocky beach, and many beaches are clearly nicer than others. In Mexico, all beaches are public property, although hotels and property owners along the beach are allowed to section off private areas and aren't required to provide beach access across their property.

BICYCLING Bike rentals are a popular recreation or transportation choice, particularly on smaller islands like Isla

BICYCLING IS PARTICULARLY POPULAR FOR GETTING AROUND ON ISLA HOLBOX'S SANDY ROADS CHIP RANKIN

READS FOR RIVIERA MAYA TRAVELERS

Give one of these perfectly apropos books a read while you're on the beach, or when you return, to ease your transition back into the real world.

Don't Stop the Carnival by Herman Wouk: If you find yourself wanting to open a hotel in the Caribbean, this meandering tale may help change your mind.

Cinnamon Skin by John D. MacDonald: A boat-bum detective travels to Cancún and the Riviera Maya to solve a crime for a friend.

A Salty Piece of Land by Jimmy Buffett: A cowboy moves to Sian Ka'an to become a fishing guide. Many Riviera Maya and Buffett song–inspired references.

A Tourist in the Yucatán by James McNay Brumfield: An action-adventure mystery set among the Mayan ruins.

Where the Sky Is Born: Living in the Land of the Maya by Jeanine Lee Kitchel: Thinking of moving to the Riviera Maya or curious about what it would be like? Learn from someone who's done it.

Wicked Spanish by Howard Tomb: This tongue-in-cheek language guide will teach you some naughty phrases and fun sayings to try out on bartenders and fellow bus passengers.

The Ruins by Scott Smith: A group of friends on holiday to Cancún and the Riviera Maya stumble across a mysterious secret in the Mayan jungle and struggle to get away. This book may make you think twice about hiking in the jungle!

Captains Outrageous by Joe R. Lansdale: A comedic and bumbling narrative of intrigue, describing travels from East Texas to the land of the Maya.

Mujeres and Isla Holbox and within larger master-planned resorts. Many hotels offer courtesy bicycles for the use of their guests.

CARIBBEAN ISLANDS The three different island destinations located off the Yucatán Peninsula each have their own distinctive character and vibe. The more developed Cozumel and the enchanting Isla Mujeres can be spotted from Playa del Carmen and Cancún, respectively, and both are accessible by ferry. The ferry to sleepy Isla Holbox lies 3 hours north of Cancún, prompting some visitors to opt for chartered air taxis.

CENOTES A rare geological feature of the Yucatán, a *cenote* (sen-NO-teh) is a freshwater sinkhole formed when the limestone ground caves in and fills with water from underground rivers. The US-based **National Speleological Society** (www.caves .org/project/qrss) has an ongoing and well-advanced project to map the extensive network of freshwater caves (see *Diving, Snorkeling & Cenotes* on page 195).

CORAL Even though it's the coral remnants that have washed ashore that give much of the region's beaches their bright-white, almost pink hue, coral itself is not to be touched. The rare piece that washes ashore will easily cut up a bare foot. More importantly for those who are diving and snorkeling, coral is very fragile, and simple contact can cause a piece to break off or commence a chemical reaction that kills organisms that took hundreds of years to form and are a critical part of the earth's ecosystem. Learn more about coral protection and conservation from the **World Wildlife Fund** (WWF) at www.panda.org/ corals.

COSTA MAYA, OR THE MAYAN COAST The region known as Riviera Maya reaches its southern border in Tulum. The Mexican Caribbean coast that stretches from that point south to Belize is known as the Costa Maya. Quieter and slower than its northern counterpart, the area is noted for its many small, ecologically themed hotels, large undeveloped areas, and protected preserves.

DIVING & SNORKELING The Mayan Riviera is one of the world's great destinations for saltwater and freshwater exploration. Check out *Diving, Snorkeling & Cenotes* on page 195 for an in-depth discussion of dive sites, scuba certification schools, and recommended dive shops throughout the region.

DOLPHINS Travelers can sign up to swim with trained dolphins in a captive environment at **Dolphin Discovery's centers** (www.dolphindiscovery.com) in Puerto Aventuras, Cozumel, Akumal, and Isla Mujeres. Other programs are available through **Delphinus** (www .delphinusworld.com) at Xcaret and Xel-Ha parks and the Cancún's Dreams Hotel, and also via **Dolphinaris** (www .dolphinaris.com) at Wet 'n Wild.

ECOLOGICAL STAYS There are a number of small ecologically themed hotels and bed-and-breakfasts in the Mayan Riviera, particularly on Isla Mujeres, Isla Holobox, and south of Tulum. Although this designation doesn't always indicate "green" facilities that offer any particular efficiency, such hotels typically feature a stronger connection to nature and often demonstrate a more conscientious behavior toward it.

GOLF The arrival of the OHL Golf Classic in 2007 clearly signaled the region's arrival as a world-class destination for championship golf. Read up on the courses and the big names who designed them in *Activities & Tours* on page 167 and visit the **Mexican Caribbean Golf Association** online (www.playgolf.mx).

GREAT MAYAN REEF The largest coral reef in North America, second in the world only to the Great Barrier Reef near Australia, is better known in scientific circles as the Mesoamerican Barrier Reef

HOLA GRINGO

In Playa, as throughout Mexico, Americans are usually referred to as *gringos*. Though it may sound a bit harsh to some Americans' ears (it does have a negative connotation in some other Latin American countries), it isn't meant as a derogatory term in Mexico. So, don't take offense. To the Mexicans, using the word *Americanos* is confusing and a bit offensive to them, since all residents of North, Central, and South America could be considered "Americans." Also, since the full name of the republic of Mexico is Los Estados Unidos de Mexico, or the United States of Mexico, it's confusing to use the textbook translation *estadounidiense*, which is essentially "United Statesian," for citizens of the USA. Americans are sometimes referred to as *norteamericanos*, which means "North Americans," but that's not quite accurate either, since that term fails to distinguish between the United States and Canada, and the latter's citizens are known simply as *canadienses*. So, embrace your inner "gringo," and don't consider it a negative label. In this book, the word American is used to refer to residents of the United States.

System. It begins off the coast of the Yucatán Peninsula near Isla Contoy and Isla Mujeres and extends south 197 miles past Belize, ending near the Bay Islands of Honduras. This living underwater environment is home to more than 600 species of fish and nearly one hundred varieties of coral.

HURRICANES With a season lasting from July through November, hurricanes have had untold impact on the Riviera Maya. Several storms—notably Hurricanes Emily and Wilma in 2005—have caused enormous destruction to beaches, buildings, and infrastructure. This damage, however, has also led developers and the Mexican government to invest billions of dollars to improve and fortify the area. The greatest risk of storms typically occurs from late August through

MEZCAL

Way cooler than its famous cousin tequila, mezcal is absolutely not the same as that bottle you might remember with the worm floating inside. While both liquors are made from agave plants, artisanal mezcal has a complex smoky flavor that you should absolutely seek out in one of the many bars and lounges around Playa.

October, although this rule of thumb is unpredictable at best. Check the **National Hurricane Center** (www .nhc.noaa.gov) for recent activity, and read about historical hurricanes in the area in the special sections throughout this book.

IGUANAS If you don't see an iguana on your vacation, you probably didn't leave your room (or the nightclubs) very often. Given the close proximity of the jungle, the prevalence of this scaly reptile, and its general indifference to people, is legendary. Iguanas are commonplace anywhere with significant vegetation. They're docile creatures, but look and don't touch. They can carry disease, and if you harass them you'll probably get hurt or into a lot of trouble.

JUNGLE Despite the beautiful white beaches and significant development around Cancún, Playa del Carmen, and Tulum, much of the region remains as the natural Yucatán Jungle. Besides iguanas, it's home to many species of flora and fauna, and at times can be unpredictable. The best way to experience the jungle is as part of a tour or excursion.

KITEBOARDING Navigating what is essentially a surfboard with a sail, novices and experts alike can sail the smooth waters of the Mexican Caribbean on kiteboards. Lessons are available, most notably with the legendary Ikarus (see *Activities & Tours* on page 167), and kiteboard rentals and limited instruction are often included at larger all-inclusive resorts.

SOME THINGS ARE STILL CHEAPER SOUTH OF THE BORDER

Though the price of meals, drinks, and many everyday purchases may be relatively close to what you'll find back home, some services are still a bargain south of the border. Here are a few ideas for ways you can save some money while you're in the Riviera Maya:

New eyeglasses: Bring a written prescription or even a pair of well-calibrated glasses, and the technicians at area eyewear shops can match your prescription in a wide variety of frames and lenses for a fraction of what you'd pay at home.

Manicures & pedicures: Want acrylic nails or just need a fresh mani/pedi? Prices at salons catering to locals are about half of what you'd pay back home.

Watch repair: If you have an old watch that needs fixing, bring it on vacation. Watch shops in Playa are common a few blocks back from the beach, and the skilled craftsmen there can fix almost anything. Drop off your broken watch and pick it up the next day. It'll be ticking like new.

Shoe repair: Shoes falling apart? Stop by a local shoe repair shop, and you can have new soles added, heels replaced, or other repairs done while you're off enjoying the ruins at Tulum. The price will be significantly less than it would be back home, and the craftsmanship is top-notch.

Prescription medications: Local pharmacies will gladly fill prescriptions from US doctors. Don't have a prescription? In many cases, one can be issued on the spot for a limited charge.

NUDE BEACHES Mexican law prohibits going nude (including topless for women) in public—and this policy extends to beaches as well. But there are several locales where officials look the other way, or pretend to. It's generally acceptable, and common, to see women sunbathing topless in areas of Playa del Carmen's beach, particularly at the beach clubs just north of Constituyentes Avenue. Several remote beach hotels cater to naturalists of varying extremes.

OCEAN PRESERVATION & PROTECTION Although it may be hard to imagine serious threats to our oceans while sunning along the Caribbean or swimming in its pristine waters, scientists estimate that, in the last 50 years alone, half of the world's coral reefs have been destroyed and more than seventy percent of the oceans' fish populations have been consumed or slaughtered through commercial fishing operations. National Geographic Society Explorer-in-Residence and renowned marine scientist Dr. Sylvia A. Earle predicts that our actions over the next couple of years will have a profound impact on the future health of the seas and the planet's ecosystems. Her frank, simple, and clear explanations of the damage, and what must be done to counter it, can be found in her 2009 book *The World Is Blue: How Our Fate and the Ocean's Are One*. It's fascinating and recommended reading for anyone moved by the beauty, wonder, and diversity of life along the Great Mayan Reef.

ART MAKES ITS WAY INTO NEARLY EVERY PART OF PLAYA LOCOGRINGO.COM

aside as a natural wilderness preserve in 1986 (www.visitsiankaan.com). An official UNESCO World Heritage site, Sian Ka'an is home to more than three hundred species of birds, a hundred types of mammals, and a diversity of geographical features (see *Activities & Tours* on page 167).

STAND-UP PADDLE BOARDING Like riding a bike on the water, stand-up paddle boards (SUP) are a great way to get some exercise while also exploring scenic waterways in the area. *Activities & Tours* on page 167 lists some of the more popular SUP excursions in the area.

UNDERWATER SCULPTURE GARDEN Artist Jason deCaires Taylor began an ambitious project in 2009, creating MUSA (www.musamexico.org), an underwater garden of hundreds of sculptures of human figures and common objects. Located near Isla Mujeres, 10 to 20 feet below the surface, MUSA (which stands for *Museo Subacuático de Arte*, or "Underwater Museum of Art") is a beautiful and eerie accomplishment. Made from a material conducive to the proliferation of coral, the statues are designed to encourage new growth and draw visitors away from fragile natural reefs.

PETS Although Mexico allows visitors to bring dogs and cats into the country temporarily, if accompanied by the required paperwork, it's rarely a good idea. Many hotels and resorts do not permit animals, and your pet will be at risk of catching diseases from local strays and other critters. Don't do it.

SEA TURTLES Nothing could be more memorable than swimming with endangered sea turtles in their natural habitat. We've listed a few adventure companies in the area (see *Activities & Tours* on page 167) who are conscious of sea turtle safety. During nesting season from May through September, **Centro Ecológico Akumal**—a local environmental group focused on sustainable tourism—organizes nightly beach walks to observe new turtle hatchlings.

WHALE SHARKS The world's largest fish is one of many reasons to visit Isla Holbox (see *Other Destinations Near Playa del Carmen* on page 139). The best time of year to swim with these peaceful, polka-dotted giants is mid-May through mid-September. Many adventure groups that lead excursions also promote efforts to protect the endangered whale sharks and their feeding habitat.

SIAN KA'AN BIOSPHERE RESERVE Located south of Tulum and covering ten percent of the state of Quintana Roo, this federal land was set

PLAYA DEL CARMEN

CHIP RANKIN

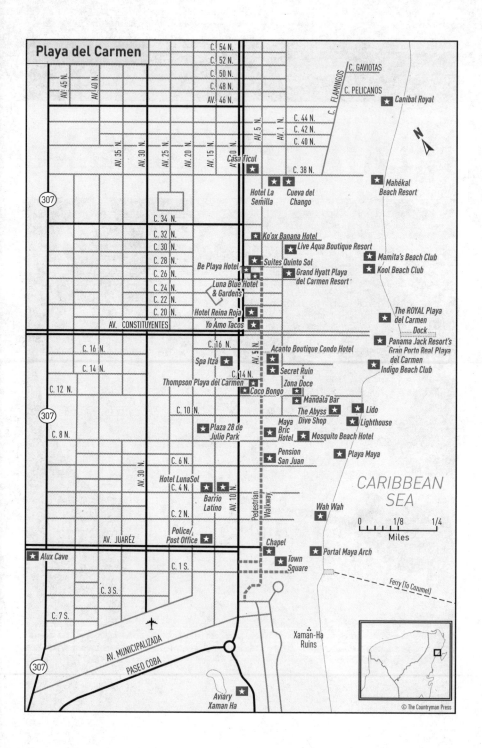

Playa del Carmen

AV. 45 N.
AV. 40 N.

C. 54 N.
C. 52 N.
C. 50 N.
C. 48 N.
AV. 46 N.

C. GAVIOTAS
C. PELICANOS

C. FLAMINGOS

★ Canibal Royal

AV. 35 N.
AV. 30 N.
AV. 25 N.
AV. 20 N.
AV. 15 N.
AV. 0 N.

AV. 5 N.
AV. 1 N.

C. 44 N.
C. 42 N.
C. 40 N.

Casa Ticul
★

C. 38 N.

★ Mahékal
Beach Resort

307

Hotel La
Semilla
★
Cueva del
Chango
★

C. 34 N.

C. 32 N.
C. 30 N.
C. 28 N.
C. 26 N.
C. 24 N.
C. 22 N.
C. 20 N.

★ Ko'ox Banana Hotel

★ Live Aqua Boutique Resort

Be Playa Hotel
★ Suites Quinto Sol
★

★ Mamita's Beach Club
★ Kool Beach Club

★ Grand Hyatt Playa
del Carmen Resort

Luna Blue Hotel
& Gardens

Hotel Reina Roja ★

★ The ROYAL Playa
del Carmen

AV. CONSTITUYENTES

Yo Amo Tacos ★

Dock

★ Panama Jack Resort's
Gran Porto Real Playa
del Carmen

C. 16 N.

C. 14 N.

C. 16 N.

AV. 5 N.

Acanto Boutique Condo Hotel

★ Indigo Beach Club

C. 12 N.

Spa Itzá ★

★ Secret Ruin

C. 14 N.

Thompson Playa del Carmen
★ Coco Bongo

Zona Doce

307

C. 8 N.

C. 10 N.

★ Plaza 28 de
Julio Park

Mandala Bar
★
The Abyss
Dive Shop
★ Lido
★ Lighthouse

AV. 30 N.

C. 6 N.

Maya
Bric
Hotel
★ Mosquito Beach Hotel

★ Playa Maya

Hotel LunaSol
C. 4 N.
★ ★

AV. 10 N.

Pension
San Juan
★

Barrio
Latino

C. 2 N.

Police/
Post Office ★

Pedestrian Walkway

★ Wah Wah

CARIBBEAN
SEA

0   1/8   1/4
Miles

AV. JUARÉZ

★ Alux Cave

C. 1 S.

Chapel
★
Town
Square
★

★ Portal Maya Arch

C. 3 S.

Ferry (To Cozumel)

C. 7 S.

AV. MUNICIPALIZADA

Xaman-Ha
Ruins

307

PASEO COBA

Aviary
Xaman Ha ★

© The Countryman Press

PLAYA DEL CARMEN

Playa del Carmen is located at the geographical center of the Riviera Maya and is the region's principal city. It's the seat of the municipal government and is home to the area's primary lodging, dining, nightlife, and shopping options.

No longer the sleepy fishing village of years past, Playa has grown into a cosmopolitan beach resort that has managed to nevertheless remain true to its origins. Its character today is typified by low-rise development, international flavor, and a casual come-as-you-are vibe. Visitors will find small local inns next to luxury resorts, taco shacks next to steakhouses, and dusty cantinas next to stylish lounges. The mix of people and cultures, the variety of tourist offerings, and the welcoming spirit of the locals make Playa a unique travel destination with few comparisons, not just within Mexico but in the entire world.

✳ To See & Do

BEACHES *Playa, plage, spiaggia,* beach: however you say it, and in whatever language, the white powdery beaches of the Riviera Maya are undeniably—and justifiably—the region's main draw. Though not quite as flour-like as the shoreline of Cancún, the crushed-shell beaches in and around Playa del Carmen are world-renowned for their softness, white color, and pristine sparkle.

WHITE SAND BEACHES, BILLOWING PALM TREES, AND TURQUOISE WATER WILL BE THE BACKDROP OF MANY VACATION PHOTOS LOCOGRINGO.COM

PLAN ON CHECKING OUT AT LEAST A FEW OF THE REGION'S MANY BEACH CLUBS FOR A FULL-SERVICE BEACH DAY

All ocean beaches in Mexico are considered federal property and are open to the public. No hotel, landowner, beach bar, or any other entity may legally restrict access to the beach. That being said, it is common for hotels to cordon off an area for the exclusive use of their guests, and this is generally accepted, as it seems to do more good than harm for the most number of people. All-inclusive hotels, for instance, may serve food and drinks on the beach, and it is helpful to the servers if their guests are slightly removed from other beachgoers. Some beach bars set up a perimeter around their beachfront tables and do not allow minors to enter. They can even charge a cover for entrance, but the restricted area cannot extend all the way to the water line or prevent non-patrons from freely passing by. In some spots, resorts will set up a roped-off area where their guests can use beach chairs and umbrellas without being hassled by vendors or other non-guests.

Licensed vendors can set up chairs and shaded *palapas* and can legally charge for their use. The general rule is, unless you're staying at the hotel that owns the facilities, you are not allowed to use them. Still, though, many tourists successfully beach-hop and visit a number of different beaches and rarely have problems using any lounge chair they happen by. Sometimes ordering a drink can earn you access to a good beach spot, and having a beach towel that matches the color of the ones the hotel provides helps, too.

Many of the main beaches, including the beach just north of the ferry dock in Playa and along the shallow cove of Akumal, are secured by federal lifeguards who are well equipped and trained to handle most emergencies. The nature parks, including Xcaret and Xel-Ha (see *Activities & Tours* on page 167), have private guards on duty to keep an eye on bathers and assist with any problems. With the lack of undertow, little poisonous marine life, clear water, and well-marked swimming areas, accidents are relatively uncommon, and the beaches are considered quite safe.

Some areas, however, do require a bit more caution. Keep an eye out for submerged rocks, shallow reefs, and off-course WaveRunners. Be careful also to avoid black spiny sea urchins, floating debris, or diving into shallow water. If you're exploring remote

OCEAN SAFETY

M any beaches along the Riviera Maya use a colored flag system to alert swimmers of the ocean's condition:

Black: No swimming allowed. Used to denote swift current, dangerous tides, lightning, or other serious problems. Seldom seen and should be taken very seriously.

Red: Caution urged. Dangerous conditions possible. Used to indicate crashing waves, presence of rocks, or other potential hazards. Common at high tide or on windy days. Strong swimmers can still enter the water but should be careful.

Yellow: Stay alert. No known issues, but swimmers should stay aware. Most common flag flown in the area. Used on all but the calmest of days. Competent swimmers should not be dissuaded from enjoying the water.

Green: Ideal conditions. Safest swimming possible. Seen only on the best of days.

areas, it's a good idea to stay in a group and not wander off alone. Even though the beaches are government property, locals may not take too kindly to tourists wandering too far from the beaten path and encroaching on their home territory. Be careful not to enter private property adjacent to the beach, and be respectful of locals who have claimed a beach area for themselves.

Petty theft can be a problem anywhere, including on the beach. Keep a watchful eye on your belongings if you stray from them, or, better yet, take turns playing in the waves and leave someone on the beach to watch your things. And don't assume that just because you're in a remote spot and can't see anyone yourself that no one can see you. Stories abound of snorkelers returning to their beach blankets after a stint on the reef only to find their bags pilfered. Playa del Carmen's most popular beach zone is just north of Constituyentes Avenue and the ROYAL Playa del Carmen (18th Street) all the way to 40th Street.

IT'S STILL POSSIBLE TO FIND A SECLUDED HIDEAWAY IN THIS POPULAR BEACH DESTINATION

QUINTA

Also known as Avenida Quinta, or 5th Avenue in English, "Quinta" is the common name for the main tourist thoroughfare in downtown Playa. All locals and many tourists refer to it this way. For purposes of clarity and consistency with other numeric street names, this book often lists it as "5th Avenue." However, if you want to speak like a local, or at least like a seasoned visitor, you'll want to say "Quinta." You're also likely to see it written as "5ta" (much like our "5th") on signs and printed materials while you're in Playa. Curiously, the name has no direct relation to the name of the state of Quintana Roo.

BEACH CLUBS The bustling **Mamita's Beach Club** (28th Street at the beach, www.mamitasbeachclub.com) attracts a trendy crowd that gathers every afternoon to soak up the sun and sip cold beers and frosty margaritas. It's usually packed with day-trippers, cruise passengers, and sun worshippers staying in Playa but not on the beach. Mamita's rents lounge chairs and umbrellas and offers beachside drink and meal service, with fish, shrimp, tacos, and other Mexican specialties topping the menu. With a separate family pool and DJ-spun music setting the scene in the upscale adult area, all manner of beachgoers are welcome here. Stretch out on a comfortable sun bed perfect for people watching and then have your wishes met with VIP service. There's also a large

AMAZING BEACHES ABOUND IN THE RIVIERA MAYA RIVIERA MAYA DESTINATION MARKETING OFFICE

48 HOURS IN PLAYA DEL CARMEN

If you're visiting a number of destinations in the Riviera Maya, or just looking for a fun-filled weekend getaway, it's easy to make reservations online for any of these two-day itineraries. Head to Playa and hit the ground running!

TWO DAYS OF FAMILY FUN

Unless your kids are teenagers, the best value for a two-day trip is to go for an all-inclusive hotel in Playacar, which is just a quick bicycle ride or taxi trip into town. Staying at an all-inclusive resort takes care of the main issues when traveling with younger children: bored kids and pleasing everyone. The variety of restaurant options at an all-inclusive will allow picky eaters to stick to their favorites, while more adventurous kids can sample some local Mexican food beyond the usual tacos and quesadillas. The kids' club also helps resolve the boredom issue, and many all-inclusives have waterslides and adventure activities that will help tire children out while parents enjoy lounging by the pool.

Plan on spending the morning of day one exploring some of the super-fun family amenities at your resort, and check breakfast and lunch off your to-do list for the day. After lunch, you'll want to head off-site and visit one of the more amazing geological wonders of the area, *cenotes*! *Cenote* Azul and *Cenote* Jardín del Eden are right next to each other and only 20 minutes from Playa del Carmen by car. You can find a tour group to take you to any of the nearby *cenotes*, or you can easily go on your own via taxi or *colectivo*. If you're looking for fewer crowds, it's best to go on a weekday in the morning before the big tour groups arrive.

Cenotes are a pretty amazing experience for kids as the fresh water is cool and completely clear, and if your little ones aren't fans of salt and sand in their eyes, then this will be one of their favorite moments of the trip. You might want to prepare everyone for the little fish that will nibble at your feet and legs. It won't hurt, but it may surprise any unsuspecting swimmers. Don't forget to pack goggles, towels, reef-safe sunscreen, and a few snacks, as most *cenotes* will not have facilities or rentals. See *Diving, Snorkeling & Cenotes* on page 195 for more options for exploring nearby *cenotes*.

Back at the hotel, plan on walking around the grounds and taking note of some of the tropical flowers and iguanas, and if you haven't ventured farther than the hotel pool yet, late afternoon is the perfect time for playing on the beach. See if you can borrow some sand toys from the kids' club, and many of the hotels will have bodyboards and snorkeling equipment available for use. Take photos of the whole family playing on the beach in Mexico in the perfect lighting, and consider your holiday card done.

THE FAMILY THAT PLAYS TOGETHER STAYS TOGETHER RIVIERA MAYA DESTINATION MARKETING OFFICE

After freshening up, find a restaurant you haven't yet tried for dinner. If the kids are still awake, check out some of the resort's nightly entertainment, or head back up to your room to get ready for your next big day.

Start your second day at **Ah Cacao** with coffee and pastries for the adults, and get the kids ready for adventure with a chocolate-fueled sugar high. Stock up on snacks (like their cacao-based energy bar) for a day of fun in the sun. You've got two choices for your day today: for zip-lining, jungle tours, and Mayan-style water sports, head to the **Xplor** eco-adventure park where you'll spend several hours in the trees and on the sand. For families with animal lovers, you can't go wrong with a trip to **Xcaret** and its varied attractions—a coral reef aquarium, butterfly pavilion, stingray adventure, waterslides, *cenotes*, and more for a day they won't soon forget. Also, the park has more than enough to do to fit in one day, so you'll likely spend the majority of your second day here. Transportation to and from your hotel is available online when you book your park tickets.

If you have time after dinner and the kids are willing, walk or take a taxi to **Quinta** so everyone can experience the magic of Playa del Carmen. Together you'll hear different languages, marvel at all of the different restaurants and street artists, and maybe head home with a few cool souvenirs for friends.

TWO DAYS OF ROMANCE

Your time in Playa is limited, so find a beachfront hotel online with the best rates for your stay. No need to go all-inclusive since you won't be spending much time at the hotel anyway. Drop your bags in your room as soon as you arrive and head straight for the beach.

Later, head north along the waterfront to 10th Street and then pick the best seat you can find at the **Lido Beach Club**. With less of a nightclub scene than some of the other beach bar options, this chill hangout with hammocks and rope swings offers a tropical, authentic vibe. Order a bucket of ice-cold Coronas, a fresh fish ceviche, and extra limes. Vacation has arrived.

Spend the afternoon enjoying the sunshine and fresh air, taking frequent dips in the ocean and applying sunscreen each time you order another round of drinks. If you're feeling ambitious, book a late afternoon paddleboarding trip with the **Aloha Paddle Club**

DINING AL FRESCO WITH CEVICHE AND A KILLER VIEW

GET SOME EXERCISE AND EXPLORE THE SIGHTS WHILE PADDLEBOARDING ALOHA PADDLE CLUB

(www.alohapaddleclub.com, 6th Street at the beach). Later that evening, head to Quinta (5th Avenue) just in time for "magic hour"—the enchanting interval just before sunset when the air cools down, the bars start to bustle, and the parade of vacationers makes its way through town.

Pick a restaurant along Quinta for a leisurely meal, then enjoy Playa's version of a pub crawl, with a stop at any bar that strikes your fancy. For a romantic setting, seek out one of Playa's many rooftop lounges like the one at the Thompson Hotel, with its view of the ocean. For late-night excitement, head to Coco Bongo and secure a spot upstairs near the DJ booth— the perfect vantage point for watching the action both on the stage and on the dance floor.

When you wake up the next morning, fix your headache with some fresh squeezed juice at 100% Natural, because there's no time to waste on day two. Sign up for a crash course in local culture in the form of a cooking class or tequila tasting. There are more than a handful of options for local cooking classes (see *Activities & Tours* on page 167 for recommendations), and the small group sizes provide a great opportunity for mingling with other couples. If cooking isn't your thing, the Tequila Academy (www.tequilatastingplaya.com) offers tequila tasting packages for couples only, or you can join others for a tequila and food pairing. Either way, you'll return home with some new dishes in your repertoire and a great story for your next dinner party.

After you've eaten, dash back to the hotel to change into your swimsuit. Your boat rental (www.getmyboat.com or see the tours listed in *Activities & Tours* on page 167) awaits. Spend your afternoon gazing at all of the amazing sea life and capture a few selfies with the turquoise water as your backdrop. And as you're headed back to Playa with the sun setting beyond the horizon, relish the magic of the moment with your partner.

For your final night in Playa del Carmen, consider lobster at the Blue Lobster downtown, or walk to the Thompson Hotel's C-Grill (at 8th Street and the beach) to sample impeccably fresh seafood and authentic Mexican cuisine with a contemporary twist. Keep the evening going at a beachfront bar, and with your toes in the sand, make plans for your next romantic adventure.

On your final vacation morning, have breakfast on 5th Avenue, then hit up the souvenir shops close to the town square. If time permits, enjoy one more visit to the beach for a final swim in the Caribbean.

clubhouse with full restrooms (including showers) and a restaurant overlooking the stunning beach.

Wah Wah (2nd Street at the beach) has plenty of beach for energetic kids to roam, while the free lounge chairs and cheap beer are big selling points for parents. You'll hear lots of English spoken here, and the kitchen serves up some quality fare. It's one of the more popular spots in town to hear some beachy live music and enjoy a fun afternoon by the shore.

Channeling 1950s Brazil, **Canibal Royale** (48th Street at the beach, www.canibalroyal.com) offers a trendy tri-level venue where you can sit by the beach, swim in the adults-only roof-top pool, and imbibe. Guests must buy food and drinks to use the facilities, but the menu—starring an outdoor stone oven perfect for pizzas—is much better than your typical local beach club fare. Refreshing juices, buckets of beer, and mixed cocktails ensure that there's a delicious beverage for every palate. There's a different DJ featured daily, making this upscale beach hangout a great place to spend the day.

Anyone looking to perfect their chillaxing should look no further than **Lido** (10th Street at the beach). Order any food or drink and your beach chair is free. Hammocks, happy citrus-colored chairs, and beach loungers all encourage lazing away the afternoon. Families easily mix with cool twenty-somethings, and the menu offers an accommodating mix of seafood, Mexican dishes, and kid-friendly fare.

Family-friendly **Kool Beach Club** (28th Street at the beach, www.koolbeachclub.com), just north of the ROYAL Playa del Carmen, offers lounge chairs and beach umbrellas for rent, plus a kids' pool, a restaurant serving seafood and Mexican food, and, of course, cold beer right on the beach. Active folks can play beach volleyball and soccer; ride WaveRunners; or go parasailing, banana-boat riding, kiteboarding, or body surfing. Massage service is provided on the beach or in a shady *cabaña*.

Located in Playa's original downtown, **Zenzi Beach Club** (10th Street and the beach, www.zenzi-playa.com) offers stylish sun beds, shades, loungers, and a cool daytime DJ-spun soundtrack. The club has a full kitchen and bar and stays open from 8 AM–2 AM most nights. Locals love their early morning breakfasts on the beach, and after 5 PM, the live music draws people in for burgers and chilling by the sea.

Indigo Beach Club (14th Street at the beach, www.indigobeach.com.mx) offers a popular breakfast buffet where you can start your day sipping green juice above a perfect white sand beach. On weekends, the club hosts differently themed events and is a popular spot for beach weddings. Though the beach is not the largest, good use is made of lounging space with parasol-shaded beds and wooden reclining chairs.

A SUNSET FACING EAST?

Facing east, the Riviera Maya isn't exactly known as the best place for witnessing a tropical sunset. However, if your beach vacation just won't be complete without watching the golden orb disappear into the horizon, there's still hope. Try these five tips for catching a sunset in the Riviera Maya.

- Take a champagne sunset cruise aboard the *Fat Cat* 41-foot catamaran in Xaac Cove near Puerto Aventuras and watch the sun sink into the Caribbean (www.fatcatsail.com).
- Walk to the point at the north end of Playa del Carmen Cove, behind the Gran Porto Real hotel, and watch the sun go down next to the lighthouse.
- Take a day trip to Isla Cozumel and stay for the sunset, then take a late ferry back to the mainland. Since the town's main beaches and town square face west, the sun sets over the ocean, just like in the postcards.
- Travel to the still charming Isla Holbox, northwest of Cancún, where you can watch the evening sun settle into the Gulf of Mexico from the island's sleepy beach (see *Other Destination near Playa del Carmen* on page 139).
- For the ultimate unobstructed sunset view, schedule a sundown skydive and look down, not up, at the setting sun (see *Activities & Tours* on page 167).

✱ Lodging

For some travelers, selecting a hotel is part of the fun of a visit to Playa del Carmen. There are more than 90,000 hotel rooms in the Riviera Maya, with many of them in the greater Playa area, and more hotels and luxury apartments changing the Playa landscape every year. Within a 2-mile radius, visitors choose from more than one hundred hotels, many of which, while not always large, would be perfectly suitable for most needs.

Accommodations range from hostels or smaller hotels with few amenities catering to budget travelers to enormous self-contained resorts with first-class facilities and services. "Concept hotels" like Live Aqua Boutique Resort or Be Playa—offering trendy accommodations (and typically nightlife) in uniquely designed surroundings—have also become an integral part of the local hospitality landscape.

Many properties provide an array of accommodations from which to choose, often offering simple beach cabañas, modern hotel rooms, and luxury villas all within the same resort. The most important criteria for any traveler to consider

are location (on the beach, on Quinta, or in town), budget, and desired atmosphere. The selections in this chapter are organized into three different price-range categories—budget ($75 or less per night), midrange ($80–$250), and luxury ($250–$1,000)—and within each category there is a wide range of choices to please a wide range of tastes. The price ranges above reflect costs for the high season, but plenty of bargains can be found in

THERE'S ALWAYS SOMETHING TO SEE ON QUINTA
CHIP RANKIN

QUINTA WALKING TOUR

Since you're already walking on Quinta anyway—enjoying the rush of locals mixed with guests of nearby hotels, day-trippers from the all-inclusive resorts along the coast, and cruise ship escapees stretching their legs—why not do a quick little walking tour for historical purposes? I promise you'll still end up back at the beach with some interesting Playa history and plenty of steps on your pedometer.

Head uphill on 10th Street to 20th Avenue and the City Hall municipal building. Turn into the main structure on your left and enter the courtyard to view a nice fountain backed by a huge colorful mural depicting life through the years in Playa del Carmen. The park across the street has a walkway with goalpost-like arches bearing the names of various towns within the Playa del Carmen municipal district, plus upright rocks displaying the state song and others showing how to count to twenty in the native Mayan language. Depending on the day, there may be a free show at the amphitheater on the northeastern corner of the park. Head back toward the beach on 10th Street and look for the Riviera Grand Casino on your left, and if it's that time of day (they open at 3 PM), stop in for a mezcal and some people watching at **Don Mezcal Bar** just down the street.

PLAYA DEL CARMEN'S ORIGINAL CHURCH IS IN THE TOWN SQUARE

After you've revived yourself with a cocktail or two, continue down 10th Street toward the beach and lighthouse that crown the beachfront condo complex. Walk down to the shore and look beyond the waves to see the hotels of northern Cozumel.

After taking in the view, walk along the beach until you hit the 12th Street party strip, or *zona doce* as I like to call it, though locals call it simply "la doce." Head uphill past the Mandala Nightclub and other patio lounges that make up Playa's trendiest district. Until recently, this area was dominated by the **Blue Parrot**. Once the king of *palapa* bars in Playa, the Blue Parrot existed for nearly 20 years as a sort of community center—with a hotel, popular lounge-chair-laden beachfront, lively meals, and nightly fire dancers that would attract tourists and locals alike to watch the spectacle. A revamped Blue Parrot reopened in 2015 in an attempt to keep pace with Playa's more upscale spots, but after the tragic shooting deaths of five people at the BPM Music Festival in January of 2017, the Blue Parrot shuttered its doors, and as of press time, it has not been replaced by another beachfront club.

If you haven't decided to give up exploring for some lounge time at the **Lido Bar** or another

REHYDRATE WITH THE FRESHEST COCONUT WATER YOU'LL EVER TASTE

A SMALL MAYAN SHRINE IS TUCKED AWAY IN AN ALLEY OFF 5TH AVENUE

THIS STATUE ON CONSTITUYENTES HONORS THE OLMEC, WHO LIVED IN THE REGION PRIOR TO THE MAYA

oceanfront beach club, head back up to Quinta between 12th and 14th Streets. Look on your right for a statue of a Mayan god with a feathered headdress. The figure marks a small passageway that leads to a nearly forgotten Mayan ruin, about the size of a Volkswagen Beetle. The site sits behind a chain-link fence, marked with a signpost from the National Institute of Archaeology, but is otherwise nondescript, with little to explain its history or any other fanfare. Even so, it's fun to try to envision how the native Mayans may have used it and interesting to see the thousands-of-years-old structures against the nearby H&M store, the bustling *Calle Corazón* shopping center, and the posh Thompson Hotel.

Keep heading north on Quinta. The big intersection ahead is Constituyentes Avenue, marked by a large Olmec (the Mayans' predecessors) head statue in the center of the traffic circle. Across the street is **Yo Amo Tacos**, which serves good tacos and great margaritas. The structures to the north of this intersection didn't exist a decade ago and now constitute the area known as the "New Playa" or the "International District," depending on who you talk to.

If you're not tired yet, keep walking north on Quinta. The primary tourist district continues for another twenty blocks or so, with dozens of restaurants, bars, and shops ripe for exploring. Turn right anywhere along this stretch and you're only two blocks from the beach. This is where Mamita's Beach Club and other popular wave-watching spots can be found.

After all that walking, I think it's time for a Corona. Or a margarita. Or a piña colada . . .

EAT AL PASTOR TACOS FREQUENTLY AND PLENTIFULLY

TEN TIPS FOR ENJOYING YOUR TRIP

Rent a car: Being mobile and independent will give you a whole new perspective on a destination. You won't need a vehicle the whole time, but get one for a few days and explore the coast on your own. Pack a cooler, a beach towel, a mask/snorkel, and a map (freebies are available at the airport and most hotels), and hit the road for Tulum, hidden beaches, and lost-in-time villages.

Learn a little Spanish: A little goes a long way, and it helps you feel like you belong. It's also a nice gesture to make to your Mexican hosts who will appreciate the effort and may be willing to take the time to teach you new words. For bonus points, learn a little Mayan. Even saying "hello" or "thank you" in the native tongue is a sure way to get smiles from locals, many of whom speak the language fluently.

Take care of yourself: Don't get dehydrated or sunburned. Drinking plenty of purified water will keep your energy level up and can prevent serious illness. Don't be stingy with the sunscreen either: a trip-ruining sunburn can happen in less than an hour if you're not used to the sun and don't protect yourself. And while you're at it, put on insect repellent before heading out at night. While others are scratching their ankles, you'll be enjoying your margarita.

Order the whole fish: Native to the region, this dish has been a favorite for hundreds of years. The fish is scaled and gutted but left whole, and it is then lightly fried and usually served with tomatoes and onions. It's a good dish to share, with each diner forking off the pieces he or she wants. Even the skin is crispy and tasty, full of healthy fish oils.

Request a mariachi song: Sure, you can hear them playing at the table across the way, but there's nothing like being surrounded by the band as they play at your very own table. It makes for great photos too, so request a song, try to sing along, and take some pictures. Tip $3–5 per song.

Check out the late-night scene: Sitting under the stars while listening to music mingling with the ocean waves is a longtime Playa tradition, and it's alive and well at the many trendy rooftop bars in town. The rooftop at the Thompson Hotel is notable for its upscale atmosphere and lounge-like vibe while the smaller and more laid back Be Playa rooftop promises a more intimate and affordable evening.

Stroll along the beach: Leave your sandals behind and take a long walk on the powdery white sand beach. If you're staying in Playacar, head south toward Xcaret and follow the beach until a rocky point bars your way, and you'll find a secluded and picturesque spot to rest before heading home. If you're staying near Quinta, head north past Mamita's Beach Club all the way to the Reef Club hotel and the deserted beach beyond (Playa Chun-Zumbul).

the area if you're willing to travel in September or October during the rainy hurricane season.

BUDGET HOTELS (AFFORDABLE, FEW FRILLS) Typically located a few blocks from the beach, between the town square and 30th Street, the properties listed here are considered clean and safe but may lack amenities that some travelers are accustomed to. Although many of these hotels still provide easy access to the beach, most will not feature swimming pools, beautiful views, or on-site restaurants, and the rooms may be without air conditioning or balconies but will make up for it in charm. Prices at many of these budget-friendly hotels are less than $75 per night, and some will also entertain discounts for long-term stays.

The eighteen-room Italian-owned **Barrio Latino Hotel** (4th Street between 10th and 15th Avenues, www.hotelbarriolatino.com) is a popular base for Europeans, student travelers, and

Visit a *cenote*: These freshwater sinkholes, unique geographical features, are a lot of fun (see *Diving, Snorkeling & Cenotes* on page 195 for more). The refreshingly cool water feels great after a day in the sun, and the virtually unlimited visibility makes you feel like you're floating in space. Many of the best spots are just a short distance from town, easily visited in an afternoon.

Snorkel or scuba dive on the Great Mayan Reef: Take the plunge for a chance to see colorful corals, tasty-looking lobsters, stern-looking barracuda, slippery eels, majestic turtles, and hundreds of tropical fish.

Get up early: Though the sun sets over Quintana Roo mainland, it rises over the Caribbean. Combined with the solitude and quiet of the early-morning hours, watching the sunrise is a spiritual and calming way to start your day. Next, head to your favorite café for a cup of coffee and some *pan dulce* (sweet pastries) as you watch the shops open up and the tourists start their rounds.

CRUISE SHIPS ARE COMMON ON THE HORIZON IN THIS PART OF THE WORLD LOCOGRINGO.COM

those who could stay at one of the more luxurious properties around town but choose the smaller inn for its character, authenticity, and family-like service. Just a block and a half from Quinta, the hotel provides quick access to the town's restaurants and nightlife. Rooms are secure and clean with private bathrooms, ceiling fans, Wi-Fi, and air conditioning. Many even offer a hammock on the patio, perfect for afternoon siestas. The proprietors are also able to book most of the same tours that larger tour agencies offer but return their sales commission to their guests, resulting in a nice discount.

A happy holdover from old school Playa, the friendly, family-run, twelve-room **Pension San Juan** (between 6th and 8th Streets, www.pensionsanjuan .com) is located right on Quinta. On a terrace overlooking the avenue, an incredibly charming outdoor kitchen is available for guest use. The experience is akin to dining in your own private café and one that conjures up the Quinta of the late '90s.

THE PENSION SAN JUAN IS A BUDGET-MINDED HOTEL ON 5TH AVENUE

proximity to the active 12th Street party zone, this hotel couldn't be described as sleepy or subdued, but it does evoke a simpler time. Rooms are modest but modern with air conditioning and ceiling fans, and the beachfront Disco Bar serves draft beer and snacks at a wooden counter with bar stools near the pool.

With twenty-three air-conditioned rooms, a common terrace, a small pool, and a rooftop sundeck, the three-story **Ko'ox Banana Hotel** (Quinta at 32nd Street, www.kooxhotels.com) has the feel of a large and friendly home. Set in the middle of the action, it's a few blocks from Kool and Mamita's beach clubs and was formerly known simply as Hotel Banana.

With shaded hammocks set amidst a lagoon-like sunken garden and waterfall, the adults-only **Luna Blue Hotel & Gardens** (26th Street between Quinta and 10th Avenue, www.lunabluehotel.com) elicits a lost in time quality not easily replicated in a modern resort destination. The hotel serves as a good example of what used to be Playa's standard a short 15 years ago.

Opened in 1984, **La Rana Cansada** (10th Street between Quinta and 10th Avenue, www.ranacansada.com) is one of Playa's oldest and most beloved hotels. Loyal guests return year after year for the consistently comfortable colonial-style accommodations, central location, authentic beach-town ambiance, and friendly service from the Swedish hosts and Mayan staff. Just a couple of blocks from the beach and a half-block from Quinta, the hotel has fifteen modest, individually-designed rooms (upgrades with air conditioning are available), a community kitchen, and a lounge area.

There's always something happening at **Siesta Fiesta** (Quinta between 8th and 10th Streets, www.siestafiestahotelplaya .com), a hot spot in the middle of Playa's busy pedestrian walkway, which could be viewed as either a good or bad thing. Fah Restaurant and Bar in the cozy courtyard

Located in the bustling northern end of Quinta, the independently owned, adults-only **Casa Ticul Hotel** (Quinta between 38th and 40th Streets, www .casaticul.com) has been delighting guests for a decade. Despite the fact that this inn takes its name from an old Yucatán city south of Merida known for clay pottery and leather shoes, the environs here are quite well-appointed. The cozy lobby calls to mind a stylish home in early twentieth-century Europe, and the quaint courtyard, small pool, and sundeck look especially charming after the sun goes down. Thoroughly modern, the twenty rooms feature dark wood furnishings, luxury bedding with pillow-top mattresses, and bathrooms with rain showers. A great stretch of beach is 2.5 blocks away.

One of the original beach hotels in Playa, the modest thirty-eight-room colonial-style **Costa del Mar** (1st Avenue between 10th and 12th Streets, www.hotelcostadelmar.com) feels like the Playa of a bygone era. Given its

TOP TEN ADULTS-ONLY RESORTS

Whether you're escaping your own kids or simply looking for an unobtrusive spot to spend your precious vacation days, any one of these adults-only resorts will ensure a relaxing and romantic getaway.

1. Royal Hideaway Playacar
2. Paradisus Playa del Carmen La Perla
3. The ROYAL Playa del Carmen
4. Iberostar Grand Hotel Paraiso
5. Platinum Yucatán Princess
6. Viceroy Riviera Maya
7. Live Aqua Boutique Resort
8. Valentin Imperial Maya
9. Secrets Maroma Beach Cancún
10. Live Aqua Cancún

Xtudio Comfort Hotel (Quinta between 4th and 6th Streets, www.xperiencehotelsresorts.com) provides ten clean, comfortable, stylish rooms and friendly staff service at an affordable price. Rooms are ample, and the décor is plain but modern. Guests have privileges at the rooftop deck at Xtudio's sister property, Hotel Illusion.

The family-owned twenty-nine-room **Maya Bric Hotel** (Quinta between 8th and 10th Streets, www.mayabric.com) earned its Playa cred as a haven for divers. Today, under new management, its focus is affordability, simplicity, and comfort, offering air-conditioned rooms, small fridges, and balconies that overlook the pool and tropical gardens.

A decade-long favorite for budget travelers, **Hotel Cielo** (4th Street between Quinta and 10th Avenue, www.hotelcielo.com) offers a great location only a block from the beach and boasts traditional architecture and Mexican décor. Standard rooms have air conditioning, and the family-style quarters for four provide ocean-view balconies, beach towels, and plenty of space.

features several hours of live music each night and a large-screen TV for live sporting events and recorded concerts. Vacation camaraderie is especially strong here, making it a great spot to meet and socialize with other travelers.

CONSTRUCTION WALLS ARE A COMMON SIGHT ALONG QUINTA AS OLD HOTELS AND STOREFRONTS MAKE WAY FOR THE NEW CHIP RANKIN

MANY OF THE GUESTS AT THE PLAYA MAYA HOTEL VISIT EACH YEAR PLAYA MAYA HOTEL

With its stucco walls, *palapa* roof, shared al fresco kitchen, and stone walkways, **Hotel LunaSol** (4th Street between 15th and 20th Avenues, www.lunasolhotel.com) charms from the moment you see it. Each of the sixteen air-conditioned rooms overlooks the inviting pool or lush courtyards, comes equipped with a small fridge, and offers a balcony with a view of the green space below.

Also from Xperience Hotels and Resorts, **Hacienda Paradise** (10th Avenue between 20th and 22nd Streets, www.xperiencehotelsresorts.com) boasts thirty-three rooms filled with hardwood furniture typical of traditional Spanish-style haciendas. Patios or balconies look out onto the garden and swimming pool. A favorite hotel among travelers seeking style and comfort at a favorable price, the hotel is also home to the restaurant Cosa Nostra and a spa. Rooms are equipped with Wi-Fi, cable TV, ceiling fans, and safes that can easily hold a laptop.

The twenty-room **Playa Maya Hotel** (on the beach between 6th Street and 8th Street, www.playamaya.com) can be reached solely from the beach, making it one of the few places in town where you get to feel the sand each time you come and go. The beachfront is the main attraction; it's one of the best in the area—with sandy water access, calm waves, and plenty of people-watching. Although the Playa Maya lists prices higher than other hotels in this section, its rooms haven't been updated since the first edition of this book. Therefore, the hotel is recommended only for its location, history, and simple charm, and to those who are willing and able to negotiate a reduced rate.

MIDRANGE HOTELS (BOUTIQUE & LOCAL EXPERIENCES) Located on or near Quinta, or even on the beach, these hotels hit the sweet spot for most travelers to Playa del Carmen—with prices ranging from $80 for a standard hotel to $250 for a property with upgraded amenities and a premier location (whether on Quinta or the beach). The options in this section are especially popular among travelers who are looking for boutique accommodations with some charm and for those who would rather explore Playa than remain secluded in their all-inclusive.

Illusion Boutique Hotel (8th Street between Quinta and the beach, www.xperiencehotelsresorts.com) from Xperience Hotels offers forty-one spacious guest rooms featuring marble floors and

IT MAY BE PARADISE, BUT IT'S STILL THE JUNGLE

Even though Playa del Carmen and the Riviera Maya are wonderful beach vacation destinations, these areas are still relatively undeveloped and exist in close proximity to the jungle. Set your expectations accordingly.

You should also remember that there are hassles and frustrations inherent to any travel situation. You're on vacation to have fun and celebrate life, so try not to let the little challenges you encounter bother you.

If a chicken walks into your beachfront restaurant and pecks at your crumbs, don't get mad—take a picture. If a gecko streaks across the wall of your hotel room, don't call the front desk—give him a name and consider him your pet. If your shower runs out of hot water, don't complain to the concierge—a cold sprinkle is good for your sunburn. And most importantly, if you find yourself at odds with your travel partner, it's time to hit the nearest bar, order a margarita, feel the warm breeze, and remember why you came here in the first place.

bathrooms adorned with precious ticul stone mined from the region. All rooms either overlook a central courtyard or the Caribbean Sea itself, just a half-block away.

Even though it's right on Quinta, **Hotel Lunata** (Quinta between 6th and 8th Streets, www.lunata.com) seems secluded once you pass through its narrow entrance, which introduces an air of privacy not found in other downtown hotels. Designed by architect Angel Isles, the décor is contemporary hacienda style—archways, earth tones and blues, river stones, dark woods, iron, and tile. With only ten rooms, the hotel has the feeling of an old-style guesthouse, and each chamber—including a four-person junior suite with a fridge and garden-view terrace—has its own distinct appeal.

Eclectic and artsy, the eighteen-room **Eclipse Hotel** (1st Avenue between 12th and 14th Streets, www.hoteleclipse .com) is something of a hodgepodge. A rustically tropical exterior gives way to rooms featuring modern décor (except for the two-story Robinson Crusoe–themed suite, which is its own thing). The courtyard features large palm trees, hammocks, and gardens, and the hotel is a favorite among traveling artists, young couples, and others who enjoy eclectic accommodations. Located just around the corner from the party on 12th Street,

the hotel makes a great home base for revelers but may be too loud for many travelers. Guests have access to Mamita's Beach Club nearby.

Highly rated by its guests, **Magic Blue Boutique Hotel** (10th Avenue between 10th and 12th Streets, www .hotelmagicblue.com) offers a modern tropical atmosphere that leans heavily

ONE OF THE MOST PHOTOGRAPHED PLACES IN PLAYA DEL CARMEN IS JUST OUTSIDE HACIENDA TEQUILA

on deeply-stained hardwoods rather than the stucco and concrete so frequently used in the region. The hotel's forty-four rooms and one master suite surround a large grassy area, swimming pool, and bar, offering up a more relaxed mood than many of the more tightly-packed properties in downtown Playa.

On a corner, just a block off Quinta, the fifty-one-room **La Tortuga Hotel & Spa** (10th Avenue and 14th Street, www .hotellatortugaspa.com) offers chic rooms and a private, upscale ambience. From the landscaping to the furnishings, this tropical hideaway provides the perfect combination of jungle atmosphere and elegance. The winding, meandering pool provides a handful of rooms with easy patio swim-up access.

The adults-only **Be Playa Hotel** (26th Street between Quinta and 10th Avenue, www.beplaya.com) provides its guest with sleek, straightforward, and stylish quarters, most of which include a large bathtub. The rooftop bar offers a pool, dining area, and—as one might anticipate—stunning Caribbean views. Be Playa is comparable to Playa Soho with regard to quality, location, look, and lifestyle.

Families seeking the vacation-making combo of fantastic beach access coupled with all the comforts of home tend to love Playa's **El Taj Oceanfront & Beachside Condos** (1st Avenue at 14th

YOUR HOME AWAY FROM HOME AT BE PLAYA HOTEL
BE PLAYA HOTEL

Street, www.eltaj.com). Bedroom suite options for one to four people include full kitchens, and guests have access to dining areas, a beachside infinity pool, and the Indigo Beach Club.

Slick and fashionable, **Suites Quinto Sol** (Quinta at 28th Street, www .suitesquintosol.com) is a complete—from the studs—modern rebuild of the former Mediterranean/Mexican hacienda-style hotel of the same name. Perched in the heart of Quinta's international section, this newly-renovated condominium hotel opened in 2016 and offers multiple room configurations with full kitchens, clean, contemporary design, and a location along one of Quinta's most elegant stretches.

With a similar Miami Beach-esque design, **The Palm at Playa** (8th Street between Quinta and 10th Avenue, www.thepalmatplaya.com) comprises sixty-nine rooms encircling a handsome courtyard filled with palm trees. Rooms are modern and luxurious. The Roof Club at the Palm additionally boasts one of the more expansive views of town and Cozumel, as well as a pool and lounge open day and night.

The Soho Playa Hotel (10th Avenue and 24th Street, www.sohoplayahotel .com) is a trendy boutique hotel with a sleek, modern tropical approach that suits Playa perfectly but would also feel right at home in Buenos Aires, Ibiza, or Miami. In addition to comfortable rooms and a rooftop pool and bar, Soho Playa features a unique artist-in-residence program and displays works by various local artists throughout the year. Guest rooms are straightforwardly inviting with comfy beds, glass-walled showers, and ample safes that can hold multiple laptops. Discounts are available at Evolve Gym down the street, which boasts a bevy of fit locals getting their sweat on.

Charming, romantic, and intimate, **Acanto Boutique Hotel** (16th Street between 1st and 5th Streets, www .acantohotels.com) is situated smack-dab in the middle of Playa, on a pleasant

THE OPEN AND MODERN LOBBY AT THE PLAYA SOHO CHIP RANKIN

side street around the corner from Quinta and one block from the beach. The hotel offers easy access to the original heart of downtown and to Quinta's stretch north of Constituyentes Avenue. Although the hotel is only a couple of blocks away from the bustling nightlife of 12th Street, the party noise abates as you turn the corner onto the side street. One-, two-, and three-bedroom condos offer convenience for families alongside all of the typical luxuries of other hotels. Acanto enforces a strict "no guests" policy, so singles expecting to make new friends and bring them back to their nearby digs should book elsewhere.

Simple, fresh, and elegant, the bed and breakfast **Hotel La Semilla** (38th Street between 5th Avenue and the beach, www.hotellasemilla.com) features nine carefully curated guest rooms furnished from the spoils of Mexico's many formerly grand haciendas. Modern comfort melds with a "rough luxe" décor that seems completely unique within Playa while also managing to fit right in. Amenities are limited to the inn's plush rooms, a covered outdoor kitchen and dining room overlooking the jungle, and a stunning garden

courtyard. You'll think you're a guest at someone's meticulously curated home, but you won't be quite sure what century you're in.

Lit up like a bright blue beacon at night, the beachfront **Carmen Hotel** (8th Street at the beach, www.carmenhotel .com) resembles a docked cruise ship. With swirling architectural lines and modern décor, this thirty-seven room adults-only hotel attracts a fun-loving crowd with its rooftop deck, hip amenities, and ocean views.

One of Playa's tallest hotels, the literally over-the-top **Hotel Reina Roja** (20th Street between Quinta and 10th Avenue, www.reinarojahotel.com), is an eye-catching union of dark hardwoods, metal cages, and lush green vines, the whole of which glows red by night. Approaching visitors will spot this marvel from a block away. Mexican-owned, the hotel evokes Amsterdam's red-light district—scantily clad mannequins adorn the balconies and lobby—and the hotel's crimson glow extends to its guest rooms. A party hotel for party people, this property features a large bar and a massive rooftop bar with city views and

THE ROOMS AND SUITES AT ACANTO BOUTIQUE CONDO HOTEL SURROUND A PEACEFUL COURTYARD STEPS AWAY FROM THE HEART OF QUINTA ACANTO BOUTIQUE CONDO HOTEL

THE ADULTS-ONLY CARMEN HOTEL IS RIGHT ON THE BEACH
AND JUST MINUTES FROM QUINTA   CHIP RANKIN

a swimming pool. Five themed rooms—
including the "After Hours Room" with
DJ booth, disco lights, dance floor, and
outdoor smoking area—are available for
the extra-indulgent. Not exactly a cozy
place, but these quarters rate high in
gimmick value.

Villas Sacbe (1st Avenue between 12th
and 14th Streets, www.villasacbe.com)
offers privately owned one- and two-bed-
room condos, each with its own unique,
tony décor. The complex has a narrow,
meandering pool and Jacuzzi, and is a
great place to stay for those seeking luxury in close proximity to the *Zona Doce*.

EXPENSIVE HOTELS (EXCLUSIVE &
LUXURY) The best of the best, these
hotels and resorts cater to international
travelers accustomed to the finer things.
Most of the larger properties have multiple swimming pools, restaurants, bars,
spas, kids' clubs, wedding services, and
are designed to wow with their all-inclusive amenities. The smaller concept
hotels are a bit lighter on the on-site
extras, but high on style and status. All
will typically boast spacious and luxurious rooms, well-designed bathrooms,
guest balconies, and on-site restaurants,
and many will likewise supply some of
the best beach access in Playa. Room
rates range from $250 per night for a
highly-rated hotel to $500 per night at a
top-of-the-line all-inclusive resort. Vacationers willing to splurge on the unforgettable can find multi-room suites
above the beach for more than $1,000 per
night.

Rising confidently above Quinta
and the remade *Calle Corazón*, the
impressive and decadent **Thompson
Playa del Carmen** (entrance on 12th
Street between Quinta and 10th Avenue, www.thompsonhotels.com) has
the highest profile in modern Playa—
literally and figuratively. Delivering
one-of-a-kind panoramic views over
Quinta and the Caribbean Sea beyond,
this luxury boutique occupies the top
three floors of a large, five-story cres-
cent-shaped building that extends from
12th to 14th Street. At ground level, the
crescent hugs *Calle Corazón*, a pedestrian offshoot of Quinta lined with
retail shops and restaurants, which
connects with the main thoroughfare at
both corners.

Situated above the charming, if rather
commercial, side street, most of the
hotel's ninety-two rooms and suites look
out over Playa and the sea from private
terraces with plunge pools or daybeds.
All rooms are opulently appointed, with
mid-century modern décor, overhead
rain showers, expansive bathrooms, and
sateen-woven bed linens. Above them,
on the fifth level, you'll find the hotel's
raison d'être. Unlike anything else in
Playa, the 30,000-square-foot lounging, dining, and entertainment space
provides unmatched views of the town
below and the sea beyond. Here's where
you'll find the rooftop infinity pool,

EVERYTHING AT THE THOMPSON HOTEL (INCLUDING THEIR SWIM-UP BAR) IS MODERN AND COOL THOMPSON HOTEL

private cabanas, an open-air restaurant and lounge, and no lack of space to lie in the sun.

With its front door opening onto 12th Street, a location just steps away from Coco Bongo, and an open-air rooftop nightclub, the Thompson is ideal for people who want to be in the heart of the action, or for those with a fear of missing out and a budget to accommodate it. Although rooms are well insulated, expect to overhear revelry well into the night. Rooms on the northern end of the hotel, toward 14th Street, are typically quieter.

For those looking for Thompson's access and style but with more beach and quiet, the low-rise sister property **Thompson Beach House** (8th Street and the beach, www.thompsonhotels.com) provides a more intimate twenty-seven-room affair with quarters and terraces opening out over a pool and direct access to the beach and oceanfront lounge. The hotel's size also makes it a good fit for destination weddings, corporate retreats, family milestone celebrations, and other special events.

All Thompson facilities are available to guests of both properties, and all-inclusive and European plan options are available.

An entirely different vacation experience can be found at **Grand Hyatt Playa del Carmen Resort** (entrance at 1st Avenue and 26th Street, www .grandhyatt.com). From the street, the massive beachfront resort is mostly concealed behind neighboring storefronts and hotels. But it wows you once you encounter its true scope. Greeted by high stone walls and hardwoods, guests pass through the entrance into a modern lobby evoking design elements typical of the Yucatán coast and present-day Mexico City. The dark wooden ceiling above

THE ROOFTOP DECK IS ONE OF THE SEE AND BE SEEN SPOTS IN TOWN CHIP RANKIN

the entryway extends toward the ocean like a pier, protecting both the open-air lobby and an undulating walkway that winds down to the pool and the beach beyond. On either side of the promenade are mangrove gardens, preserved during the hotel's construction and a rare sight within Playa proper.

Named *El Paseo*, the walkway is a nod to nearby Quinta, housing the hotel's retail and souvenir shop, coffee counter, dessert café, and poolside bar along the route. Like a bridge hovering above the open view to the beach is the hotel's fifth floor, with rooms and suites directly facing the sea.

The hotel's 314 rooms and 36 suites (some of which include swim-up access) are oriented around the perimeter of the massive property and overlook the mangrove garden and ocean. The hotel's fifth floor hovers above the pool area like a bridge, with rooms and suites directly facing the sea and featuring open views of the beach. Crisp and modern, all quarters feature furnished balconies, walk-in rain showers, ample bathrooms, and plenty of in-room amenities. The hotel's infinity pool sits one floor above the property's 460-foot stretch of white sand beach, with The ROYAL Playa del Carmen off to the south and the popular Coralina, Kool, and Mamita's beach clubs immediately to the north.

Grand Hyatt is ideal for travelers looking for a thoroughly comfortable resort experience as well as direct access to the heart of Playa del Carmen and Quinta just beyond the door. Everything in central Playa is within easy walking distance or a quick cab ride, yet the hotel

and its many rooms are nevertheless far enough removed to ensure a quiet night's sleep.

A few blocks away, on the other side of the Grand Hyatt, is the upscale, adults-only, all-inclusive **The ROYAL Playa del Carmen** (Constituyentes between 1st Avenue and the beach, www.realresorts .com). With 518 rooms and a grand portico reminiscent of Cancún, or perhaps even Las Vegas, this elder statesman remains the largest resort within the heart of Playa del Carmen.

The ROYAL's is one of the better beaches in the area—the sand here is exceptional and the water is calm. Perhaps unsurprisingly, it's the site of many weddings, which make for a fun distraction for the sun-worshippers who perennially populate the waterfront area. Beyond its fantastic beach, the ROYAL boasts six restaurants, four bars, a massive pool, an ultra-luxe day spa, a *temazcal* sweat lodge, and a full fitness center that offers daily spinning and Pilates classes. The hotel was also among the first resorts in the region to offer online check-in 24 hours before arrival, permitting guests to select their rooms from available options the day before they arrive.

Across the street—and curiously constructed on the former site of Playa's original nudist beach—sits the family-friendly, all-inclusive, 287-room **Panama Jack Resorts Gran Porto Real Playa del Carmen** (Constituyentes Avenue at the beach, www.playaresorts.com), which was the first large-scale hotel built along the town's tourist strip instead of in Playacar. The ROYAL's sister resort, Gran Porto Real sports a Mediterranean-esque exterior and overlooks a waveless cove at the southern end of Playa's central beach.

Inside the resort, however, some changes have been afoot (or shall we say "a hat"?). In 2017, the property was rebranded to become one of the first two Panama Jack Resorts. Still welcoming all ages, the remodeled interior now reflects a more laidback sensibility, combining a ambiance authentic to the Yucatán with a mood typical of surf and seaside culture across Central America, California, and the Caribbean.

There are five restaurants, four bars, a nice pool, a car rental desk, a day spa, and a kids' club. Guest favorites include the 24-Hour Room that's always stocked with snacks, drinks, and even bottles of booze, and the resort's thatched-roof beach bar, complete with rope-swing barstools and a panoramic view of the main bay. This is also one of the very few hotels in the area situated so as to provide a view of the sunset over the ocean.

The oceanfront **Mahékal Beach Resort** (38th Street and Quinta, www .mahekalplaya.com) is laid out like an old Mayan village, with low-rise, thatched-roof *cabañas* making up the preponderance of its lodging quarters. One of the earliest resorts constructed in the area and renovated for a new concept, Mahékal has retained its local charm while keeping its facilities up-to-date. Five restaurants, a signature spa, a painting room, and three enormous pools help pepper the resort's authentic grounds with luxurious amenities, making it a favorite of brides and grooms in search of a beachfront wedding. As one of the final properties on the northern edge of town, this nearly remote resort provides a sense of privacy and luxury.

If you want to stay technically within Playa's city limits but still experience the full escapism of a pampering all-inclusive, **Paradisus Playa del Carmen** (Quinta between 108th and 110th Streets, www.paradisus.com) offers a wholly insulated escape, with two separate resorts for adults and for families. The two facilities are connected by means of a few overlapping centrally-located amenities, but while adults staying at either resort are welcome to cross over the threshold whenever they please, kids are restricted to the family resort at all times. This arrangement makes for a welcome solution for multi-generational families and groups whose members want to spend time together but differ on accommodation preferences. Food, drink, and entertainment are all included throughout the resort.

The family-oriented, 510-room **Paradisus La Esmeralda** features a massive 57,000-square-foot pool adorned with slides—one from a pirate ship and another from a hippo's mouth—as well as a kids' club and family activities and lessons. Half of the resort's shared restaurants are on the family-oriented side, including its vast buffets as well as its sit-down restaurants serving traditional Mexican and Mediterranean specialties.

Paradisus La Perla, the adults-only resort, has 394 suites and is predictably more serene than its frenetic family-oriented sibling. Swim-up bars within its lavish, sleek pool are particularly popular here. All amenities, bars, clubs, and restaurants on this side of the resort are designated solely for adults, including the resort's signature restaurant Passion, created by Michelin-starred Chef Martin Berasategui of Spain (unlike all other restaurants and bars, dinner at Passion requires an additional fee).

All rooms and suites are well-appointed with a fresh, contemporary décor. Options include swim-up terraces. The white sand beach, also more or less divided between families and adults, is a naturally stunning and popular spot for weddings. Tour desks can help plan excursions and day trips, and it's easy to get a cab into town if you want to explore old school Playa.

On the opposite end of the all-inclusive spectrum, the intimate, strictly adult **Live Aqua Boutique Resort** (1st

THE ROOFTOP POOL AND LOUNGE AT LIVE AQUA LIVE AQUA BOUTIQUE RESORT

Avenue between 30th and 32nd Streets, www.liveaqua.com) occupies prime real estate above Quinta. Modern lines, sultry textures, soothing earth tones, intricate mosaic details, artistic splashes, and quirky details (such as an old-school VW Bug sliced in two and adorned with shells) distinguish the sixty-room hotel from the busy bustle outside its large open-air courtyard. Although the main entrance is on tranquil 1st Avenue, another entrance offers direct access to the crux of the action within Quinta's International Zone.

The expansive rooftop terrace and pool impresses with views of both the sea and the city. The roof is also home to one of the most photogenic bars in Playa (covered with mismatched tiles that look even more beautiful together than they do individually) as well as a deck sporting daybeds and an enclosed, air-conditioned gym.

Like most of Playa's higher-end properties, rooms are handsomely modern and inviting, with a few light regional touches. Although the hotel is not on the beach, it does provide discounted access to the Mamita's and Kool beach clubs for all-inclusive guests and is a perfect fit for someone who desires contemporary elegance within a few steps of one of Playa's most stylish intersections. Although the hotel focuses on all-inclusive guests, European plan packages are often available.

✳ Where to Eat

Playa del Carmen is home to an incredibly wide variety of cuisines and dining establishments. From hole-in-the-wall taco shacks offering complete meals for less than $5 and traditional Mexican steakhouses serving fine cuts of Angus beef and live lobster to stylish

THE OPEN AIR LOBBY BALANCES MODERN DESIGN WITH RAW, NATURAL ELEMENTS

lounge-style restaurants serving Mediterranean and international cuisine, Playa is sure to please every palate.

Restaurants have a tendency to come and go in Playa, especially on the very busy and popular Quinta, where property owners routinely raise their rents. Even with all this change, however, much remains the same, and many old favorites have endured. In truth, it's hard to go wrong dining out in Playa and strolling down Quinta. In fact, walking around and considering the options just might become one of your favorite evening rituals.

Breakfasts are normally inexpensive, with many restaurants posting their specials on a chalkboard out front. Choices include traditional Mexican dishes such as *pan dulce* (sweet pastries), *huevos rancheros* (ranch-style eggs), and *huevos Mexicanos* (Mexican-style eggs), but you'll also find American favorites like pancakes, omelets, steak and eggs, or bagels and lox, as well as European options such as croissants and crêpes.

Lunch is generally quite casual, as many travelers choose to eat fresh

AVOID WALKING IN CIRCLES

The best way to plan your meals for the day is to have a loose idea of what and where you'd like to eat since there are now so many options in town. Download the Maps.me app for a fully operational map to your destination which you can access without having to use up your data or order a beer at a random place just for some Wi-Fi. It will also help to know the name of the place where you plan to go, but Maps.me (or any other offline map you download) will help with street-by-street directions to restaurants or attractions you're trying to find around Playa del Carmen.

seafood, sandwiches, or burgers on the beach or next to their hotel pool. Most restaurants in town, however, are also open for lunch, with happy-hour specials starting early and plenty of seating available at the sidewalk restaurants along Quinta.

Once the sun goes down and the stars come out, the lights of the restaurants,

NOT SURE WHAT TO EAT? STROLL DOWN QUINTA FOR SOME INSPIRATION RICARDO VAGG

bars, and shops of Playa's main street start to twinkle, and candlelight glows from many eateries. The town begins to feel a bit like an international bazaar, with restaurants competing for your business, hawking their specials, offering free drinks with a meal purchase, and tempting diners with live music, wafting smells, and pleasant hostesses.

For some, choosing where to eat is half the fun, and often visitors will make several laps to check out the night's offerings and take in the scene. Many restaurants assemble sample entrées and display them next to their menus, showcasing the exact size of their plump steaks, lobster tails, giant shrimp, or fish fillets. Depending on what you're in the mood for, each block will have several options to choose from. You can expect to find restaurants along Quinta from 12th Street all the way through 32nd Street.

If you're not sure what you'd like to eat or if you're with a group of travelers with varied tastes, you're in luck, as many restaurants have extensive menus with an array of alternatives spanning from tacos to pasta, from fish to steak, and from pizza to burgers. The average dinner bill at an inexpensive restaurant is less than $8 per person. Costs for a meal at a moderately priced restaurant range from $8–$20. Expensive restaurants offer meals starting at $21.

All of the locations in the *Budget Dining* section are casual eateries catering to locals and value-minded travelers in the know. They're good places to sample the regional fare and use your Spanish. Many don't accept credit cards and may have restrooms that aren't up to the cleanliness standards of some travelers. Even so, they're all regulated by the health department and serve only purified ice and water.

BUDGET DINING A top pick among locals and ex-pats, the *palapa*-shaded **La Vagabunda** (Quinta between 24th and

GRAB A CHEAP BITE AT LA VAGABUNDA

PESO-PINCHING ACTIVITIES

Traveling on a budget? Try these free and fun activities:

- Snorkel the protected cove at Akumal Bay and catch a glimpse of stingrays and sea turtles lurking in the shallows.
- Visit the Xaman-Ha ruins, just south of the Playacar Palace Hotel (see *The Riviera Maya— South of Playa del Carmen* on page 89).
- Head to the beach and build a sandcastle in the shape of the great pyramid at Chichén Itzá.
- Get up early to watch the sun rise over the Caribbean. Some people enjoy this experience even more than watching a sunset.
- If you're venturing out in the early morning, challenge yourself to a bit of a hike along Quinta. Keep heading north until about 106th street, and you'll find the Punta Esmeralda public beach. Visit on a weekday, and you'll likely have this natural wonder—where the cold waters of a *cenote* meet the sea—all to yourself.
- Take advantage of the free appetizer/drink coupons furnished by many restaurants along Quinta in Playa del Carmen. Then sit and enjoy the people-watching along this bustling street.
- Hang out in the renovated Parque Fundadores in the heart of town, where you can marvel at the amazing art (see *History* on page 210), let the kids blow off steam at the playscape, or enjoy one of the many cultural performances held here regularly.
- Buy your coworkers a fun trinket from Mexico at the Sunday flea market on 54th Street between Avenues 10 and 30. Or just enjoy perusing the market. After all, browsing is always free.

26th Streets, www.vagabundaplaya.com) and its sister location La Vagabunda Centro (Quinta between 4th and 6th Streets) serves traditional American and Mexican breakfasts, crêpes, omelets, pastas, and cappuccino.

Popular with locals and tourists alike since 2011, **Kaxapa Factory** (10th Street at the Plaza 28 de Julio, www.kaxapa factory.com) is a small spot near City Hall serving up affordable, homemade Venezuelan fare. With just nine tables and a small patio, it's easy to take a peek at other patrons' plates to help determine your order. Favorite entrées include sweet corn pancakes called *cachapa*; deep fried plantains; *arepas* filled with manchego cheese; and a variety of meats, empanadas, and freshly squeezed juices. Care and attention are given to gluten-free and vegetarian diners.

Early risers will delight in the options available at **Madrez Café** (Quinta at 8th Street). This teeny-tiny sidewalk café across the street from the Frida Kahlo Museum is especially packed at brunch, so plan accordingly if you want one of their heavenly waffles. Granola and yogurt and hearty bagel sandwiches are also offered to go, so don't let the small dining area keep you from stopping by.

For a taste of Playa from way, way back, head to **La Tarraya** (2nd Street and the beach, www.captaintarraya.com), which has been welcoming guests to the same beachfront establishment since 1968. The open-air, family-oriented restaurant serves up fresh seafood, Mexican dishes, and cold beer. Tables spill out onto the sand, where La Tarraya also manages a small beach club. Everything is good and inexpensive with no frills. Curiously, kid-appropriate coloring books featuring local history lessons and the adventures of colorful Captain Tarraya (evidently based on the owner) are available online in English and Spanish at the restaurant's website.

Ah Carbón! (22nd Street at Quinta) is another solid option for an authentic and inexpensive taco experience in Playa. Build-your-own tacos, thin grilled steaks, and a handful of vegetarian offerings are all tasty, but don't miss the al pastor,

TOP TACO SPOTS

There are as many tacos in Playa as there are bikinis, but these four eateries are must-tries while you're in town. They're popular, modestly priced, and make for a totally addictive handheld meal.

El Fogón (30th Avenue between 4th and 6th Streets) serves a mixed-grill plate (*parrillada mixta*) big enough to serve three people, but the al pastor and chorizo tacos are hard to stop eating in the al fresco setting. This is arguably the most visited taco place in town, so expect a wait at peak mealtimes.

Grab the bull by the horns at Don Sirloin (Constituyentes at 25th Avenue), where the al pastor is shaved to order, the *queso fundido* (melted cheese) is gooey and divine, and the sirloin is grilled to perfection. Draft beer and cocktails round out the meal. Cash only.

Just like the busy taco stands near where the locals live, the popular Yo Amo Tacos (Constituyentes at Quinta), Spanish for "I Love Tacos," serves fresh, hot tacos al pastor (cut right from the fire), beef tacos, and cheese tacos. The combos and happy hour make for a great value if you have a big group to feed.

Expect the menu at Tacontenedor (Constituyentes between Quinta and 10th Avenue) to hold its own against the hip and thoughtful design (tacos are served from a shipping container). Dishes highlight fresh seafood and include ceviche, seafood burgers, and specialty tacos like lobster and fish al pastor. An amazing cocktail menu—don't miss out on the potent Coco Loco served in a coconut.

ENJOY THE VIEW AT YO AMO TACOS

which you can order on everything from nachos to baked potatoes.

Brochetas (28th Street and the beach, www.brochetas.mx) serves up delicious skewers of steak, chicken, and seafood at reasonable prices. Located across from Mamita's Beach Club.

Cheap eats in Mexico don't have the same dearth of nutritional value as American "fast food," so count on the Big Gulp–sized smoothies at the bright and colorful **Nativo** (30th Avenue between 20th and 22nd Streets) to fix your tequila headache. The rest of the menu has a similar healthy, fresh focus with vegetable-laden entrées, crêpes, fish tacos, enchiladas, and hearty soups. A second smaller location is just a block down the street.

Los Hijos de la Tostada (Quinta between 38th and 40th Streets) is a youthful sidewalk spot that concentrates on seafood, local beers, and a lively atmosphere. Obviously, the tostadas are the star of the show—crispy flat tortillas topped with heaping mounds of either hot or cold seafood combinations. Other menu highlights include a tuna burger lightly seared with crispy onion rings, ceviche, and *aguachiles* on top.

If you're tired of tacos, slices start at $1.50 at **Pizza Pazza** (Quinta at 14th Street; 10th Avenue between 8th and 10th Streets), and combos that include a drink are also available. Open late, this place is a favorite for satisfying after-party munchies.

MEXICAN & MAYAN **Micaela's** (Quinta at 28th Street) provides some prime people-watching opportunities and a warm and inviting atmosphere that often makes diners want to linger and soak it all in. Authentic Mexican cuisine, tableside guacamole, and tourist-friendly breakfasts top the menu. Diners are frequently drawn to the combination of traditional and whimsical décor, but it's the food that brings them back a second time. Seating is available indoors in the glass-walled and deliciously

DRINK SOMETHING THAT'S ACTUALLY GOOD FOR YOU AT NATIVO

air-conditioned dining room or outside on the pedestrian walkway.

Since opening in 2014, **Axiote Cocina de Mexico** (34th Street between 5th and 10th Avenues, www.axiote.rest) has been pleasing diners with tasty takes on Mayan and Mexican dishes in an intimate space lined with hardwoods and featuring a cool bar and open kitchen. At night, the restaurant's signature red hue glimmers into the street, enticing passersby. Specialties include duck tacos with three chiles, *cochinita pibil* tacos, and octopus- and shrimp-stuffed chiles. The bar also serves specialty cocktails made from mezcal, rum, and other popular fixings.

Both locations of **Mi Pueblo** (Quinta and 8th Street, www.grupoazotea.com) serve up fresh and tasty Mexican fare that doesn't intimidate. The newer northern location is particularly spacious with a large outdoor patio surrounded by overgrown jungle.

La Cueva del Chango (38th Street between Quinta and the beach, www .lacuevadelchango.com), or the "Monkey Cave," is an eccentric spot that manages to come across as rustic, funky, and romantic all at the same time. Candlelit tables populate a jungle-like atmosphere, establishing a mood that's both soothing and exotic, making it ideal for both a special occasion or a simple night out. The menu features several cuts of steak, fajitas, and other Mexican specialties, alongside fresh salsas served in authentic pottery. There are likewise vegetarian and vegan menu options, and breakfast here is especially popular with locals, keeping the blender busy crafting fresh juices.

With a multifaceted eye-catching design, the open-air, two-level Mexican gastropub **Caguameria De Esquina** (1st Avenue and 20th Street, www .caguameriadeesquina.com) easily attracts interest. It also pleases diners

with signature dishes like its tuna and watermelon tostadas, lobster burritos, pizzas, and anything else that acquires a heap of flavor from the restaurant's brick oven.

With its Spanish-tiled roof and strolling mariachi bands, **La Parrilla** (Constituyentes at Quinta, www .laparrilla.com.mx) puts diners in the mood for good Mexican meals, and it delivers. Its best dishes include beef fajitas, grilled shrimp, and *chiles relle-nos*, and there are also fresh salads and vegetarian dishes. Save room for the flambé desserts and flaming coffees, prepared tableside.

The oceanfront C-Grill at the **Thompson Beach House** (8th Street and the beach, www.thompsonhotels.com) puts a modern spin on authentic local and Mexican fare. Food is responsibly sourced from local farmers, fishermen, and suppliers to create entrées like fresh ceviche, lamb tamal, cauliflower steak with almond mole sauce, and more. The al

THERE'S NO OTHER DINING ROOM LIKE THE ONE AT LA CUEVA DEL CHANGO

MAYAN CUISINE

Contributed by Destination Riviera Maya magazine

Traditional Mayan cuisine integrates the delights of land and ocean: the beans, vegetables, and fruits cultivated in the region combine with the rewards from fishing and hunting, a cultural embodiment of a centuries-old society. Corn, chocolate, honey, and turkey are not only the main ingredients of delicious meals and beverages but also play an integral part in Mayan religious rituals, where chocolate is known as the "drink from the gods." Numerous spices such as peppercorn, coriander, *achiote* (similar to paprika), and cinnamon are used to make *recados*, special seasoning pastes that enliven chicken, fish, or beef dishes. Some significant traditional Mayan plates include the following:

Cochinita pibil. The word *pibil* means "to roast in a hole," but fortunately, modern cooks have devised a method that requires no shovel. The dish is typically made with pork and marinated with red *recado* and bitter orange, which is wrapped in banana leaves with onions and either steamed or roasted, and then served with onions marinated in vinaigrette.

Poc chuc. Chargrilled pork marinated in sour orange with black beans, purple onion, tomato, and Mayan spices.

Papadzules. Tortillas stuffed with hard-boiled eggs in a pumpkin seed broth and topped with roasted tomato sauce.

Frijol con puerco. Pork and black bean stew served with chopped radish, onion, tomato, and pieces of lime. Eaten with a corn tortilla.

Relleno negro. Turkey, ground beef, and hard-boiled eggs in a blackened chile sauce.

Tikinxic. A whole fish marinated in achiote and sour orange with tomato, white onion, and green pepper slices, then wrapped and grilled in a banana leaf.

Panuchos. A fried tortilla filled with refried beans, pieces of turkey or chicken, lettuce, tomato, onion, and avocado.

---

fresco dining room faces a beautiful and active section of the beach. Those who are not guests at the hotel are welcome and may enter through the lobby on 8th Street or from the beach itself.

La Perla Pixán Cuisine and Mezcal Store (34th Street between 5th and 10th Avenues) offers up traditional Oaxacan dishes and unique mezcal combinations in a simple but charming covered outdoor restaurant. Although only a few doors west of Quinta, the place emanates a remote, tropical vibe. It's enough to make you wonder if some magical ingredient might have been slipped into those fine mezcals and delectable original sauces (think flavors like prickly pear and habanero, mole with almonds, and a cheese sauce infused with mezcal). Live local music is a constant here (and is usually quite good), and you're as likely to mix with locals as with other travelers if you stop by.

A sports bar and Mexican cantina, **Pez Vela** (Quinta at 2nd Street, www .pezvela.com) has several settings in one spot: a bar with swinging bar stools, a

BIKES ARE A POPULAR TRANSPORTATION CHOICE FOR TOURISTS AND LOCALS IN THE RIVIERA MAYA CHIP RANKIN

DON'T LET THE STUNNING OCEAN VIEWS DISTRACT YOU FROM YOUR DINNER AT C-GRILL

central dining area with plastic tables, a few sidewalk tables, and some TV-front tables, perfect for watching live sports games, which seem to always be on. The menu, which trades in tacos, grilled shrimp, and burgers, is inexpensive and quite satisfactory for the price. For the best deal, order beer by the bucket (five bottles) and you'll soon know why this is one of the older locales on Quinta.

DON'T SIT, SWING AT THE BAR AT PEZ VELA

Aldea Corazón (Quinta and 14th Street, www.aldeacorazon.com) is a secret oasis in the middle of town. The menu offers a modern, refined spin on traditional Mexican cuisine and margaritas. For a romantic dinner setting like nothing you've experienced at home, be sure to opt for a table in the back of the restaurant in the peaceful jungle garden next to the *cenote*.

Restaurante Frida Kahlo (Quinta and 8th Street, www.fridakahlorestaurante .com) and its one-of-a-kind multimedia dining experience are welcome additions to Quinta's original stretch. The late, iconic Mexican artist's larger-than-life visage draws fans and passers-by for selfies and sustenance. The menu takes an appropriately creative and flavorful approach to traditional Mexican and Latin dishes, and also provides vegetarian, vegan, and gluten-free alternatives. Overlooking Quinta, the restaurant sits above the affiliated Frida Kahlo Museum.

ITALIAN At **La Famiglia** (10th Avenue at 10th Street, www.lafamiglia.mx) you'll think you've been transported to an Italian beach town, where you've stumbled upon a friendly neighborhood restaurant where everybody knows each other. Tables line the sidewalk and the second-floor covered terrace (which is also air conditioned) and are filled each evening with families and devoted regulars munching on pizza, handmade pasta, and seafood dishes.

Popular pizza spot **Don Chendo** (30th Avenue between 24th and 26th Street, www.don-chendo.com) isn't for anyone who's in a rush. Everything here takes time and is made to order, including the towering Chicago-style deep dish pizzas and homemade pastas.

Serving three meals a day, the sidewalk café **Il Baretto** (Quinta at 26th Street) is also something of a headquarters for Italians residing in Quinta's international neighborhood. But it's not merely Italian ex-pats who frequent Il Baretto for its pasta, pizza, and seafood dishes, and the multicultural dinner crowd makes for a lively atmosphere, luring in passersby. The restaurant also serves imported coffee

drinks, espresso, and cappuccino, and is likewise known for sumptuous desserts. Sister restaurant **Eat Italy** (Quinta at 8th Street) supplies a more casual setting, with pastas and wood-fired pizzas served up with a side of people-watching from the checkered-tablecloth-covered tables.

Ambasciata D'Italia (Quinta at 24th Street, www.ambasciataditalia.com) has proven a popular date spot on Quinta since 2009. In an elegant setting along the busy pedestrian path, the restaurant features a well-explained variety of fresh pastas, deeply flavorful seafood dishes, and creative antipasti. The wine list is extensive. Younger diners will appreciate the cheese pizza.

Piola Playa del Carmen (38th Street and 1st Avenue, www.piola.it), the local outpost of the beloved Italian pizza and gnocchi chain, serves up fresh slices, pasta dishes, and tiramisu in a crisp modern setting. The restaurant is set back, slightly obscured behind some natural jungle.

An old Playa favorite, **Ristorante Da Bruno** (Quinta at 12th Street, www.grupoazotea.com) is known for both its authentic Italian menu and its premium

THE FOOD IS AS COLORFUL AS THE ART AT RESTAURANTE FRIDA KAHLO CHIP RANKIN

people-watching perch in the heart of Quinta's *Zona Doce*. With the new Thompson boutique hotel looming across the street, there is more to observe than ever. The owners and chefs are Italian, the pasta is made in-house, and the food tastes fresh and hearty. Top dishes include gnocchi, pizza, ravioli, antipasti, prosciutto, mahi-mahi, lobster, and, of course, tiramisu for dessert.

A newer Italian favorite in Playa, **Cenacolo** (Quinta and 28th Street, www.cenacolo.com.mx) offers a modern gastronomical journey based on traditional Italian philosophies in a sleek, upscale, and modern setting.

Long a destination restaurant in Cozumel, Cancún, and Isla Mujeres, **Rolandi's** (Paseo del Carmen Mall, www.rolandirestaurants.com) outpost in Playa offers a casual ambience with upscale flair. Wood-oven-fired pizzas stand out on the menu, alongside pastas and desserts.

INTERNATIONAL The French-owned gourmet restaurant and wine bar **Byblos** (10th Avenue at 24th Street) is one of few spots in town where you can enjoy an exquisite meal in an air-conditioned dining room with white linen tablecloths and outstanding service. Menu highlights include carpaccio, foie gras, pasta, risotto, grilled fish, flambéed lobster, veal chops, rabbit, New Zealand beef and lamb, duck, apple tarts, and crêpes flambéed with Grand Marnier.

You've heard of cave diving, but **Alux** (Avenue Juárez between 65th and 70th Avenues, just west of Highway 307, www.aluxrestaurant.com) offers cave dining. Housed deep within a natural cave formed thousands of years ago, and featuring live music nightly, this restaurant makes for a romantic spot for dinner or a drink. The food is not the best in town, but the novelty of the experience more than makes up for it. Local promoters occasionally host all-night rave parties here, which can get extremely crowded and are best avoided if you're prone to claustrophobia.

With fewer than ten tables and located off the beaten path, the upscale eatery **Oh Lala Cuisine by George** (14th Street between 10th and 15th Avenues, www.ohlalabygeorge.com) works hard to deliver an exceptional meal and experience. The attentive staff, fresh delicious dishes, and modern space make this restaurant worth seeking out.

Much more casual and lively is **Karen's Seafood, Steakhouse, and Pizzas** (Quinta between 2nd and 4th Streets) which boasts live music nightly and one of Playa's most all-encompassing menus. Crowds tend to linger in the joyful atmosphere, so arriving early for a good table is recommended.

A swanky lounge/restaurant with indoor seating, candlelit tables, comfy sofas, and sidewalk tables facing Quinta, **Di Vino** (Quinta at 12th Street, www.divino.com.mx) offers deluxe selections like grilled fish, steak, and lobster. As the night carries on, diners swap out for drinkers, and a lounge scene emerges. As the swank factor multiplies, the indoor couches become the favored seats, ideal for candlelit canoodling. Food is served late into the night, but you'll spot more swizzle sticks than butter knives as the evening goes on. This place is a great spot to woo a date or to show your feelings to a special someone.

Como Como (10th Avenue between 12th and 14th Streets, www.comocomo.mx) offers seasonal Mediterranean flavors, warm décor, and solid service that keep ex-pats and international locals coming back. Reservations can be easily made online.

Linen tablecloths and leather banquettes set the tone at upscale **Imprevist** (1st Avenue at 16th Street, www.imprevist.mx) where the Asian fusion menu and decadent desserts may entice you to take a break from Quinta and stay a while. The prix fixe breakfast is also a great bet for regional specialties, fresh

NIGHTLIGHTS OF PLAYA DEL CARMEN

Each night, numerous points of light blink into existence up and down 5th Avenue, in hotels and along the beach. They give Playa a new overlay, setting the stage for evening romance, laughter, and adventure.

Jellyfish Lamps. These showstopper lanterns adorn shops, restaurants, and hotels, collectively giving Playa a distinctive sense of place. The strings of shells that hang from many of the lamps earned them their name.

Catholic Votive Candles. These tall candles—usually displaying important religious figures—are traditionally lit in prayer for and remembrance of departed family. They make for an artistic and easy gift for any of your cool friends back home.

Wall Sconces & Tin Lamps. Often spied in courtyards, restaurants, lobbies, and condos, these clay, metal, and wooden shades make popular design accents and—hanging on your deck or patio back home—would remind you of your beach trip.

Fire Lanterns. Wielded in the region's infamous fire-dancing spectacles, these lanterns are literally set aflame and swung at the end of chains. During performances, dancers paint vivid, overlapping circular patterns in the air and around themselves.

squeezed juices, and comforting brunch classics.

Mar de Olivos (26th Street between Quinta and 10th Avenue) serves creative Spanish fare, including squid ink paella, fresh seafood, and authentic tapas. A handful of candlelit tables spill out onto the curb, making it one of the more relaxing spots to linger for dinner off busy Quinta.

ASIAN & SUSHI **Babe's Noodles & Bar** (10th Street between Quinta and 10th Avenue, www.babesnoodlesandbar.com) supplies affordable and well-portioned Asian and Thai cuisine for lunch and dinner. Thai-style noodles are the house specialty, but the menu also features a nod to the European-born owners with classic comfort food favorites, like Swedish meatballs.

The Buenos Aires–based **Sushi Club** (10th Avenue and 26th Street) can be found in an uber-slick space on the ground floor of the Be Playa hotel. The restaurant offers sushi as well as a mix of Japanese and Asian fusion dishes.

Locals and visitors enjoy consistently good Thai food—think pad Thai, curry, chicken satay, and pork dumplings—at **Gluay Muai Thai** (38th Street between

Quinta and the beach), a crisp, modern, and casual eatery.

Officially part of The ROYAL, the Asian fusion restaurant **Asiana** (Constituyentes and 1st Avenues, www.realresorts.com) is also open to non-resort guests. It serves lunch and dinner in a bright environment featuring contemporary design and strong lime-green accents.

STEAK With its wide and undulating staircase opening up on a prominent corner of Quinta, **Madre Tierra** (Quinta and 14th Street) is hard to miss. The steakhouse, which also has an extensive seafood menu, exudes a warm and inviting atmosphere that reaches out from its open-air, minimalist second-story *palapa* and down into the street below.

Small, locally owned **500 Gramos Grill** (Quinta between 34th and 38th Streets) is one of those in-the-know places you'll talk about long after your trip. Affordable and top-notch steaks (T-bone, filet, and ribeye) are grilled to perfection in the casual open-air eatery. It's not a romantic date-night dining room, but the lights of Plaza San Pedro are pretty and you'll have a quality meal for a fraction of what you would normally pay. Cash only.

On the opposite end of the ambiance spectrum is the ultra-posh **Harry's Playa del Carmen** (Quinta between 12th and 14th Streets, www.harrys.com.mx) in the glittering and commercial Calle Corazón. The restaurant's raw bar is unmatched, and steaks from the wood-fired grill (including Japanese wagyu and a Fred Flintstone–like, sharable tomahawk cut) are first-rate. Fantastic giant shrimp and lobster are just two of the amazing seafood offerings. If you feel like getting dressed up and treating yourself to something fancy, Harry's does fine dining well. Reservations are easily made online.

Located on a charming street across from Acanto Boutique Condo Hotel, the cool and upscale **Plank** (16th Street between Quinta and 1st Street, www.plank.mx) offers fresh USDA-certified beef, chicken, and fish, as well as grilled vegetables and gourmet flatbreads, cooked on wooden and Himalayan salt planks.

The two-level **Sur Steakhouse** (Quinta at Calle Corazón, between 12th and 14th Streets, www.grupoazotea.com) carries on the present-day Playa trend of putting both Quinta and its diners on display. The Argentinian grill is big and open and has a décor that's slick and mod, with indirect lighting, soothing lounge music, and a strong Mediterranean vibe.

SEAFOOD Perched on the Thompson hotel's sweeping rooftop **CATCH** (12th Street between Quinta and 10th Avenue, www.thompsonhotels.com) is the seaside sibling of the NYC rooftop hotspot of the same name. The restaurant and bar serves up delicious seafood and contemporary fare alongside sweeping views of the city and the Caribbean sea. Modern Playa's grandest dining location, it's frequented for breakfast, brunch, lunch, and dinner by fashionable locals and travelers alike. From a dedicated entrance next to the hotel entrance on 12th Street, non-hotel guests are whisked to the rooftop by elevator. From there, you can soak in the scene at the nearby pool and survey the foot traffic on Quinta and Calle Corazón below. Sushi fans should try the

SEAFOOD AND STUNNING ROOFTOP VIEWS ARE ON THE MENU AT CATCH THOMPSON HOTEL

Hellfire Roll (made with spicy Bluefin tuna flown in from Ensenada, green apples, and balsamic vinegar) and the Truffle Sashimi (tuna, Hamachi, chili oil, ponzu, American caviar, and shaved black truffles).

The laid-back, casual sidewalk setting of the small **El Muelle** (Quinta at 32nd Street, www.elmuelledeplaya.com) offers only the slightest hint as to the complexity of the restaurant's menu. Super fresh seafood is the star, whether grilled, fried, or baked. The ceviche is likewise some of the best in town, and if you've never tried octopus before, it's one of the house specialties.

Another affordable seafood option is the popular **Puerto Cocina Urbana** (Quinta between 34th and 38th Streets) in Plaza San Pedro. Quirky, delightful cocktails, local and regional craft beers, and modestly priced seafood make this place a must find for lunch or dinner. Go hungry, as you'll want to try all of the mouthwatering tacos, especially the octopus al pastor, pan-fried fish with mango and potato, and Ensenada-style shrimp. Seafood cocktails and nearly a dozen styles of ceviche are also worth a try, including a Peruvian ceviche with habanero that will have you ordering another beer right away.

Right in the middle of Quinta, **La Fishería** (Quinta between 24th and 26th Streets, www.lafisheriaplaya.mx) combines a prime location with celebrity chef buzz. From executive chef Aquiles Chavez, expect some culinary surprises like shrimp pizza, grilled octopus tacos, and a creative catch of the day.

Located next to the Playa town square, gourmet **La Casa del Agua** (Quinta at 2nd Street, www .lacasadelagua.com) offers up European and Latin fusion cuisine with a menu focusing on fresh fish and shellfish, Angus beef, and a few traditional Mexican dishes. Water features decorate the dining room, and candlelit tables are covered in white linen, creating a contemporary, romantic feel.

A SIDEWALK SERENADE AT BLUE LOBSTER RESTAURANT

One of Playa's older restaurants, the two-story **Blue Lobster** (Quinta at 12th Street, www.bluelobster.com.mx) opened in 1991 and specializes in seafood and live lobster (including a daily $19 lobster special), plus a few unusual plates like octopus puffs or fish with curry and anisette. The key lime pie is popular here, and there's live music in the evenings.

With its new location on 12th Street and its original spot by the highway, **El Oasis Mariscos** (12th Street between Quinta and 10th Avenue, 22nd Street and Highway 307, www.eloasismariscos .com) remains popular with local expats, natives, and travelers. The menu features shrimp tacos, fish tacos, ceviche, and other seafood and Mexican dishes. At its original location by the highway, the *palapa*-style dining room is large, and the décor decidedly Mexican. In keeping with its surroundings, the 12th Street location is smaller, with a more tropical

Playa look that complements the In Fashion Boutique Hotel next door.

Another spot frequented by expats in the know, **Los Aguaschiles** (Constituyentes between Quinta and 1st Avenues), offers great seafood, tacos, and ceviche, as well as an array of delicious sauces and drink specials. You can't go wrong with one of the ceviche plates or Los Aguaschiles' fresh take on traditional tacos.

Situated on a high-profile corner of Quinta, **Almirante Pech** (Quinta and 30th Street) will catch your attention if only because it emanates *cool*. The restaurant's elegant menu concentrates on contemporary seafood and Mexican fusion cuisine, but it's the creative cocktail menu (especially anything featuring mezcal) that has made this spot a date-night favorite. Even if you don't eat there, you'll likely be drawn in to have a drink at the bar.

CAFÉS & LIGHT FARE From its original location (facing the Olmec statue and fountain at one of Playa's busiest intersections), **Ah Cacao Chocolate Café** (Constituyentes at Quinta, www.ahcacao .com) has expanded north to new outposts (Quinta at 30th Street, Quinta between 38th and 40th Streets). Sought after by both locals and tourists, Ah

100% NATURAL RESTAURANT HAS FRESH FRUIT SMOOTHIES AND HEALTHY MEALS

Cacao whips up all sorts of chocolate delicacies—including hot/cold drinks, to-die-for brownies, ice cream, cookies, and old-fashioned chocolate bars. It's also a purveyor of gourmet coffees from around Mexico. Be sure to pick up one of their Kicao cacao-based energy bars for your day's excursion. TOP TIP: From shampoo and moisturizers to oils and raw cacao, you'll have no trouble finding a unique gift that soothes the soul at this local java shop.

For a bit of clean eating in Playa, head to **The Pitted Date** (26th Street between Quinta and 10th Avenue) for vegan bakery goodies and a meat-free breakfast menu of hearty burritos, bagel sandwiches, and fresh squeezed juices.

Open for breakfast, lunch, and dinner, **100% Natural** (Quinta between 8th and 10th Streets, www.100natural.com.mx) is a chain restaurant that feels completely local. There are several different eating areas, from sidewalk seats and others next to a waterfall to covered tables with ceiling fans upstairs. The menu features omelets, enchiladas, sandwiches, seafood, steak, and other dishes. The fresh fruit juices and smoothies are delicious and good for what ails you. Special concoctions that claim to lower cholesterol, boost energy, cure hangovers, and improve memory are popular. Prices are reasonable, and the food is always fresh and tasty.

Chez Céline (Quinta and 34th Street, www.chezceline.com.mx) is a perfectly traditional yet modern French boulangerie and pâtisserie with a patio and indoor seating. In addition to sweets, pastries, frozen lemonades, teas, and coffees, the café also furnishes a full menu of salads and sandwiches. If you're taking your treats to go, head directly to the counter to order. If you plan to eat there, grab a seat and a server will find you.

On the south side of downtown Playa, about 100 feet west of the ferry dock, you'll find the diminutive **Café Antoinette** (South 1st Street, between Quinta and the ferry dock, www.café-antoinette

LOCAL FOOD DELIVERY

While less relevant for those staying at an all-inclusive resort, having meals or groceries delivered to your hotel or rental property is one of the more convenient modern amenities to take full advantage of when on vacation. "I can't wait to spend the first day of my vacation going back and forth to the grocery store to stock up the fridge," said nobody, ever.

- **A Bit of Home in Mexico** (www.abitofhomeinmexico.com) requires some planning before you leave for your vacation (at least 72 hours is needed for processing orders), but this full-service option will really help you feel like you're in for a carefree getaway. The company's site has easily downloadable forms to order your groceries, non-food kitchen items like soap and trash bags, alcohol, and any extras you might need. Submit your order online, and they'll contact you to confirm your shopping list. The cost is merely the cost of groceries plus a 20 percent service charge, and payments are made securely online through PayPal. Delivery arrangements are typically made with the property manager prior to your arrival, so you'll start your vacation with a fully stocked kitchen. Paradise!
- **Deli to Go** (www.delitogo.mx/en/playa-del-carmen) looks like the real deal, with their well-designed website and easy navigation. Select from a wide offering of restaurant menus, and choose to pay via credit card, PayPal, or with cash on delivery. There's also a free app and delivery service is available daily from 8:30 AM–10:30 PM in Playa del Carmen or Cancún.
- **LoQsea** (www.loqsea.com) is a total game changer for anyone renting a house for any length of time. Grocery delivery is available for Playa del Carmen, Cancún, Puerto Aventuras, and Tulum. Their English-language website offers easy categories of food (both fresh and frozen), cleaning supplies, personal hygiene items, and fresh bouquets of flowers, as well as beer, wine, and liquor. There are also categories for organic, gluten-free, and other specialty foods. Select your delivery window and pay securely online via credit card or PayPal. TOP TIP: Their Welcome Kits offer a hassle-free selection of basic groceries, milk, and coffee. The Hurricane Pack and Healthy Pack are worth a look for their creative combo of goodies.
- **Playita Express** (www.playitaexpress.com) provides food delivery to hotels, condos, and other locations throughout Playa del Carmen. The service works with a wide variety of local restaurants, including Yo Amo Tacos, Ah Cacao, and even McDonald's and Subway. Contact them via Skype or WhatsApp to place your order. Delivery is available Mondays from 1 PM–10:30 PM and Tuesdays through Sundays from 10 AM–10:30 PM.
- **Playa Now** (www.playanow.com) supplies restaurant delivery service daily from 9 AM–12 AM. Select from a large alphabetical list of local Playa del Carmen restaurants, choose your items, and then place your order via phone using Skype. Playa Now will contact the restaurant for you (ideal for anyone with limited Spanish) to order your food. Online payment options are coming soon, but for now, the Playa Now service requires cash on delivery.

.com). With a perfectly crisp, low-hanging awning, the café appears as though lifted from a Parisian storybook. In truth, it's an expansion outpost from the popular French bakery and café in Cancún and serves up fresh, rich, and buttery pastries, croissants, crêpes, and other goodies. Coffees (arguably some of the best in town), bottled drinks, and *vino* are all on the menu as well. The small interior is clean and simple, and a nice spot to hideaway from the heat or activity on the busy street.

✳ Bars & Nightlife

When the sun goes down, the action on Quinta heats up. Tourists hit the town with their sun-kissed skin and newly

THE BREAKFAST SPREAD AT CHEZ CELINE

heyday and ushered in a new era of mass international tourism that continues to reshape this once-sleepy fishing town. Though smaller than its sister club up the coast in Cancún, it's still Playa's largest and most extravagant nightspot and, in truth, deserves to be viewed more as a must-see tourist attraction than merely another nightclub. Live performances, including lip-syncing celebrity looka-likes, flair bartenders, DJs, dancers, and—most notably—high-flying acrobats keep the audience entertained all night long, making it feel like New Year's Eve every night of the year. Smoke machines, a video wall, laser light shows, balloon drops, confetti explosions, and compressed air blasts help ensure that there's always something pumping energy into the crowd. The cover charge is $70 and includes an open bar with

purchased tropical outfits to enjoy the evening breeze, have dinner, gaze at the twinkling lights, and then, quite frequently, have a few drinks. Fortunately, there are plenty of options for nightlife on and around Quinta and the beach. Whether you're looking for a casual beach bar, live music, TV sports, or a cosmopolitan lounge, you'll find what you're looking for in Playa. There are clubs and bars all along Quinta and at various spots along the beach, but the most popular area for nightlife is 12th Street, sometimes known as the *Zona Doce,* where bars and clubs line both sides of the road all the way from 10th Avenue to the beach. Many travelers will take a few laps around town to see what's going on before settling on a particular place to spend the evening. As the night carries on, the crowd thins a bit, becomes less populated with Americans, and funnels into the after-hours clubs, some of which continue serving drinks until sunup.

TRENDY CLUBS The 2008 opening of **Coco Bongo Playa del Carmen** (12th Street between Quinta and 10th Avenue, www.cocobongo.com.mx) marked Playa's unofficial departure from its hippie

COCO BONGO IS ONE OF PLAYA'S OLDEST AND LARGEST NIGHTCLUBS

LOCAL LINGO—OUT ON THE TOWN

2 x 1: Look for this sign at the entrance to a bar, and you'll know that their two-for-one happy hour has begun! Don't see the sign? Try asking the bartender for "dos por uno" anyway—you might get lucky.

Anejo con coca: Anejo is a golden blend of aged rum, and it goes great with a Coke, making it a bit of an upgrade from a standard *Cuba libre*. To order one in a loud bar, grasp your chin and move your hand downward, as if stroking a beard. Then, with the same hand, hold your pinkie under your nose for a moment, then wipe it away, as if you're snorting a powdered Colombian export from under your fingernail.

Barra libre: Some bars offer *barra libre* nights, where your cover charge includes an open bar, or put more bluntly, all you care to drink. This charge normally includes bottled water, so it's a good chance to hydrate as well.

Cantinero: Spanish for "bartender."

Chela/chelada/michelada/chamochela: *Chela* is colloquially used to mean "beer." A *chelada* is a beer served in a glass of fresh lime juice and salt. For a real local treat, try a *michelada*—a *chelada* plus Worcestershire, Tabasco sauce, and tomato juice. A recent twist, a *chamochela*, adds a tamarind-like fruit called chamoy to the traditional *michelada*.

Consumo minimo: Translating from Spanish into "minimum consumption," it's a common policy at popular bars and clubs, where instead of a cover charge, your entry fee includes drink coupons equivalent in value to the amount you pay to get in. Such a policy keeps out patrons who just want to socialize and dance but not buy anything.

Cuba libre: "One revolution is still necessary: the one that will not end with the rule of its leader," wrote Cuban spiritualist Jose Marti, describing his desire for a free Cuba, which in Spanish is *Cuba libre*. It's also the name used locally for a rum and Coke served with a wedge of lime. In the Riviera Maya, bartenders will still understand if you just order a "Cuba."

Desechable: Remember, no bottles on the street, so if you want your drink to go, ask for it in a *desechable*, and it will come in a Styrofoam cup. Many bars also have a stack of them at the exit, so if you've got one for the road, leave your glass behind.

En las rocas: Spanish for "on the rocks." Try your margarita *en las rocas* and earn a bit of respect from your *cantinero*.

Lager: Used when ordering a Dos Equis (XX) beer in the green bottle, as opposed to the XX Amber, which is the dark beer in the tinted bottle. You can also hold your index fingers together to form an "X" in front of you, then pump your hands twice, indicating *dos equis*, or "two Xs." To order two or more Dos Equis, first flash the number of drinks you want with your fingers, then proceed to make the "X" sign.

Nohoch: The Mayan word for "big." Order your favorite cocktail *nohoch*, and it'll be served in a tall glass.

domestic beer and liquor drinks. Open nightly from 10:30 PM–5 AM.

Situated next to Coco Bongo, and almost as popular, **Palazzo** (12th Street between Quinta and 10th Avenue, www .palazzodisco.com) is a more traditional nightclub than its neighbor. Upon entering the club, visitors travel to the second floor, where they make their grand entrance with the dance floor below them. The club is filled with light shows,

dancing, drink specials, and frenzied patrons. Open Thursday through Saturday from 10:30 PM–6 AM.

La Bodeguita del Medio (Quinta at 34th Street, www.labodeguitadelmedio .com.mx) is a Cuba-themed restaurant during the day and evening, but its crowd grows rowdier and the music gets louder as the night goes on. Live salsa music is featured most nights. For a break from the crowd, seek respite

TOP TEN SONGS TO ADD TO YOUR PLAYLIST

The right song can help secure a memory, make good times even better, or help share an experience with friends. Try some of these to capture the spirit of the Riviera Maya:

"Margaritaville" by Jimmy Buffett: Said to have been written on a flight from Cozumel to Houston, it's a song about a mythical island at the bottom of a Cuervo bottle.

"Mexico" by James Taylor: This is a classic tale of an extended vacation: "The sun's so hot, I forgot to go home."

"Stays in Mexico" by Toby Keith: A countrified reminder to keep your vacation exploits to yourself.

"Mexico" by Nash Girls: Young women having fun at the beach.

"Married in Mexico" by Mark Wills: A south-of-the-border romance complete with beachfront nuptials.

"I Got Mexico" by Eddy Raven: Sometimes, that's all you need.

"Blame It on Mexico" by George Strait: "Too much guitar music, tequila, salt, and lime." I know I've used this excuse before.

"Ten Rounds with Jose Cuervo" by Tracy Byrd: Crazy things can happen with tequila, especially after ten rounds.

"Mail Myself to Mexico" by Buddy Jewell: Vacation fantasies go postal.

"One Step Closer to Cancún" by Elmer Thudd: Inspirational song about an upcoming vacation.

on the back patio overlooking a steep, rocky arroyo, and ask for a marker to add your name to the wall of fame. Originally founded in Havana, Cuba in 1942, where the bar earned fame as one of Ernest Hemingway's favorite watering holes, the Playa locale boasts a slightly kitschy décor with Cuban art, flags, and paraphernalia.

During the day, **Mandala Bar** (12th Street at 1st Avenue, www .mandalanightclub.com) may look as though it closed down a month ago, but come 10:30 PM and on into the early morning, the red-hued club blasts its music into the street, and the party set crowds its dance floor. The multilevel bar is popular with revelers from around the world, emanating a vibe that's more Miami Beach–chic than Playa-casual. The centerpiece is a large dance floor that fills up as the evening goes on. The sexy crowd here is far less pretentious than one would guess by its appearance alone, making this one of the hipper places to linger over cocktails and dance through the night. Open bar costs $55, and Mandala is open until 5 AM.

La Vaquita (12th Street at Quinta, www.lavaquitadisco.com), like many of the clubs along the *Zona Doce,* is largely open-air. Expect sexy club-goers to provide a show for the passersby on 12th Street and, for those in the club, the passing crowd outside provides a similar spectacle. DJs spin lounge and EDM, and the dance floor gets increasingly packed as the night presses on. A second-floor balcony is reserved for VIP and bottle service. In accordance with its name, the bovine theme is carried over into the club by means of dancing cows and scantily clad cowgirls.

See and be seen at the swanky open-air **Abolengo Bartina** (12th Street at 1st Avenue, www.abolengobartina.com) as you sip cocktails and party with the pretty people. During the day, the prime corner space serves up an accommodating mix of American classics like burgers and chicken wings, and mainstream Mexican classics like nachos, quesadillas, and burritos. After ten, the scene makes a serious switch to a hip, intimate nightspot which has become a favorite first stop on the *Zona Doce.* The club stays open until 5 AM, and 2 hours of open bar will cost you $35.

CASUAL DRINKS Visitors looking for a shady spot to sip a cold drink can discover what the guests of the La Rana Cansada hotel already know regarding **Bar Ranita** (10th Street between Quinta and 10th Avenue, www.ranacansada .com). Patrons will feel at home in this traditional rustic Mexican setting that emphatically whispers "beach town cantina." Choose between a seat at the bar, in the lounge area, or out in the courtyard surrounded by flowering tropical plants.

A more intimate night out calls for **Don Mezcal** (10th Street between Quinta and 10th Avenue), which offers a break from the thumping noise on Quinta. Mezcal-based shots, mixed cocktails, frozen drinks, and beer constitute the majority of the menu options, but some tacos and tostadas will help soak up the potent drinks. As the night goes on, the music gets a little louder (with live DJs some nights), and the crowd can often spill out onto 10th Street, but the hard partying set usually treat this bar as a first stop only, leaving it vacant for lovers of mezcal and low-key hangout spots.

Popular with day-trippers, cruise passengers, and Mexico first-timers, **Señor Frog's** (Plaza Marina, at the ferry dock, www.senorfrogs.com) is always a good bet for cover bands, goofy contests, and a bit of risqué fun. It is built out over the sand and has a great view of the Palace Resort beach and the ferry dock. The menu features Mexican standards plus pasta, seafood, and burgers.

Beer lovers will start a fiesta at **Club de la Cerveza** (Quinta at 38th Street, www.clubdelacerveza.mx) with the variety of smaller batch and microbrews available from Mexico and craft beers from around the world. Tucked a bit off of Quinta, the patio still provides for

SEXY NIGHT SPOT MANDALA BAR IS ALWAYS A GOOD CHOICE CHIP RANKIN

REQUESTING A MARIACHI SONG

The strolling mariachis you see in the restaurants, walking down Quinta, or sometimes even on the beach work for tips. The typical price per song is $3–5, but ask ahead to be sure. Duos can cost less, and larger groups cost more. Not sure which song to request? Here are a few longtime favorites to choose from:

"El Son de la Negra": This raucous song is often the first song played when the mariachis make their grand entrance. It's also a lively, joyful song to play any time a room needs a lift.

"La Bamba": Everybody knows the words—at least some of them. This is an uplifting song of hope and can really get the crowd going.

"La Cucaracha": The sad tale of a bad day for a cockroach. It's a funny and entertaining song that's easy to sing along with. Kids love it, too.

"Las Golondrinas": A sad ballad about migrating swallows often played when someone is gone or going away.

"Las Mañanitas": This is the song played for birthdays and celebrations. Request it for a friend who is celebrating something special.

"Maria Isabel": An easy song to sing along to, it tells the story of lovers on the beach. It has a happy tropical sound that you'll remember for a long time and is especially popular in Cozumel.

some excellent people-watching, and the relaxed atmosphere encourages lingering over a pint or two ... or three, since you're walking. Expect a menu of dishes tailored for beer drinking—sausages, bruschetta, tacos, and other appetizers. Cocktails are also on the menu, but it's the taps that tempt the regulars and tourists looking for something more nuanced than Corona.

If you've been to Spain and loved the sidewalk café culture there, then stop by **La Verbena** (34th Street between Quinta and 10th Avenue) for some *botanas* (snacks) and a lively atmosphere. A favorite of locals, the *palapa*-shaded sidewalk bar boasts a tropical vibe complete with plants hanging from the ceiling. If the tables out front are full, venture back into the courtyard for more seating options and an ample stage for live music.

Offering a taste of the rainforest to the sidewalk bar scene, **Living Garden Bar** (Quinta between 14th and 16th Streets) is part of the Tukan Hotel & Beach Club but open to anyone seeking a nice place to chill for a while and grab a snack. Some tables front 5th Avenue,

but others are set back, shaded by trees and surrounded by tropical plants, dappled lighting, and jungle décor. The mojitos are a favorite, and there's always something entertaining on the large flat-screen TVs. Best of all, the temperature seems to drop about ten degrees as soon as you step inside.

Anyone with a penchant for wrestling (*lucha libre* in Mexico) is likely to find a soft spot for **Las Helodias** (28th Street between Calle Cozumel and 1st Avenue, www.lashelodias.com). Sample the menu of seafood (cocktails, ceviche, and *aguachiles*) and tacos under the masked gaze of the *luchadores*. Fit in with the locals, and try one of the many tasty versions of *micheladas*. Every Wednesday is two for one from 10 PM–2 AM.

If chilling to live music sounds like the makings of a fun night, then check out **Kitxen** (Quinta between Constituyentes and 20th Street) for a live music experience not typical on Quinta. This longtime local favorite gets crowded later in the evening, or when the band on the open air stage plays classic rock hits that lure passersby on Quinta. Grab a table for prime people-watching and a varied menu of regional and American-friendly dishes. Cash only.

✳ Selective Shopping

While Playa's streets are overflowing with shops, and your hotel concierge can always point you in the right direction for a quick sundry and supply run, a few stores in town present something unique or at least atypical. In short, they're pure Playa del Carmen and miles above any of the tacky souvenir shops advertising bargains galore.

Overwhelmed by all of the options or not much of a shopper? Some tried and true gifts from Mexico include the ubiquitous wobbly-headed wooden animals, Mexican blankets (skip any with words and stick to neutral colors), a bottle of tequila or mezcal, Mexican pottery (especially house numbers, colorful tiles, or small boxes), a hand-embroidered blouse (called a *huipil*), and Cuban cigars.

Jellyfish Lamp Shop (4th Street at Quinta, www.jellyfish.com.mx) spills onto the sidewalk, showcasing the tropical lanterns seen adorning many restaurants and bars. They're made

DRINK LIKE A LOCAL

If you're not in the mood for a tall tropical drink with a paper umbrella, try ordering one of these local cocktails for far fewer calories and a whole lot more "street cred."

Paloma: Similar to a Salty Dog (which is made with vodka or gin), this refreshing mix of fresh grapefruit juice, tequila, a splash of soda, and a salted rim is arguably the most popular cocktail nationally. And since we're talking about tequila, go ahead and order your margarita *en las rocas*, or on the rocks, so you look more like a local.

Mojito: Though born in Cuba, this highball cocktail is popular in Mexico. White rum is poured into a glass packed with ice and fresh mint, sugar, lime juice, and soda water. The perfect drink for an afternoon of poolside lounging.

Michelada: This is the ultimate cool-guy drink in Mexico. A mix of beer (which is called a *chela* colloquially and typically a Modelo), lime, tomato or Clamato juice, and a few splashes of hot sauce, Worcestershire sauce, Maggi sauce, and a seasoned or salted rim. You might never drink a Bloody Mary again.

LOCAL ARTISANS HANDCRAFT THESE CANDLES FROM DRIED ORANGE PEELS CHIP RANKIN

COMMON BEERS OF THE RIVIERA MAYA

Bohemia: Served in a dark bottle with gold foil on the neck, Bohemia is a bit more expensive than other beers. With a robust taste, it's a bit of a status symbol.

Bohemia Dark: Introduced to the Riviera Maya in 2008, this darker cousin of Bohemia offers a richer head and a creamier, almost stout-like finish.

Corona: Though it's brewed in Mexico, it seems to be more common in the States. Not all bars carry it, so if you're normally a Corona drinker, it may be time to expand your horizons. Normally served with a slice of lime.

Dos Equis: Advertised on billboards throughout the region, Dos Equis (XX) comes in lager (green bottle) and amber (tinted bottle). The lager is much more common and goes better with lime.

Leon Negra: Somewhat of a microbrew, this dark and flavorful beer is locally brewed in Mérida, the capital of the state of Yucatán. Sometimes hard to find.

Modelo Especial: Sold by the bottle or in single cans at convenience stores, this light-bodied lager is favored by many locals and goes nicely in a beach cooler.

Montejo: Crafted at the same Mérida brewery as Leon Negra, this beer, when available, adds a touch of class to any bar experience.

Negra Modelo: A dark beer sometimes sold at a slightly higher price than others, it's normally served in a glass and goes great with steak.

Noche Buena: From the makers of Bohemia, this dark seasonal brew is available only in the winter holiday season. The name means, essentially, "Christmas Eve."

Sol: Commonly found at beach bars and nightclubs, Sol is what most Corona drinkers opt for when their usual beer is not on the menu. Frequently served with lime.

Superior: Served in a dark tinted bottle—which helps keep it from getting skunked in a cooler on a sunny day—this full-bodied beer is sold at a discount in grocery stores and is available mostly at bars favoring locals.

Tecate: Most commonly served in cans, Tecate is best enjoyed with plenty of salt and lime. Popular at sports bars.

Victoria: Brewed by Grupo Modelo, the same company that makes Corona and other local favorites, this is a hoppy pilsner that isn't generally exported, so it's fun to see it and then try a few.

THE MEXICAN FLAG FLIES PROUDLY OVER THE MUNICIPAL BUILDING IN DOWNTOWN PLAYA BRIAN E. MILLER PHOTOGRAPHY/WWW.LOMIMONK.COM

from coconuts or similarly shaped gourds adorned with jewels, whimsical designs, and streamers that make them look like jellyfish with dangling tentacles. They range from baseball-sized lanterns selling for a few dollars to basketball-sized works of art selling for more than $100.

Original works of art made by hand in Mexico can also be found at the small **Artesanias La Catrina** (14th Street between Quinta and 10th Avenue). Proprietor Ariadne Gamas curates popular items from local artists and creates many of the heart-shaped works herself. Expect to find traditional Mexican handicrafts with modern twists and surprises, such as photos of graffiti poetry from around Mexico rendered onto small canvases or images of Frida Kahlo wearing a Daft Punk T-shirt.

The only shops dedicated to rewarding the little ones you left at home (or with a sitter at the hotel), **Caribbean Puzzles** (storefronts and kiosks roughly every five blocks along Quinta) sells unique, brightly colored, wooden puzzles and other fun stuff for the kiddos. Most of the stock is of the educational variety—nothing makes loud noises or goes fast—and much of it derives from local culture and geography.

WHERE DO JELLYFISH LAMPS COME FROM?

Exclusive to Playa del Carmen, these gourd lanterns are sold at shops and featured in restaurants and bars throughout downtown Playa. Carved from local gourds and jicaras, they're often adorned with tendrils of natural materials like seeds and shells and sometimes inset with stained glass panes and marbles.

Local artisans and entrepreneurs are responsible for the production of these lanterns, which by necessity are all made by hand. The proprietors of The Jellyfish Lamp shop have gone so far as to implement a rigorous training and certification program for local artisans.

Through their program, Mayan workers received training for a four-year period before earning the designation of Master Crafter. Starting out, they make the hanging tendrils that fall from the bottom of the lamp. From there, artisans focus on one of three specialties: designing, cutting, and encrusting stain glass, or polishing and finishing the gourds themselves. Four workshops are located throughout the Riviera Maya, including one in Playa del Carmen.

Guests who don't want to be responsible for toting a lantern back home, can also order them online from the Jellyfish Lamp Shop (www.jellyfish.com.mx).

SOME OF THE FUN AND FUNKY PUZZLES AT CARIBBEAN PUZZLES CHIP RANKIN

Guayaberas Dexorden (16th Street between 1st Avenue and Quinta) is an elegant shop for authentic *guayaberas* (an embroidered men's shirt popular in the Caribbean) also known as a Mexican wedding shirt. Straw hats, accessories, handmade artisanal jewelry, colorful hand-beaded purses, and women's clothing with a decidedly boho vibe all make for a great shopping experience.

Hacienda Tequila (Quinta at 14th Street) is the perfect one-stop shop for souvenirs and spectacularly chilly air conditioning. Find hand-painted pottery (look for "lead free" on the underside if you plan on using the dishes for food), cute kids' T-shirts, beachwear, liquor, and Mexican blankets. The large tequila barrels and life-sized skeletons (*calacas*) at the back of the store provide a cute photo op. Keep your eyes open for one of the store's random tequila tastings. TOP TIP: One of the most photographed spots in Playa is at the front of Hacienda Tequila, so be sure to take a seat next to the bronze cowboy (*vaquero*) on the bench.

The charming neighborhood farmers' market, **DAC Market** (30th Avenue near Constituyentes Avenue, www.dacplaya .com), keeps locals stocked with regional grocery items including produce, dried herbs, fresh bread, and tortillas. Tourists will love the handcrafted gifts and popular La Ceiba restaurant in front of the bustling market.

LOCALLY MADE CRAFTS, FRESH MARKET PRODUCE, AND A RESTAURANT ARE JUST A FEW OF THE OPTIONS AT DAC MARKET

One of the most meaningful and long-lived ways of remembering your vacation is to purchase local art. Every Thursday evening on Quinta, regional artists display their work, so you can meander down the street and enjoy the al fresco gallery of Caminarte. The art reflects a variety of styles, and there is likely something to suit everyone's taste and budget.

✳ Services

FITNESS & SPAS The word *temazcal* means "bath house" in the Nahuatl language of the ancient Aztecs, and the centuries-old *temazcal* sweat-lodge ceremony hasn't changed much over the years. The ritual, performed by a shaman or trained healer, is designed to serve both spiritual and medical purposes. Native women were known to give birth inside the dark, warm environment of the *temazcal*, thus making the transition from the womb more gradual. The sweat-lodge ceremony takes place in a stone or adobe hut, dug into the earth and

GET SOME SERIOUS SOUVENIR SHOPPING DONE WHILE ENJOYING SOME AIR CONDITIONING

CUBAN CIGARS: DON'T GET RIPPED OFF

Courtesy of SeePlaya

For many travelers, the question of where to find authentic Cuban cigars comes up at least once during their trip to the Riviera Maya. A little information can go a long way toward losing your hard-earned pesos on fake Cohibas on Playa del Carmen's Quinta Avenida.

COUNTERFEITS ABOUND

First, be aware that the majority of so-called "Cuban" cigars you'll see in Playa are counterfeit, even those sold in cigar stores. If you see a Cohiba sitting in a jar next to a cash register it is almost certainly fake. The scam here is that the store owners know that visiting Americans will pay high prices for authentic Cubans, so they re-label secondhand cigars (factory rejects) or cheaper brands.

DON'T buy so-called "Cuban" cigars from any shop or vendor unless the box has a holographic sticker of authenticity attached. The Cuban government now places a hologram on genuine boxes (or the three- and five-packs) of legitimate Cuban cigars. Even the Montecristos at the high-end resorts usually don't have these holograms, and most are just pretty good-looking fakes.

WHERE TO FIND AUTHENTIC CUBAN CIGARS

La Casa del Habano on Quinta between 26th and 28th Streets and inside the Paseo del Carmen shopping mall (www.lacasadelhabanoplayadelcarmen.com) is one of the more popular sources in Playa for authentic Cuban cigars. The Quinta location offers a cigar bar with patio tables ideal for lingering over a cocktail and puffing away.

BRINGING CIGARS HOME

According to the US Department of the Treasury, Americans can now return to the US with Cuban cigars as long as they are for personal use and not for resale. So, stock up on those authentic Cuban cigars as gifts from your Mexico vacation, because Cuban cigars are still not sold in the United States.

TOBACCO LEAVES AWAIT THEIR TURN WITH THE HAND ROLLERS

forming a dome large enough for about a dozen participants. Before entering the *temazcal*, all those who will participate reflect on the four cardinal points and are cleansed with incense. Volcanic stones are heated in a wood fire, carried into the *temazcal*, and placed in the center of the floor.

Each participant sits behind a clay pot full of water, and the door is closed and sealed, making the inside completely dark and very hot. The leader pours water onto the rocks, creating steam that fills the *temazcal* and helps partakers liberate their minds, bodies, and souls. Ancient chants are repeated, songs are sung, and participants are led through a cleansing ritual. In some versions, regional fruits are passed around to be tasted and rubbed on the skin. Modern-day participants generally wear their bathing suits and can splash water on themselves to regulate their breathing and prevent overheating.

Many people have visions and even see an animal or other creature rising from the glowing rocks. The ceremony leader can help interpret whatever you may see. At the end of the ceremony, it is customary to run to the ocean and bathe in the shallows, letting the cool water wash away the sweat and complete the renewal process. Next, a soothing herbal tea helps lock in the benefits reaped during the ceremony. It's a wonderfully spiritual experience that can leave

THE ROYAL PLAYA DEL CARMEN OFFERS A TOUCH OF LUXURY WITH THE TEMAZCAL EXPERIENCE ROYAL RESORT PLAYA DEL CARMEN

LEGAL REQUIREMENTS FOR GETTING MARRIED

At least two days before the ceremony, the couple must go to the local courthouse and present:

1. A valid tourist card (your temporary visa, issued at the airport) plus a valid passport.
2. A notarized copy of each person's birth certificate (must have a raised seal).
3. An official Spanish translation of the birth certificate (should be done locally by a court-approved translator).
4. A health certificate certifying blood type and AIDS/STD status. (The tests must be performed and certified by a court-approved facility.)
5. The proper court documents if either person is divorced or widowed. If not applicable, then a single status affidavit or Single Status Statutory Declaration is required.
6. Four witnesses, with valid passports showing name, age, address, and nationality. They will also need to arrive in Mexico at least three weekdays (working days) before the ceremony.
7. Basic fees, which total about $475.

you energized and refreshed for hours afterward.

Places in the Riviera Maya with *temazcal* facilities include the Belmond Maroma Resort & Spa, Punta Maroma, The ROYAL Playa del Carmen, Hotel Grand Sunset Princess, Playa del Carmen, Viceroy Riviera Maya (Playa Xcalacoco), Cenote Encantado (Tulum), and at Xcaret three times daily for an additional fee.

Founded by veteran Californian holistic health practitioner Sharon Sedgwick, the modern **Spa Itzá** (Calle Corazón and 14th Street, near Quinta, on the Calle Corazón pedestrian walk, www.spaitza .com) takes a traditional approach to body treatments, accenting its services with ancient Mayan healing principles. Their full- and half-day spa packages promise the ultimate in a relaxing getaway, plus the five-hour bridal package can help brides-to-be feel beautiful on their big day.

Located at the ROYAL Playa del Carmen, **SPAzul** (Constituyentes between 1st Avenue and the beach, www .realresorts.com) is open to the public and offers a fantastic *temazcal*, a sweat lodge, a great whirlpool room, plunge pools, and therapy rooms. One of their more popular treatment packages offers couples a romantic moonlight massage

on the beach accompanied by chocolate dipped strawberries.

Yoga by the Sea (46th Street between Quinta and 10th Avenue, www .morethanyoga.com) offers daily Hatha yoga classes, yoga retreats, specialized programs, and meditation and relaxation techniques. They have special yoga programs for couples, divers, and golfers, and their private yoga classes are perfect for special vacations like a girls' getaway or a romantic yoga honeymoon.

Modern and upscale, **The Gym** (1st Avenue between Constituyentes and 16th Street, www.thegymplaya.com) offers top-of-the-line weight and cardiovascular equipment, spin and kickboxing classes, and personal training. Day passes or ten-visit cards are perfect for those wanting to remain active while on vacation.

Evolve Gym (24 Street, between Quinta and 10th Avenue, www .evolvefitness.com.mx) has multiple locations across town, but the 24th Street location is the flagship and still provides the best value in terms of amenities. Top-of-the line machines, tons of weights, and some great classes are coupled with a juice bar and sauna. The gym offers Pilates, yoga, spinning, and cardio kickboxing instruction.

TOP FIVE PLACES TO POP THE QUESTION

Courtesy of Brenda Alfaro, long-time Playa entrepreneur and humanitarian

1. The cliffs at the Mayan ruins of Tulum
2. On a private sailboat in Soliman Bay
3. On the beach at Playa Maroma
4. On top of the rocks at the Xaman Ha Beach in Playacar
5. In the canals of the Sian Ka'an Biosphere

TOP TEN BEACH WEDDING VENUES

You could get married at any hotel or beach in the Riviera Maya and have an amazing experience, but for the best of the best, these ten luxury resorts have wedding packages that promise an unforgettable destination wedding.

1. Rosewood Mayakoba
2. Grand Velas Riviera Maya
3. Secrets Maroma Beach Riviera Maya
4. Viceroy Riviera Maya
5. Banyan Tree Mayakoba
6. Fairmont Mayakoba
7. Azul Fives Hotel
8. The ROYAL Playa del Carmen
9. Paradisus Playa del Carmen La Perla
10. Sandos Playacar

WEDDINGS If your idea of the perfect wedding is a beachside ceremony, exchanging vows as the sun goes down, tropical flowers forming the aisle, a Mexican trio providing romantic music, and your guests dancing the salsa while they sip tequila, then getting married in the Riviera Maya may be for you.

Though most weddings in the region are fairly casual outdoor affairs, the facilities and services exist to put on a spectacular formal ceremony for hundreds of guests, complete with all the traditions and comforts of a wedding in your own hometown. Both civil and religious ceremonies can be planned (as of press time, same-sex marriages are not legally recognized in the state of Quintana Roo), depending on the couple's preference, but the civil ceremony conducted by a judge will be the only one recognized as legal once you return home. You will need to register your marriage certificate at your local City Hall to have your marriage recognized in the United States. And don't forget to have the marriage document certified with an apostille, or stamp, before leaving Mexico.

There are several independent wedding planners in town, in addition to the on-staff planners at the larger hotels. They can assist with all of the details—from cakes to flowers, from hotels to photography, and from rehearsals to receptions. Due to the legal requirements for foreigners getting married in Mexico, it is recommended that the couple arrive in Playa del Carmen at least three business days prior to their wedding day to file the necessary paperwork. Also worth noting is that all the paperwork will be in Spanish, but your actual ceremony can be performed in English so you know what you're getting yourself into.

✳ Extend Your Stay

If you're lucky enough to have more than a couple weeks to spend in the Riviera Maya, you'll have the chance to explore well beyond the traditional tourist attractions.

KOHUNLICH These Mayan ruins are located near the border of Belize. Since the location is quite remote, the site remains in excellent condition, and it's worth the trip.

THE RIVIERA MAYA: A LAND OF BUSINESS OPPORTUNITIES

by Brenda Alfaro

Great business opportunities abound in the Riviera Maya, and with careful consideration and planning, foreigners can invest successfully in this growth. Doing business in Mexico is not for the faint of heart, however. It requires moxie and experienced advice to be successful. Having a local on your side is always a plus, especially in Latin America, where polite business relationships guide you through the maze of paperwork, labor relationships, and license requirements. Patience is also a must-have virtue for coping with the laid-back, *mañana* Latin style.

Where do you start to create a business in Mexico?

- First, look for someone who has been successful in creating lasting and meaningful professional relationaships.
- Second, before making a substantial investment, do some research online and make sure you understand the legal system and labor relationships in Mexico. Mexican law is based on the Napoleonic Code and resembles that of France or Louisiana in the United States. Mexican employees know their rights and use them effectively—as do the lawyers representing them.
- Third, take note of the important role of the Mexican notary, a powerful appointed position in Mexico. Notaries create most of the official legal documents in Mexico, including paperwork for establishing corporations, buy-sell agreements, and real estate transactions. No contract or agreement is considered legally binding in Mexico unless it has been officially registered. All parties to an agreement must sign it in front of a notary, and that document must then be registered in the municipality's official records.
- Fourth, before you agree to sign anything, seek the advice of a person who is completely independent of the parties involved and someone you can trust to translate the documents for you accurately. I am always amazed when I hear that someone is using a lawyer or notary who was recommended by those who stand to benefit from the transaction, such as a seller or a real estate agent. A good rule of thumb: if you would not do this in your own country, you should not do it here.
- Fifth, contract an accountant to keep you current with your tax filings and license requirements. Be careful about whom you hire and seek the advice of those who have experience doing business in Mexico.
- Sixth, avoid all lawsuits and labor board actions. Swallow your pride or anger and settle with an employee who is leaving or involved in a legal situation. In the end, it will save you money and stress and allow you to focus on your business at hand rather than a need for revenge or a compelling desire to "win." If you do end up needing a lawyer, find one who actually knows the law and has solid legal contacts.
- Seventh, be polite and patient—always! Mexican citizens are intelligent and are part of a formal, polite society. Do not underestimate their abilities or insult them. Stop, listen, and think before you answer or react. Directness is not a business asset in Mexico. Talk, smile, and never argue or raise your voice. If you do, the costs will be great.
- Eighth, follow the rules. It is so much easier when you remain always in compliance, which means no extra favors need to be made to run your business. Remember, the person who receives a favor will be out of power in a few months or years, and the new official will expect the same or more—so why begin down that road? And get your FM3, a resident work visa, to avoid any risk of deportation.

- Ninth, treat your employees with respect, learn the labor laws, and make use of employee contracts. Talk with business owners in your field and understand your labor base. Call for references before hiring someone. Identify any "professional labor board employees" who move from business to business collecting labor settlements. Look prospective employees in the eye—if they do not look back or if they seem distrustful, do not hire them. Trust your instincts.
- Tenth, enjoy the experience. When your patience begins to wear thin, escape to the beach to relax, recharge, and remember why you chose to live and work in this paradise in the first place.

Brenda Long Alfaro is a long-time business owner and entrepreneur in Playa.

BACALAR This ice-blue freshwater lagoon is one of the main attractions on the Mayan Coast. Bacalar can be done as a day trip from the southern Riviera Maya, but if you're able to spend several days, there are plenty of other nearby sites to explore.

MERIDA The capital city of Yucatán state is a wonderful place to learn more about Mayan culture and experience the slow pace of a modern Mexican city with deep roots in the past.

HAVANA, CUBA There are regular flights from Cancún to Havana. Package deals, including airfare and hotel, are available for less than $350 and can be booked at local travel agencies around Playa del Carmen and even at many hotel tour desks.

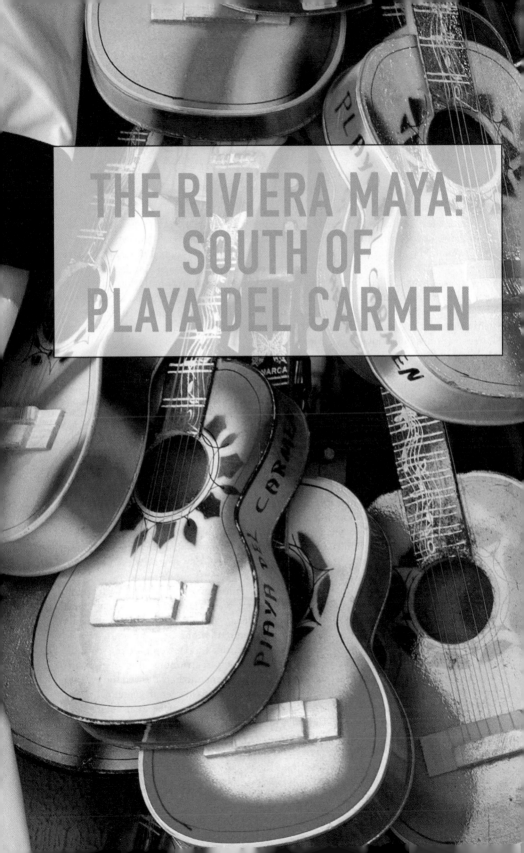

THE RIVIERA MAYA:
SOUTH OF
PLAYA DEL CARMEN

THE RIVIERA MAYA: SOUTH OF PLAYA DEL CARMEN

Travelers venturing further south of Playa del Carmen will find a striking variety of options for lodging and recreation. Ultimately, the further south you go, the more remote, unspoiled, and adventurous things become. A stone's throw from Playa del Carmen, Playacar is home to a winning collection of all-inclusive resorts, where travelers from around the world visit to play golf, lie on the beach, and be pampered in every way possible. The beachfront towns of Puerto Aventuras and Akumal beckon scuba divers and fishing enthusiasts with excellent conditions year-round, while the abundant *cenotes*, hidden beaches, eco-adventure parks, and Mayan ruins provide venturesome travelers with the kind of vacation experiences that turn postcards home into exotic tales of intrigue and exploration.

Many of the hotels and resorts south of Playa are all-inclusives, with vast campuses featuring luxurious accommodations, multiple dining options, on-site nightlife, spas, recreational activities, and everything else guests need to spend a week of fun in the sun without ever getting into a car. Other lodging options in this area include eco-conscious *cabañas* that offer opportunities to commune with nature alongside modern amenities and private rental properties, many of which are beachfront and perfect for families or anyone with more than four vacation days in a row.

PLAYACAR

Just south of Playa del Carmen (literally on the other side of the ferry dock and the outdoor Paseo del Carmen shopping mall), off Highway 307, at km 285, the large-scale, gated resort community of Playacar surrounds the ancient Mayan ruins of Xaman-Ha and is composed of resort hotels, condos, private residences, shopping plazas, restaurants, a golf course, activity centers, and one of the most pristine stretches of beach in the whole Riviera Maya.

The creation of Playacar was the single most important event in the development of large-scale tourism in the region. Before its existence, travelers were content with small, locally owned hotels, relatively few services, and European plan (no meals included) rates. Aside from a few standouts, accommodations were generally simple affairs, providing basic amenities and very few luxuries but a strong feeling of tradition and harmony with the surroundings. Strict density restrictions in Playa del Carmen made the town ill-suited for large resort development and had allowed the town to grow slowly and organically, unlike the rampant development seen in Cancún.

In the early 1990s, though, things started to change. Mexico's real estate conglomerate Grupo Situr purchased a huge plot of barren beachfront land just south of Avenida Juárez and christened it Playacar, a term deemed more marketable and English-friendly than the name *Playa del Carmen* itself. Since the area was beyond jurisdiction of the development restrictions, the Riviera Maya had its first opportunity to build international-class hotels, which needed a larger scale and higher volume of guests to turn a profit.

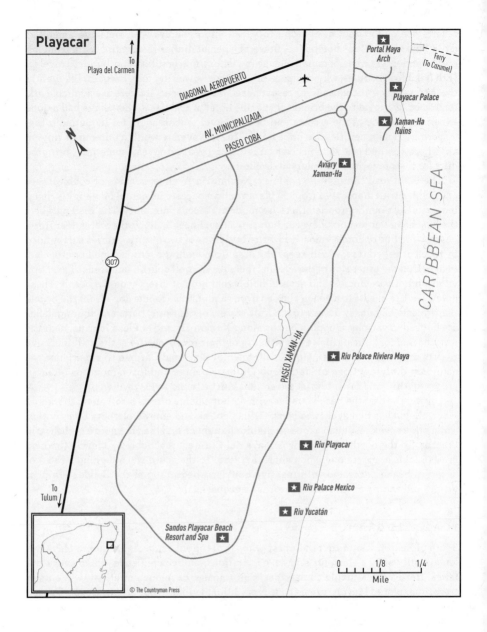

Playacar

To Playa del Carmen

DIAGONAL AEROPUERTO

AV. MUNICIPALIZADA

PASEO COBA

PASEO XAMAN-HA

307

To Tulum

Portal Maya Arch

Ferry (To Cozumel)

★ Playacar Palace

★ Xaman-Ha Ruins

Aviary ★ Xaman-Ha

★ Riu Palace Riviera Maya

★ Riu Playacar

★ Riu Palace Mexico

★ Riu Yucatán

Sandos Playacar Beach Resort and Spa ★

CARIBBEAN SEA

0   1/8   1/4
Mile

© The Countryman Press

Today, there are more than a dozen large resorts owned by international corporations, averaging some three hundred rooms each. Unlike the small inns and guest houses of years past, these resorts offer a vast array of services and luxuries, including imported linens, efficient air conditioning, luxurious spas, water-sports centers, on-site scuba training, dry-cleaning service, Jacuzzi tubs, tennis courts, swimming pools, and kids' clubs. Most are operated as all-inclusives, where guests pay one price that includes accommodations plus all meals, drinks, and activities. Many hotels have on-site gourmet restaurants, multiple bars, and even amphitheaters and nightclubs.

The area has become a playground for tourists from the United States, Canada, and Europe. It is an extremely popular wedding and honeymoon destination, and the resorts are quite adept at catering to vacationing couples with welcome amenities (fruit baskets, chilled champagne, flowers), special dinner reservations, and couples' spa treatments. Other common Playacar visitors are families and budget travelers with flexible schedules, who compare prices weekly, waiting for a bargain. Frequently, these travelers will choose their resort based on what special offers are available and tend to be less loyal to the brands of specific hotel properties. Others have had a good experience at one of the resorts and become avid ambassadors for it, claiming that its services and amenities are unbeatable. These travelers wouldn't dream of staying anywhere else and pride themselves on returning year after year, sometimes bringing gifts for their favorite bartenders and waiters.

The main road through the complex, Xaman-Ha Avenue, is made of cobblestones and is lined with manicured tropical plants and an occasional actual Mayan ruin, lending a timeless quality to the otherwise modern resort community. The road parallels the beachfront and splits Playacar into two sides. Phase I, along the water, features a nearly solid line of hotels—mostly low-rise buildings of two or three stories surrounded by tropical vegetation, which keeps the area from feeling overdeveloped or crowded. Phase II, on the other side of the avenue, includes the golf course, hundreds of vacation villas and private homes, and several hotels that are not directly on the beach. These hotels shuttle guests to a beach club, so even though their rooms don't front the beach, their guests have easy access to it. Craft stores, restaurants, bars, and tour agencies are housed in various shopping plazas along Xaman-Ha and at Plaza Marina, near the ferry dock. Most guests, however, either take their meals on-site at their all-inclusive resorts or venture into the neighboring town of Playa del Carmen to experience the abundant dining options offered along Quinta Avenida and throughout town. Shopping, nightlife, and other tourist attractions can be found in Playa as well.

During the day, the beach bustles with activity. Some guests stroll along the water, play volleyball, sail, kayak, windsurf, swim, Jet Ski, and enjoy a plethora of activities, while others seek respite in a lounge chair or hammock and read or snooze in the warm breezes. To the north of Playacar is Playa del Carmen, reachable by bicycle (loaners are available at most hotels) or a short taxi ride. To the south is a mile-long stretch of deserted beach decorated with massive boulders, beginning at the Sandos Playacar Resort and ending at the Xcaret resort and ecopark.

XCARET TO PAAMUL

South of Xcaret, visitors get their first glimpse of the wild side of the Riviera Maya. No longer will you see souvenir stands, gas stations, and convenience stores every few miles. Here a thick jungle canopy has kept tourism development at bay, while palm trees, unexplored Mayan ruins, and tiny traditional villages dot the landscape. To visit this part of the Yucatán, travelers either take a shuttle bus from the airport or rent a car so they can go where they choose. Public bus service is spotty and will let travelers off only along the main road, while most of the hotels and attractions are located along the beach several miles away. Tourists either take their meals on-property at their resort or, if staying at an EP hotel or condo, stop off at the supermarket in Playa del Carmen to stock up on foodstuffs and other essential supplies.

PUERTO AVENTURAS (HIGHWAY 307, KM 269)

The exclusive resort town of Puerto Aventuras is the only true sheltered marina in the Riviera Maya. It was also the first major development south of Cancún but hasn't seen the rapid growth of Playa del Carmen. If you talk to the local residents, they'll tell you

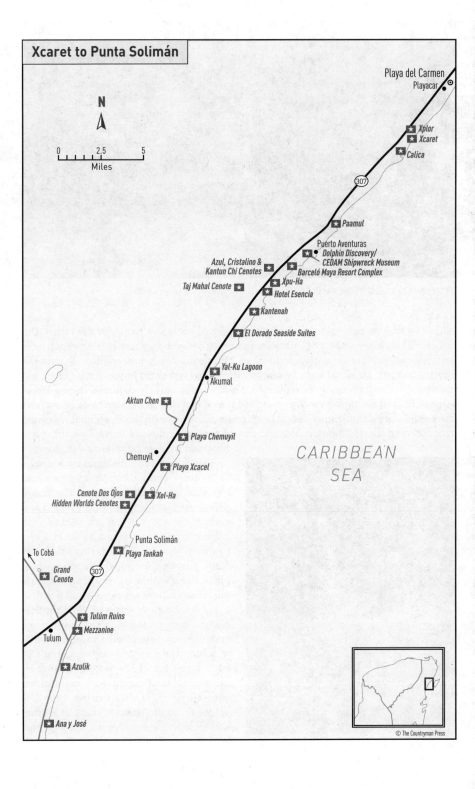

Xcaret to Punta Solimán

N

0   2.5   5
Miles

Playa del Carmen
Playacar

Xplor
Xcaret
Calica

307

Paamul

Puerto Aventuras
Dolphin Discovery/
CEDAM Shipwreck Museum
Azul, Cristalino &
Kantun Chi Cenotes
Barceló Maya Resort Complex
Xpu-Ha
Taj Mahal Cenote
Hotel Esencia

Kantenah

El Dorado Seaside Suites

Yal-Ku Lagoon
Akumal

Aktun Chen

CARIBBEAN
SEA

Playa Chemuyil
Chemuyil
Playa Xcacel

Cenote Dos Ojos
Hidden Worlds Cenotes
Xel-Ha

Punta Solimán
To Cobá
Playa Tankah
Grand
Cenote
307

Tulúm Ruins
Mezzanine
Tulum

Azulik

Ana y José

© The Countryman Press

XCARET OFFERS A SENSE OF THE MAYAN PAST RIVIERA MAYA DESTINATION MARKETING OFFICE

this is by design, to retain the small-town feel and exclusive nature of the resort. But it's also likely a by-product of a gated community designed with attracting expatriates and relocating Mexican nationals in mind. Hurricane Emily passed directly over the marina in 2005, sinking boats, beaching others, and wreaking havoc across town, but thousands of palm trees were replanted, and the area quickly regained its pre-storm appeal. In fact, the town's recovery and resilience resulted in a condo sales boom, and the community's challenge became keeping its small-town luster. The global recession that followed the 2008 financial crisis cooled that growth, but Puerto Aventuras has regained modest popularity with foreign investors and well-off Mexican nationals.

Visitors enter through a large security gate just off Highway 307. The stone-paved road winds down to the beach and ends at the 250-slip marina, packed with fishing boats, dive boats, sailboats, and pleasure yachts. The marina channels wind through an open-air pedestrian plaza, lined with restaurants, shops, bars, pharmacies, internet cafés, and a few grocery/convenience stores. A Dolphin Discovery location is built into the marina, and visitors can stroll the plaza while watching the dolphins cavort, swim, and even jump out of the water. Given how pleasantly landscaped and maintained everything is, it's surprising how few places there are to stay. There is a nine-hole golf course, a museum, a crafts market, tennis courts, and a beautiful beach where the reef is close to shore.

PUERTO AVENTURAS IS BUILT AROUND A CENTRAL LAGOON FILLED WITH DOLPHINS

XPU-HA (HIGHWAY 307, KM 264)

Several different access roads lead from Highway 307 to Xpu-Ha beach, making for fun exploration of the various areas. The picturesque beach is low-key and features a wide bay, coconut palms, and a shallow reef good for snorkeling. To find the best spots, walk to the north near the Xpu-Ha Palace Resort, where the water is calm and the access easier. (The beach to the south is not as sandy and is spotted with rocks, vegetation, and seaweed.) Conveniently, there are a few small family-run restaurants serving fresh fish and cold drinks on the beach, and one renting snorkeling equipment and WaveRunners. For overnight stays, choose among several major resorts and a handful of *cabañas* and villas for rent. On the west side of the highway, across from the Xpu-Ha turnoff, are a pair of small but swimmable *cenotes*.

KANTENAH

A small sign on Highway 307 at km 262 points the way to Kantenah beach, which is a couple miles down a washboard road. There are many coconut trees and a quiet bay with a shallow reef for snorkeling. Near the beach, there is a large handicrafts market with better prices than in Cancún or even Playa del Carmen, and there's another one on the highway, at km 259.5, with a large assortment of pots, rugs, and blankets.

AKUMAL (HIGHWAY 307, KM 255)

Five separate highway exits lead to this marina town, whose name translates into "Place of the Turtles." It is known as a family-friendly resort area with calm and shallow coves, dozens of nearby dive sites, superior sportfishing, pleasant pedestrian plazas,

DISCOVER TRUE TRANQUILITY ON XPU-HA'S BEAUTIFUL BEACHES LOCOGRINGO.COM

quality restaurants, lively bars, and a variety of accommodation options. The area consists of three separate bays: Half Moon, Akumal, and Aventuras. The late author John D. McDonald wrote several of the books in his famous Travis McGee series of boat-bum/private detective novels while lounging on these beaches.

The area remains a nesting ground for sea turtles, which are now closely protected by the government and privately funded preservation organizations. Visitors can take guided tours to observe the turtle nests and, if the timing is right, witness the turtles laying their eggs or watch the hatchlings returning to the water. An information center at the main entrance can book tours, provide directions, and reserve accommodations ranging from simple hotel rooms to large private villas. There are several grocery stores, an internet café, a dive center, a kiteboarding office, and handicrafts available near the main entrance. There's free parking in a safe lot just before the gate if you're visiting only for the day. The best beach within a short walking distance is just beyond the dive shop.

XCACEL (HIGHWAY 307, KM 247; BETWEEN CHEMUYIL AND XEL-HA)

A popular nesting ground for loggerhead and green turtles, Xcacel has very few services and no electricity. The area is a nature preserve with skunks, snakes, and other animals—some of them protected species, as well as a combination of beaches, cenotes, mangroves, and jungle terrain. The turtles are most common in the warmer part of the year, from May to October. If visiting during this time, it's very important to avoid the nests and not to bother any of the turtles. A cenote large enough to swim in is on the southern end of the beach (walk to the right, as you're facing the ocean). A small path leads from the beach to the cenote; look for a small, wooden sign. To the north, the reef comes close to the beach, making it a good site for snorkeling. A primitive camping facility offers a place to pitch a tent.

PUNTA SOLIMAN (HIGHWAY 307, KM 240)

A quiet beach good for jogging, sunbathing, and shell collecting, Soliman, as the locals call it, is the kind of place where you feel compelled to arrange your Corona bottles and lime on the table and take a picture with the sundown in the background. In fact, this beach has become famous for having been featured in a popular series of Corona beer commercials.

Although technically part of the Riviera Maya, Soliman hotels and businesses tend to label themselves as destinations within Tulum in their marketing materials, given the town's massive popularity and genuine proximity a few miles north.

If you're staying in Soliman and want to primarily stick to your hotel but make a few excursions into Tulum's pueblo and hotel zone, you will be perfectly content. If you're seeking a full-on Tulum experience, then turn to the next chapter for Tulum-proper recommendations.

TANKAH (HIGHWAY 307, KM 237; BETWEEN XEL-HA AND TULUM)

Tankah is located on a small bay. Once an important ceremonial site for the ancient Mayans, the area is home to minor ruins still being explored by archaeologists (and therefore not open to the public). The main road parallels the beach, where several guesthouses and inns can be found. One of the largest is Casa Cenote, located between the beach and a large freshwater lagoon called Manatee Cenote, which is rumored to lodge a resident manatee, though locals report not having seen one in recent years. The *cenote* has a channel that leads underground, below the road and the hotel, and ends 100 feet offshore from the beach. Only experienced cave divers should attempt the swim, however.

✳ To See & Do

PLAYACAR

Guests at Playacar resorts can spend an entire week without leaving the complex while having all their needs and whims catered to. Others, however, like to visit Playa del Carmen in the evening to go shopping, stroll the tourist plazas, try some local foods, and enjoy the nightlife.

PUERTO AVENTURAS (HIGHWAY 307, KM 269)

Aventuras's attractions are also found around the marina. Visit the small **CEDAM Shipwreck Museum**, operated by the Club de Exploraciones y Deportes Acuáticos de México (Water Sports & Exploration Club), which is responsible for locating and protecting the region's wrecks. Founded in 1959 by Pablo Bush Romero, the museum displays many artifacts recovered from shipwrecks off the Mexican coast and from around the world, explaining how the ships were excavated and how materials were recovered and restored. Free to the public (donations accepted). Closed Sundays.

NOBODY CAN RESIST A KISS FROM A DOLPHIN DELPHINIUS & THE WILKERSON FAMILY

GET A JOB & STAY A WHILE

Though it's not always easy to make the transition from tourist to local, it is possible. With a bit of determination and luck, you can find a job and live in paradise. The Mexican government requires that all foreign workers have an FM3 visa, which your employer must obtain for you. Fluency in Spanish is required, though exceptions are sometimes made. And don't expect to make anything near what you could earn back home: the minimum wage in Mexico is about $10 per day, and most jobs available to foreigners generally pay around $1,000 per month. Depending on the job, sales commission, bonuses, room and board, and other perks can help sweeten the pot. The cost of living can be much less than in the States, but only if you plan on living like a local. If you're looking for a permanent vacation and expecting to work during the day and party at tourist clubs every night, you'll probably need additional financial resources.

Adventurous travelers can interact with dolphins at **Dolphin Discovery** (www
.dolphindiscovery.com), which offers several different packages ranging from simple contact to being propelled through the water by two dolphins.

CHEMUYIL (HIGHWAY 307, KM 249)

Known in the native Mayan language as *kuxi k'aax*, the **Jungle Place** (east of Highway 307, km 248, just inland from Chemuyil, www.thejungleplace.com) is a sanctuary for the endangered spider monkey, specifically monkeys who were rescued from the illegal pet trade, poaching, and habitat destruction and then brought here for rehabilitation. "Monkey Tours" are available to see the creatures' home and the care these unique animals receive—animals that would be unable to care for themselves back in the wild. Tours are very limited and must be scheduled in advance. A minimum $80 donation per person is required for each tour, and all funds raised go directly to the care and feeding of the monkeys.

Not really a tourist town, the dusty beachfront village of Chemuyil hosts many of the service workers for nearby Akumal and other developments. It has a gated entry, and the guards are not necessarily welcoming of foreign adventure-seekers, but if you can't get enough of the Riviera Maya beaches and you won't be content until you see them all, you should be able to talk your way in and make your way to the beach for a look.

The beach itself is relatively clean, and the water is very calm and shallow since the reef reaches all the way to the surface, acting as a breakwater that keeps out waves. A couple of private campsites and some basic hotels accommodate the few backpackers, naturalists, and escape artists who find their way here, and there's a handful of beachside restaurants and bars.

XCACEL (HIGHWAY 307, KM 247; BETWEEN CHEMUYIL AND XEL-HA)

The public beach is home to the **Santuario de la Tortuga Marina**, or Sea Turtle Sanctuary. While few tourists see it, this beach is the top destination for sea turtles in the Riviera Maya. The turtles visit in the spring to lay their eggs, which then hatch in the fall when large groups of baby turtles make for the sea. The sanctuary equally protects the beach, the turtles, and their nests throughout the year. A small donation is required, typically 20 pesos, to visit this nearly spotless beach and experience the majestic sea turtles.

PUNTA SOLIMAN (HIGHWAY 307, KM 240)

If you continue the half-mile to the end of Soliman's unnamed beachfront road, you'll discover the lively and colorful **Playa Virgen**. From the sand parking lot, you'll spy a beach littered with palm trees, a small abandoned boat covered from bow to stern in vivid graffiti art, rustic volleyball courts, a food counter, and more. On a nice day, the beach is busy with locals and tourists staying nearby, but given its tucked away location, it is not overrun. A perfectly enjoyable, authentic, public Mexican beach (rather than a pristine, resort-landscaped one), Playa Virgen runs high on charm and character, while still offering primo views of Soliman Bay.

TANKAH (HIGHWAY 307, KM 237; BETWEEN XEL-HA AND TULUM)

Tankah Natural Park (east side of Highway 307, km 233, www.tankah.com.mx), sometimes known as Cenotes Tankah online, is a simple, charming, and mostly natural destination. Attractions include a natural, crystal-clear *cenote* swimming hole (complete with a two-story cliff you can use to jump in), a fun three-part zip-line tour over water (good for families and novices), canoeing, and a modest Mayan village.

ONCE IN A LIFETIME TRIPS

Whether you're celebrating a honeymoon or a quarter-century of marriage, set the scene for some amazing memories and splurge at one of these Top 10 Riviera Maya luxury resorts:

- Nizuc Resort & Spa (Cancún)
- Banyan Tree Mayakoba (Punta Bete)
- Viceroy Riviera Maya (Punta Bete)
- Rosewood Mayakoba (Punta Bete)
- El Dorado Maroma's Palafitos Overwater Bungalows (Punta Maroma)
- Fairmont Mayakoba (Punta Bete)
- Royal Hideaway Playacar (Playacar)
- Grand Velas Riviera Maya (Playa del Carmen)
- Ritz Carlton Cancún (Cancún)
- Secrets Maroma Beach (Punta Maroma)

✳ Lodging

BEST PLACES TO STAY IN AND AROUND PLAYACAR

It can be a bit difficult to differentiate among the various all-inclusive resorts of Playacar. For the most part, the hotels share a common beach, which is just about perfect anywhere along the stretch and ideal for families or couples looking for a romantic getaway. The hotels themselves are large-scale affairs with comparable pools, gyms, restaurants, bars, and activities programs. Most have bicycles for guest use, which makes the couple-mile trip into Playa del Carmen a breeze. The main considerations and differentiating factors are the size of the resort, whether or not it's adults-only, whether it's located on the beach or the golf course, and the price. As the cost goes up, generally speaking, the rooms will be larger, the grounds better maintained, food and beverages will be of a higher quality, and the vibe will feel more exclusive.

Adjacent to the Cozumel ferry dock and the Playa del Carmen town plaza, the chic **Playacar Palace** (north end of Paseo Xaman-Ha, www.palaceresorts.com) is a good spot for travelers seeking the luxury of Playacar but with ready access to downtown Playa. Playacar's original flagship resort, the structure was its first large hotel and was completely renovated in 2005. Kids stay for free at this can't-miss all-inclusive, and parents can still enjoy romantic dinners on the

BUILDING A LIFE, AN ECOSYSTEM, AND FLOATING ISLANDS

The incredible tale of one man, two floating islands, and 300,000 recycled plastic bottles

After Hurricane Emily ended a unique chapter in the history of Puerto Aventuras in July 2005, a new chapter in floating-debris lifestyles was launched near Isla Mujeres.

The story began in 1998, when British ex-pat, artist, and musician Richy Sowa (or "Reishee," as the locals call him) moved to the Riviera Maya with a dream of living a life of relaxation and simplicity based around recycling and low-impact survival. He started collecting empty water bottles and loading them into fishing nets, which were arranged in a spiral pattern to create an artificial island, which he then cast adrift in Puerto Aventuras. On it, he planted mangroves and fruit trees, added some ten tons of sand, and built a house from discarded wood, bamboo, and thatched palm.

The size of half a basketball court, the island could be maneuvered around the marina with an outboard boat motor attached to one end. Built on a foundation of more than 250,000 plastic bottles, it had a solar cooker (with reflectors laid out in a spiral) and a self-composting toilet and was home to several cats, dogs, and an occasional stray duck. Sowa's recycled island was featured on *Ripley's Believe It or Not!* in 2000. His self-stated, long-term goal for the project was to "use the waste from this world as a foundation to create a tranquil piece of paradise and sail around the earth on a floating island with the message of love and faith."

When Hurricane Emily hit in 2005, Richy and his animal friends took shelter on the mainland. When morning dawned, his island lay in ruins, ripped apart and beached on the sand. Despite the total destruction of the island's surface, the mangrove roots held much of the fishing nets and bottles together.

In late 2007, he began construction of a second island in a bay on Isla Mujeres, once again building on a foundation of plastic bottles. This time he grouped them together in vegetable sacks, and at last count, the island makes use of about 160,000 plastic bottles.

Joyxee Island opened for tours in 2008, charging visitors 50 pesos to come aboard and inspect Sowa's ingenuity, which produced an island home that boasts three beaches, a house, two ponds, a solar-powered waterfall and river, a wave-powered washing machine, and even air conditioning in the bedroom should the need arise. If you find the idea of spending a night or two on a recycled island captivating, you can sometimes find and rent Joyxee Island on the Airbnb website.

property while their children play at the kids' club.

At Playacar's far southern end, **Sandos Playacar Beach Resort and Spa** (Paseo Xaman-Ha, www.sandos.com) offers families access to a perfect beach, a kids' club, and a mini ecopark. Bordered by natural mangroves, the beach to the south of Sandos remains very natural, with no other resort developments between it and Xcaret, miles away.

Spanish-owned **Riu Hotels and Resorts** (Paseo Xaman-Ha, www.riu.com) has six all-inclusive properties on Playacar's southern end. Guests staying at one hotel can enjoy the facilities at the others, including the restaurants and nightclub, which is located at the party-friendly Riu Tequila (well, that makes sense!). Just a 5-minute walk toward the water is the hacienda-style Hotel Riu Yucatán, with a super cool waterpark, a kid's club that provides endless entertainment and free childcare, and nightly entertainment. Activities like snorkeling, kayaking, and SUP are included.

Home rental powerhouse **Airbnb** (www.airbnb.com) usually has more than 1,000 condos, homes, apartments, and private rooms available for rent in Playa del Carmen and Playacar. Vacation rental websites **VRBO** (www.vrbo.com) and **Home Away** (www.homeaway.com)

each list more than 150 condos and villas in Playacar alone, including locations on the beach, on the golf course, and around the development. Both websites list all properties and amenities to help you select the vacation rental that best suits your needs.

XCARET TO PAAMUL

Located adjacent to the Xcaret ecology park, the 769-room **Occidental at Grand Xcaret Destination** (Highway 307, km 282, www.barcelo.com) is a wondrous, all-inclusive playground catering to families and travelers looking for a lot of activities. Rooms at the massive resort are housed in low-rise buildings surrounded by five free-form swimming pools, winding rivers, and tropical gardens. If you're seeking greater exclusivity, the resort's Royal Level features thirty-eight suites with extra amenities. Packages offering unlimited use of Xcaret's parks are also available.

The Paamul Hotel & Cabanas (Highway 307, km 273, www.paamul.com) has twenty-five rooms and cabins on the pristine Paamul Beach. The destination has become popular with day-trippers who come to see the sea turtles nest, go snorkeling or diving, or lounge on the beach. The main road is lined with RV shelters, some of which have been there for years, and the hotel still operates its original RV Park, back behind the seaside development. Visitors can camp on the beach or stay at the small hotel, and there are a few super-casual beachside restaurants. The rocky beach along this shallow bay is not the best for swimming but makes for some great photos.

STEP OFF THE STREET AND EXPLORE THIS SMALL MAYAN STRUCTURE LOCATED ACROSS THE STREET FROM PLAYACAR PALACE CHIP RANKIN

HOTEL CHOICES: ALL-INCLUSIVE OR EUROPEAN PLAN

Courtesy of SeePlaya

One of the first decisions travelers have to make when planning their trip is whether to stay in an all-inclusive (AI) or European Plan (EP) hotel. AI resorts generally include all food and drinks consumed on site, plus a variety of non-motorized watersports, activity programs, and fitness centers. Some even include premium alcohol, gourmet a la carte meals, stocked minibars, and other amenities. European Plan (EP) hotels frequently have their own restaurants and bars as well, but guests have to pay for any meals or drinks that they have.

The Riviera Maya has a growing number of all-inclusive resorts, practically pioneering the concept in Mexico. Most of the large-scale, full-service beachfront resorts are operated as AIs, while the smaller, independently run hotels along the beach and near Playa del Carmen's Quinta Avenida are operated on an EP basis.

Overall, the decision on whether to go for an AI or an EP is up to the traveler. There are positives and negatives to both choices.

AI RESORTS ARE GENERALLY GOOD IF:

You don't want to do much planning. AIs generally have a higher price than hotels because all the meals, activities, and alcohol are included. However, the food and activity choices can get tiresome, and some guests complain that their mixed drinks are watered down, though this is certainly not always the case.

EP HOTELS ARE GENERALLY GOOD IF:

You are a little more adventuresome. You will pay less on average but will need to make arrangements for meals, drinks, and activities yourself. Since you'll likely be spending more time away from the hotel, you're also more likely to have a more authentic Mexican experience.

Now let's get into the details.

Food

Obviously, meals are included at AIs, while they are an extra expense for those staying in hotels. AIs generally have limited choices, and, unless you go for the very expensive resorts, the quality of the food can range from poor to very good. Most AIs have a main dining room where meals are served buffet-style and a small selection of a la carte restaurants available on site for little or no extra charge. Reservations are usually required for the a la carte restaurants and can be difficult to get if the resort is busy. It is not unusual for guests at AIs to report that they get tired of the food choices by the end of their stay.

On the other hand, most Playa hotels have limited menus, meaning you'll either have to go grocery shopping at the local supermarket or eat out at the surrounding restaurants. The quality and prices of Playa del Carmen's restaurants vary widely, but exploring the town in search of a good place to eat can also be a lot of fun.

Drinks

AIs include unlimited drinks—including water, juices, sodas, beer, and mixed drinks—which is one of their main selling points. This is unfortunately not always as good of a deal as it sounds. In Mexico, the same brands of liquor are available in different "grades," where each grade carries a different level of alcohol. The liquor you find in the AIs is generally of the lowest grade, and some guests report that drinks sometimes taste watered down.

If you stay at an EP hotel, you will generally purchase your drinks at local bars, restaurants, or from the in-room minibar. The prices for liquor vary by location, but you are generally ensured high quality. If you really want to save money, take a trip over to Walmart and stock up on the cheapest liquor in town.

Activities

Most AIs have a variety of activities tailored to their clientele: sports, exercise classes, dance classes, arts and crafts, pool games, and team sports are common offerings. It is less common for EP hotels to have these options.

One problem with AI-sponsored activities can be that these resorts tend to draw a very motley crowd. Visitors are encouraged to research their resort fully, since you will spend most of your time there and likely end up socializing with other guests.

Bringing the Family?

Although parents should always know where their children are, the setup of an AI resort, with their kids' clubs and activity programs, may allow parents to give children more freedom than they would get in a hotel that has a lot of casual traffic. This can be a big plus for AIs when parents and children are interested in doing different things. Again, parents should never get too lax about their children's safety while on vacation.

Convenience

Many people like the convenience of not having to carry money to pay for meals and activities. This is a nice perk of AIs.

Rooms

There is a wide range of accommodation quality at both AI resorts and EP hotels. If having a very nice room is important, you should make sure you do your research carefully. Don't make the mistake of thinking that an AI will automatically be nicer than a nearby EP hotel; the quality of both varies greatly.

Cost

Although many believe AIs are cheaper than EP hotels, this may vary depending on the vacationer and what kinds of activities they do while on vacation. Travelers who spend most of their time at the resort and partake in the free activities will probably find that an all-inclusive is the more economical choice. Vacationers who plan to take several tours and spend a lot of time outside the resort will probably find that an EP hotel is the lower-cost alternative.

Still unsure? Here's a helpful rule of thumb: if you have read this far, it means you like to do your research and enjoy learning about new things, and you should therefore almost certainly stay at an EP hotel.

MI CASA ES SU CASA—VACATION HOME RENTALS

For years, shrewd travelers to Mexico have chosen private condos and homes over hotels. As the popularity of these vacation rentals has soared internationally and development in Riviera Maya has multiplied, there are more options than ever. Some of the more popular spots for vacation rentals—Akumal, Puerto Aventuras, Puerto Morelos, Playacar, Soliman Bay, and others—are all good bets if your vacation will last longer than the standard four nights or if you're looking for a more immersive experience.

Private rentals can often accommodate larger groups at a lower overall price, and they feature kitchens and amenities that permit guests to dine in while also affording a greater degree of privacy than a hotel. Housekeeping is often included, and optional in-house chef services may be as well.

As with hotels, both quality and pricing range from budget to deluxe. You'll want to see as many photos as possible of the actual unit you'll be staying in, have a clear idea of its exact location, and review a full list of amenities and restrictions.

Most rental services offer private accommodations designed for vacation rental. However, the popularity of Airbnb has also introduced and popularized the concept of renting private rooms in shared homes. These are generally cheaper options and appeal to younger travelers (and homeowners or renters) who are on a tighter budget or who are seeking to get to know local residents (or foreigners, as the case may be).

Airbnb (Airbnb.com) has rental listings across the state of Quintana Roo that include private homes, condos, apartments, and shared rooms where guests stay with the owner. Terms and conditions vary from listing to listing.

HomeAway (www.HomeAway.com) has done much to market the private vacation home–rental approach in recent years, and its website offers thousands of rental listings across Cancún, Playa, and Tulum.

VRBO (www.VRBO.com), or Vacation Rental by Owner, is owned by HomeAway but has a separate listing service that features a vast selection of additional properties across the region. Many listings are exclusive, so you'll want to check both HomeAway and VRBO for the most comprehensive selection.

Tripping (www.Tripping.com) is a solid option for long- or short-term rentals in the region. With more than 15,000 rentals, the site is easy to search by price, ratings, and other amenities, and its partnership with Booking.com makes it even easier to find your perfect home away from home.

FlipKey (www.FlipKey.com) is owned by TripAdvisor, and their international listings are searchable by time-saving parameters like "family friendly" or "beach," which helps make browsing the more than 5,000 available options in the region a snap.

PUERTO AVENTURAS (HIGHWAY 307, KM 269)

On a beach south of the marina and 1 mile from Puerto Aventuras' main plaza, the upscale and very exclusive **Casa del Agua** (Highway 307, km 268, www.casadelagua.com) has four rooms right on a perfect, quiet beach in a residential area. Formerly a private residence, the décor is contemporary Mexican with handcrafted furniture, colorful Mexican textiles, and original artwork throughout. A good option for guests seeking simplicity, luxury, romance, and privacy. Latin superstar Marc Anthony showcased the property when filming the music video for his 2014 hit song *Cambio de Piel*. Search for it on YouTube for an extended view of the accommodations.

Adjacent to the white sandy beach and the commercial marina, the luxurious **Omni Puerto Aventuras Hotel Beach Resort** (Highway 307, km 269, www

.omnihotels.com) is placed at the center of activity in town. The hotel consists of just thirty rooms, but the amenities offered here are comparable to a hotel five times its size. Calm and peaceful, just like the surrounding neighborhood, it's popular with families, couples, and others looking to spend quality time with their travel companions.

Upscale and family-friendly, the 324-room, all-inclusive **Catalonia Riviera Maya** (Avenue Xcacel, Lot 1, off Highway 307, near km 271, www.hoteles-catalonia.com) gives guests a taste of the Mexican Caribbean while still providing high-end resort luxuries.

Bordering Puerto Aventuras to the north, you'll find the 1,264-room **Hard Rock Hotel Riviera Maya** (Highway 307, km 270, www.hrrivieramaya.com) occupying eight-five tropical acres along the beach. The combined resort features an exclusive adults-only section, Heaven at Hard Rock, that puts an extra degree of swank on display. Built around a natural ocean inlet, the resort is ideal for protected-water snorkeling, swimming, and sunbathing. It regularly hosts concerts with internationally celebrated pop and rock celebrities (you'll see the billboards up and down the highway). The Hard Rock Hacienda next door is a perfect spot for cool kids and their folks, complete with adult-free zones and activity clubs for both kids and tweens.

XPU-HA (HIGHWAY 307, KM 264)

A unique resort built on fifty secluded beachfront acres, **Hotel Esencia** (Highway 307, km 264, www.hotelesencia.com) has hosted many celebrities and is more of an opulent private residence than it is a hotel. Once the home of an Italian duchess, it comprises twenty-nine luxurious rooms and is notable for its ultra-cool Italian-Mexican décor. The property has large breezy terraces, an idyllic beachfront, high ceilings, an organic spa, a fitness center, and an on-site *cenote*.

LIVE LIKE A CELEBRITY FOR A WEEK

If hotels and condos aren't your thing but you still want to experience the Riviera Maya with first-class luxury and privacy, consider renting a beach house for your visit. Akumal Villas (www.akumal-villas.com) manages a collection of some of the finest private rental homes and villas in the area, with properties in Puerto Aventuras, Akumal, Jade Bay, South Akumal, Soliman Bay, and Tankah. These homes have one to six bedrooms and feature swimming pools, hammocks, full kitchens, purified water, safes, balconies, satellite TV, and other amenities. Full-time maids, caretakers, and on-call chefs and massage therapists are also provided.

Rooms feature premium bedding and liquor (including full-size bottles).

Next door, the small private **Al Cielo Hotel** (Highway 307, km 264.5, www.alcielohotel.com) provides a handful of suites and villas right on the beach, with easy access to the water. There's a small beach club and a gourmet restaurant specializing in fresh seafood and steaks. An on-site spa offers shiatsu, Reiki, reflexology, and face and skin treatments.

The Barcelo Maya Resort Complex (Highway 307, km 265, direct entrance from the highway, www.barcelo.com) is composed of more than two thousand rooms in five different hotels (Tropical, Beach, Caribe, Colonial, Maya Palace Deluxe). They're very popular for group trips, corporate-incentive travel, family reunions, weddings, honeymoons, and other occasions. The complex's scale makes it a great choice for first-time Riviera Maya travelers who would feel most comfortable surrounded by similar vacationers, rather than immersing themselves in the local culture. The more exclusive Royal Level offers additional amenities in a separate, dedicated area of the resort.

THE BEACH CABANAS AT HOTEL ESENCIA ARE PERFECTLY DESIGNED

The all-inclusive, 144-room **Bel Air Collection Xpu-Ha Riviera Maya** (Highway 307, km 265, www.belairxpuha.com) provides beachfront accommodations to families and couples who refuse to travel without their pets.

KANTENAH

Since it opened in early 2017, the luxurious, adults-only, all-inclusive **Unico 20°87°** (Highway 307, km 262, www.unicohotelrivieramaya.com) has racked up serious accolades from *Condé Nast Traveler*, *AFAR*, *Cosmopolitan*, TripAdvisor, and others for the quality of its accommodations, food, experiences, and programming. With a name that plays on the resort's latitude and longitude, Unico offers dedicated butler service for each room, curated shopping experiences, and a restaurant that revolves annually to feature the work of a new, notable chef.

The adults-only, 573-room, all-inclusive **El Dorado Seaside Suites** (9 Highway 307, km 262, www.karismahotels.com) is a popular destination for honeymooners, couples, and even families with adult children seeking to experience the Riviera Maya's less populated areas without sacrificing first-class service, comfort, and convenience. Ten restaurants serve Asian, Mexican, and other international cuisines (and no buffets). Ten bars and five pools are likewise sprinkled throughout the property. Guests can opt for the hotel's original 133-room property, now known as the Palm, or the newer six-story Infinity, with swim-up pool access on the ground floor. El Dorado Guests can pay a day-use fee to visit the clothing-optional Hidden Beach hotel next door.

The 414-room, all-inclusive, family-friendly **Grand Palladium Kantenah Resort & Spa** (Highway 307, km 260, www.palladiumhotelgroup.com) features Mayan-inspired architecture well-suited to its natural surroundings. The resort complex also incorporates two sister properties, Grand Palladium's Colonial and White Sand resorts. A staff biologist monitors the hotel's impact on the environment and advises on ways to preserve indigenous flora and fauna. As a result, there are many trees, tropical gardens, and native animals on the property. A half-mile stretch of open beach is perfect for jogging, swimming, and sun-worshipping.

The upscale forty-two-room, all-inclusive, clothing-optional **Hidden Beach Resort Au Naturel Resort** by Karisma (Highway 307, km 262, www.hiddenbeachresort.com) boasts a pool, hot tub, and beach *cabañas*. Guests can enjoy nude dining, sunbathing, and ocean swimming (though expect more rocks than sandy ocean floor). The hotel's gourmet restaurant serves three meals per day, either in the shaded dining room or al fresco, next to the pool. There is a swim-up bar, where bartenders (clothed, for the most part) are happy to mix up special drinks. At night, guests head to the on-site mini-discotheque for nude salsa lessons, dance music, and socializing. This is not a swingers resort and doesn't allow public displays of anything that would be deemed impermissible at a clothed hotel. Single travelers and gay couples are both welcome.

AKUMAL (HIGHWAY 307, KM 255)

Accommodations at the sprawling beach-front **Del Sol Beachfront Condos & Hotel** (Half Moon Bay, www.delsolbeachfront.com) range from a basic hotel room to a three-room condo at the water's edge that's darn near luxurious.

With 241 rooms and a broad white-sand beach, the all-inclusive **Akumal Beach Resort** (Highway 307, km 255, www.akumalbeachresort.com) is ideal for families and couples seeking casual and comfortable surroundings without superfluous amenities.

Open since the early 1990s, the family-friendly, all-inclusive **Gran Bahia Principe** (Highway 307, km 250, www.bahia-principe.es) is a massive upscale complex (more than two thousand rooms) that includes the Tulum, Akumal, and Cobá resorts and a central plaza with resort shops, a tour desk, and most of the popular nightlife attractions. The more upscale, modern, and adults-only Sian Ka'an sits in the middle of the new twenty-seven-hole, Robert Trent Jones II–designed Bahia Principe golf course.

Set upon Yalku Lagoon, the extremely basic, nine-room **Posada Que Onda** (on Caleta Yalku street, north of Half Moon Bay) offers charming and affordable accommodations, plus a large pool and the beach a mere 10-minute walk away. The on-site Italian restaurant serves seafood and homemade pasta under a large *palapa* roof.

CHEMUYIL (HIGHWAY 307, KM 249)

Although there have been plans for a luxury retreat in the area, nothing has yet been built. You can typically find at least twenty private homes or vacation rentals in Chemuyil listed on either **VRBO** (www.vrbo.com) or **Airbnb** (www.airbnb.com).

PUNTA SOLIMAN (HIGHWAY 307, KM 240)

After bouncing along the bumpy, mile-long dirt road from the highway, **Jashita Hotel** (Highway 307, km 241, www.jashitahotel.com) emerges as a boutique seaside oasis set on what's possibly the most coveted beach in the entire Caribbean. With its light Saharan motif, Moroccan influences, and modern vibe, the hotel is an ideal destination for pilgrims seeking an escape from the real world back home. Its beach may or may not be the exact filming location of the famous Corona commercials, but it's still picture-perfect and ideal for recreating the ads in style. With just seventeen rooms and suites, the luxury boutique resort's small inventory of rooms belies its ample facilities, which include a beachside pool for families and another for adults, a rooftop deck with its own bar and pool, and a café serving tasty Italian and other international fare with style. A curated shop sells a limited number of wraps, accessories, home goods, and other items culturally typical to Tulum, which is just 10 miles down the highway.

TANKAH (HIGHWAY 307, KM 237; BETWEEN XEL-HA AND TULUM)

The tiny **Blue Sky Resort** (Highway 307, km 237, on the beach, just past the *cenote* in Tankah, www.blueskytulum.com.mx) offers ten modern rooms and a small pool in the courtyard, right by the beach. An on-site restaurant serves a varied international menu and is open to the public.

A charming collection of casitas, **Casa Cenote** (Highway 307, km 237, on the beach next to Blue Sky Resort, www.casacenote.com) sits on the beach between the calm waters of Tankah Bay and Manatee Cenote. The rooms are

along the beach and have terra-cotta tile floors, local artwork, and ceiling fans; some also have air conditioning. The main hotel has a small restaurant and bar with a *palapa* roof and grill and several plastic tables on the beach.

✳ Where to Eat

PUERTO AVENTURAS (HIGHWAY 307, KM 269)

The majority of restaurants in Puerto Aventuras are located around the central marina plaza, overlooking the Dolphin Discovery waterway, and most have small interior dining rooms and patios with shaded tables. All in close proximity, it's easy to walk from one to the next, checking to see what looks good. Prices are a bit higher than in other areas of the region due to the resort's enclosed, exclusive nature and lower volume of visitors.

RELAX AND ENJOY THE NATURAL BEAUTY AROUND YOU IN PUERTO AVENTURAS CHIP RANKIN

Hippo Marina Lounge (www.hippos
.com.mx) is an eclectic marina-side
affair offering chimichangas, waffles,
seafood, and other delightful dishes. It's
a good spot to catch your favorite game,
toast your friends, or have an afternoon
cocktail.

Other notable options include **Dos
Chiles**, offering good basic Mexican
fare—shrimp, fajitas, tacos—in a casual
outdoor eatery, and **The Pub**, a popular
sports bar surrounded by shady trees
and serving inexpensive breakfast,
pizzas, fresh fish, tacos, enchiladas, and
shepherd's pie. **Restaurante 081** offers
better-than-you're-expecting Italian food
from a Neapolitan chef. From the same
country, although somewhat pricier,
Ristorante Massimo specializes in Italian food, including beef lasagna, pizzas,
pastas, and a good selection of ice cream
and desserts. **Aventura Gelato** (www
.aventuragelato.com) also delights the
sweet tooth with an array of Italian ices,
sorbets, and gelatos.

A WAITER DELIVERS DRINKS TO ONE OF THE ELEVATED
TABLES AT LA BUENA VIDA

XPU-HA (HIGHWAY 307, KM 264)

On the grounds of the Al Cielo hotel,
the casually upscale beachfront **Restaurante al Cielo** (Highway 307, km 264.5,
www.alcielohotel.com) has a *palapa*
roof and several tables right next to the
sand. The internationally trained chef
prepares shrimp, seafood paella, Angus
beef, duck, quail, and lamb. No credit
cards.

Created by chef Dimitris Katrivesis,
Mistura at Hotel Esencia (Highway 307,
km 265, www.hotelesencia.com) focuses
on seafood, featuring a fusion of Peruvian and Japanese flavors made with
organic ingredients native to the region.
The hotel also serves more traditional
Mexican and Yucatán cuisine at its Garden Restaurant.

The family-owned **La Playa** (Highway
307, km 265, www.laplayaxpuha.com)
offers hammocks, chairs, or several
palapa-shaded tables right on the beach.
Enjoy fresh seafood or kid-friendly

dishes while spending a day at the
full-service beach club.

AKUMAL (HIGHWAY 307, KM 255)

Just inside the main entry gate to
Akumal, you'll find a cluster of restaurants and shops. **Turtle Bay Café** (www
.turtlebaycafe.com) offers a little of
everything in a small, homey building
with a large *palapa* out front. With several ceiling fans, it's often one of the
cooler spots in town and is frequented by
local expats and villa owners.

The ultracasual and delightfully
rustic beach bar **La Buena Vida** (on
the beach of Half Moon Bay, www
.labuenavidarestaurant.com), or "The
Good Life" in English, has chair swings,
a long happy hour, good music, and an
upstairs indoor dining room with a nice
view of the beach, serving seafood, burgers, and steaks. Treehouse seating 20
feet above ground is accessible via ladders, and waiters will even climb up the
ladders carrying trays full of drinks.

The casual **La Lunita Restaurant** (at La Tortuga Condos on the beachfront a half-mile south of the marina, Half Moon Bay) serves international and Mexican dishes for breakfast and dinner.

PUNTA SOLIMAN (HIGHWAY 307, KM 240)

Set right along the highway and directly across the street from the Soliman Bay entrance, **Oscar y Lalo's** (Highway 307, km 241, www.oscarandlalo.com) serves delicious fresh seafood and standard Mexican favorites, including great ceviche and fish fillets. The best thing on the menu is the fried whole fish, large enough for two. Don't let the roadside location fool you; once you pass through its hacienda-like gate, the restaurant's traditional Mexican design and shaded tropical gardens (complete with a footbridge over a fish pond) enchant completely.

Sahara Cafè (Highway 307, km 241, www.jashitahotel.com), inside the Jashita Hotel, features Italian, Mediterranean, and international cuisine. Fresh fish carpaccio and lobster spaghetti are popular favorites. The restaurant has its own entrance, and both Soliman residents and visitors are welcome.

TULUM &
THE MAYAN COAST

TULUM & THE MAYAN COAST

Once just a dusty, often overlooked bookend to the Riviera Maya, Tulum is now an important international landmark along Mexico's Caribbean coast. Among many international circles, it's arguably more noteworthy than Playa. The hippies and adventurous backpackers of yesteryear are still there, but they've been joined by sun worshippers, yoga enthusiasts, and in-the-know travelers looking for a unique destination on pristine natural beaches.

Tulum is also the gateway for exploring most of the more rugged and lesser-known parts of the state of Quintana Roo. The Riviera Maya officially ends at the edge of the city, where Highway 307 intersects the road to Cobá, just south of the turnoff to the Tulum ruins. Turn west at the crossroads, and the town of Cobá, a picturesque lagoon, and the Mayan ruins of the same name will be about an hour away.

Turn to the east and away from Cobá on the same road, and you'll come to a T-intersection with QROO 15, the two-lane road through Tulum's bohemian hotel zone, which dots the coast to your left and right. If you turn left and pass the final Tulum hotel, you'll soon find yourself on a dirt road in **Sian Ka'an**—a massive 780,000-acre reserve, set aside for preservation and scientific study, with a few tropical outposts of civilization along its starkly beautiful coast.

If you opt to take the highway straight through the actual town of Tulum, the busy *pueblo*, then your southward journey will lead you to the Mayan Coast, also called the Sun Coast. The road bypasses Laguna Bacalar as it skirts the Sian Ka'an biosphere, offers a connection to the quietly hip Mahahual, continues toward Kohunlich and on to Chetumal, and eventually leads to the beach town of Xcalak and the border of Belize.

TULUM (HIGHWAY 307, KM 230)

Once known for its photo-friendly beachside Mayan ruins and its bohemian amenity-light eco-lodges, modern Tulum has evolved. Celebrated in the *New York Times*, *Travel + Leisure*, and *Robb Report*, Tulum is now officially a destination unto itself. Even as Playa del Carmen has emerged as the antithesis of Cancún, a visit to Tulum offers yet another immersive experience that's unlike either. Not only unique in Mexico, Tulum stands out within the greater Caribbean, all of Latin America, and perhaps even the world.

Depending on your point of view and choice of accommodation, Tulum may seem rustic, avant-garde, trendy, timeless, spiritual, showy, simple, high-profile, forgotten, embracing, and/or standoffish. The mix can be intoxicating. Its allure stems from its slam-dunk perfect beaches, dense natural vegetation (you can actually hear the jungle at night), low-impact development, jungle-luxe style, remote sense of adventure, and tropical otherworldliness.

Tulum's (boutique) hotel zone is unlike any of the densely packed *zonas* to the north. Even with light development, Tulum's coastal road feels authentically organic. A single two-lane road runs parallel to the sea and serves as the only artery for taxis, delivery trucks, mopeds, bicycles, and pedestrians. But instead of congested gridlock, the

VIDAS—HELPING PETS AND PEOPLE IN THE RIVIERA MAYA

A group of volunteer animal lovers called International Veterinarians Dedicated to Animal Health (VIDAS) travels each year to the Riviera Maya, providing education and free veterinary care in an effort to fight pet overpopulation, which leads to starvation, disease, and other health problems. They work with local communities to improve the lives of pets and the people who love them. Their first trip, in 2002, involved two vets and six students and resulted in the sterilization of one hundred cats and dogs over five days in Playa del Carmen. Since then, more than 5,000 animals have been sterilized and vaccinated throughout the Yucatán peninsula.

If you'd like to help the group by sponsoring a pet, making a contribution, or otherwise participating, log on to www.vidas.org.

modest traffic actually ebbs and flows, moving at a reasonably cautious pace (small, frequently-placed speed bumps help).

Palm trees, mangroves, bamboo, and other vegetation still dominate the street, often working together to shade the roadway and people below. Boutique hotel entrances and jungle fences line most of the coastal side of the road, offering peeks of their enticing beaches. On the west side of the road, small outdoor restaurant patios and Lululemon-esque shops in thatched, air-conditioned huts dot the path. Just about everything exists on a small, intimate scale, and stretches along this 6.5-mile route are often lined only with undeveloped tropical forest.

Much of this natural greenery can be chalked up to a desire to preserve Tulum's distinct character, but it's also due to the town's proximity to the Sian Ka'an Biosphere Reserve and the massive, encroaching jungle that extends to the north and between the hotel zone and the *pueblo* 2 miles west. With only a small, narrow footprint of development hugging the coast, the thick, untouched forest beyond to the west is a genuine presence. Many say it infuses Tulum with life and energy, making it feel like an exceptionally special place.

It might be true. At night, the stars are deep and bright, with the dense jungle and small development keeping light pollution at bay. In fact, outside of the hotels, restaurants, and occasional shops, there's no stationary nighttime lighting in the hotel zone. Passing cabs or bikes with generators cast passing lights on the road, reminding you of the thick jungle several meters away. While it could be

IN TULUM, THE COMMUTER TRAFFIC LOOKS A LOT LIKE THIS CHIP RANKIN

surreally unnerving to visitors from big cities, the quietness is not a sign of danger, just remoteness.

GETTING THERE Tulum lies about 80 miles south of the Cancún airport. Most hotels featured in this guidebook include airport transfers in their rates, and it's easy to arrange a taxi to Tulum or rent a car from tourist areas around the Riviera Maya.

Highway 307 leads straight through Tulum proper, and turning east onto the Cobá highway leads one directly to the *zona hotelera*. Once at the crossroads of Tulum's beachfront artery, most hotels, restaurants, and shops lie to the south. However, there are still great hotels and beaches to the north as well.

BOCA PAILA, SIAN KA'AN, & PUNTA ALLEN

Very few travelers will ever have the chance to visit a place as remote—and as starkly beautiful—as the **Sian Ka'an Biosphere Reserve** (www.visitsiankaan) in their entire lives. Meaning "gift from the sky" or "the sky's beginning" (depending on which translation you believe), Sian Ka'an was officially designated a nature reserve in 1986. It spans more than 1.25 million acres, represents ten percent of the land in the state of Quintana Roo, and is an official UNESCO World Heritage site. Don't expect to find picnic tables, public bathrooms, concession stands, or beach bars—this is not a nature park like Xcaret or Xel-Ha. This land is remote and does not have any of the facilities or services that travelers sometimes associate with the word "park." Once Sian Ka'an became a federal reserve, all development was frozen and all activities strictly regulated in order to protect the wild diversity of flora, fauna, and ecosystems found within the reserve. There are more than three hundred species of birds (including herons, ibis, roseate spoonbills, and parrots), at least one hundred species of mammals (wild cats, monkeys, coatimundis, and deer, among others), and geographical features including barrier reefs, mangrove swamps, lagoons, marshes, and tropical forests. There are also more than twenty-five Mayan relics, small native villages, and ruins of abandoned ranches, hotels, restaurants, and homes.

The goal of the reserve is to provide a place where nature can thrive on its own, absent the negative impacts associated with the presence of humans and the development that so often seems to follow. A portion of this biosphere is completely restricted, but much of it is open to exploration, so long as visitors follow the reserve's strict rules about low- or no-impact adventuring. A rocky and sometimes sandy road passes through the area, and vehicles may not depart from the path. There is no inland fishing or scuba diving permitted, but snorkeling is still allowed, which has a lower impact on the reefs. A handful of fishing lodges and rustic hotels do operate in the reserve but must provide their own water and electricity because there are no utilities in the area.

There is a $3-per-person fee to enter the park, and all travelers must check in at the visitors center. Jeeps and four-wheel-drive vehicles are recommended, as the road is heavily rutted, rocky, and sometimes muddy. Taking a regular rental sedan on the road makes for slow going and may violate your renter's agreement, nullifying any sort of insurance you may have purchased, so it's best to check in advance. There are plenty of picturesque and totally deserted beaches where you can stop for a bit of beachcombing, picture-taking, and stretching. Unfortunately, since the beach is not attended to, as it is at the resorts, years of washed-up trash remain at the high-tide mark, making a silent yet very compelling case for the need for more awareness of garbage-dumping in the world's oceans.

At the southern end of the road, you'll reach the tiny village of **Punta Allen**. And no, some gringo named Allen doesn't own the town. The name comes from the Mayan

HOW GREEN WAS MY GETAWAY?

Evaluating Ecological and Sustainable Marketing Claims

Since 2006, many hotels and tourism businesses have been championing themselves as environmentally sensitive. Terms like *green, sustainability, carbon offsets,* and *eco-friendly* appear with increasing frequency.

Once companies became aware of the marketing advantages of an environmentally and culturally conscious brand, the claims came fast and furious. Many are genuine. Many are superficial. And many lie somewhere in between.

No hotel or company on Earth has perfected its sustainability program, so if a business makes a genuine effort today, and seeks to improve it, that represents progress.

If you're booking a trip and want to stay in sustainable properties, it can be hard to determine just how valid a company's assertions might be. Here are a few rules of thumb that should help you gauge their authenticity.

Seek specific details. If a hotel or business is actively making an effort to engage in real sustainability programs, they'll be glad to share particulars. You'll often see them articulated on their website. If not, sending an email asking for specifics will usually reveal what you want to know.

Make sure they aren't just focused on your sacrifice. If green programs are based on your willingness to make a sacrifice, then that business isn't doing very much. All hotels want you to limit the number of items you send through their laundry and to reduce your consumption of their energy and resources. It costs them less. And while it's great that they may want to educate you about recycling once you return home, that doesn't take much effort on their part. If they aren't actively engaging in daily practices and programs themselves, then their marketing claims are hardly genuine.

It's not all about LEED certification. In the US, a LEED-certified (Leadership in Energy and Environmental Design) building shows the builder's observation of environmental principles. But LEED is an American program and is often unrecognized overseas. Even with certification, ongoing operations involving energy conservation, recycling, use of environmentally safe cleaning agents, and buying food and resources from local producers can have a much larger impact.

Be forgiving with smaller, established "ecological" hotels. Although all the above points hold true, the term "ecological" has been in use for a long time in Latin America and the Caribbean, signifying a smaller, rustic, low-impact property. Some hotels of this type continue to use the term without intentionally engaging in any new specific efforts toward sustainability. Often, it's the context of the word that's changed on *them*. But even without specific programs, these smaller hotels do produce a correspondingly smaller environmental footprint, and their overall negative impacts are typically much lower than those of the concrete box resorts found along the beach.

word *allin*, which means "crocodile." The village is home to six-hundred inhabitants, said to originate from ninety original families. There are a handful of lodges, a couple of restaurants, a bar, and a general store called Tienda Socorro where travelers can purchase basic supplies.

With mangrove swamps, shallow lagoons, and a barrier reef that comes quite close to the beach, this region is a favorite for birdwatchers, anglers, and shell collectors. Crocodiles and manatees also make their home here, which adds to the overall excitement and improves your chance for a once-in-a-lifetime natural encounter. Jimmy Buffett fans will recognize this area as the setting for the singer's novel *A Salty Piece of Land*, which chronicles an American expatriate cowboy who sails with his horse to the fictitious island of Punta Margarita (sound familiar?) in Ascension Bay and becomes a fishing guide.

GETTING THERE Take Highway 307, the main highway along the Riviera Maya, south from Playa del Carmen to the town of Tulum, about 45 minutes away. At the main Cobá crossroads, one stoplight past the turnoff to the Tulum ruins, turn east and follow the paved road a couple of miles to the end, and then turn right, to the south, and parallel the beach. After passing the Tulum beach hotel zone, you'll cross a usually empty guard post marking the unofficial beginning of the Sian Ka'an biosphere reserve. Three miles later, you'll come to an arch across the road and the official, always-manned entrance. All vehicles must stop to be logged in and to pay a $2-per-person fee to enter. Once inside the park, follow the road along the beach for another 10 miles (about 45 minutes' worth of bumping up and down), and you will reach Boca Paila, marked by twin bridges—one wooden, one concrete, built in 2005—over the lagoon. Twenty miles into the trip, you'll come across a small, unmarked Mayan temple partially hidden in the scrub brush next to the road on its west side. Several miles later, the road ends at the town of Punta Allen. Once you've left Tulum, the next gas station is in Punta Allen, which is 40 miles and about an hour and a half away (in good conditions), so don't leave without filling up.

Colectivo shuttle service is available from Tulum to Punta Allen, departing from a garage on Highway 307, two blocks north of the Weary Traveler. It leaves daily at 2 PM.

THE MAYAN COAST—SOUTH OF THE RIVIERA MAYA, TULUM, & SIAN KA'AN

South of the Riviera Maya, beyond Tulum and the nearby Sian Ka'an reserve, are some curious and quirky hideaways few travelers venture to see, including the stunning Lake of Seven Colors and the emerging town of Mahahual, which just may become the quirky, upscale getaway that today's toddlers favor in 20 years.

The road to the Mayan Coast is the same Highway 307 that takes travelers into Tulum. After continuing through the center of downtown Tulum, the highway skirts to the west, going around the Sian Ka'an Biosphere Reserve. The road into the reserve dead-ends at Punta Allen, so it's not possible to reach the places in this chapter from there unless you also have access to a boat or airplane.

MAHAHUAL

When you arrive in Mahahual, you'll immediately notice its laid-back atmosphere but possibly also that things may be changing. More villas and small inns continue to pop up, and the town is slowly developing a rustic yet upscale tone, similar to Playa del Carmen in its earlier days. There are a few sandy streets and several open-air restaurants, and hotels and private homes are stretched out along the beach.

The shallow reefs of the Chinchorro Banks are known for being the healthiest in the area, with huge sea fans, sponges, anemones, sea cucumbers, arrow crabs, and seahorses. There are also hundreds of species of fish (including large barracuda), sea turtles, and even dolphins, which sometimes follow dive boats and play in the wake.

In 2000, Mahahual completed construction of a cruise ship terminal, and each month there seem to be increasing arrivals, which are steadily changing the face of the town. The cruise dock is only five blocks from the town center, and the streets have become lined with new restaurants, bars, and souvenir shops. When the boats are in town, the beach is full of day-trippers snorkeling, swimming, riding WaveRunners, and enjoying the day. The rest of the time the village is noticeably more mellow, with locals talking in the storefronts, tourists lingering at the beachside restaurants, and only a few people relaxing on the beach.

GETTING THERE To get to Mahahual by car from anywhere along the Riviera Maya, take Highway 307 south toward Chetumal. Fill up with gas when you go through the town of Carillo Puerto, as there are few stations in this area. Once you pass the village of Limones (about 2.5 miles south of Playa), you'll go approximately 2 more miles, and then you should see a sign for Mahahual and the Cafetal exit. Turn left and head east to the beach. From this point, Mahahual is still about an hour away. About half-way down this road, you'll arrive at a military checkpoint, so don't be alarmed if you see men in uniform carrying machine guns. They may search your car for drugs, but they are courteous and won't cause any problems—as long as you don't. The road is a fairly straight shot through the jungle before arriving finally at the small beach town of Mahahual. Most hotels, restaurants, dive shops, and other attractions are located proximally to where the main road meets the beach.

To get to Mahahual by bus, from the Cancún station take a bus to Limones, either a direct route or a bus to Chetumal that stops there. Because not all buses to Chetumal stop in Limones, be sure to verify that yours will. From there, transfer to a Mahahual bus, which leaves every hour or so from Limones.

LAGUNA BACALAR

About 2.5 hours south of Playa del Carmen is Laguna Bacalar, a freshwater lake just east of Highway 307 that feeds into Chetumal Bay. With crystal-clear water and gleaming white sands, it's a rare jewel in the jungle. The lake presents a dramatic setting and has varying depths, which causes the color of the water to change from spot to spot—hence its nickname, the Lake of Seven Colors. It's a prime spot for snorkeling, bird-watching, swimming, and photography.

✳ To See & Do

TULUM (HIGHWAY 307, KM 230)

Beachfront Maya Spa (adjacent to the Azulik hotel, www.maya-spa.com) offers daily yoga classes, lucid dreaming courses, and a *temazcal*, a Mayan-style sweat lodge. Local shamans perform traditional Mayan treatments, and local healers use native plants and herbs to perform various therapeutic ceremonies. Other services include body wraps, Reiki, aesthetic treatments, Mayan massage, and flotation-chamber therapy.

There are multiple hip hotels, complete with interior bars and lounges for those looking to keep their evening going, but collectively these spots do not constitute anything like a nightclub or even a meet-up scene. Whether between couples, friends, families, or visitors with common interests (like a yoga camp), nights end quietly in Tulum. Given the spectacular sunsets, it's not surprising.

BOCA PAILA, SIAN KA'AN, & PUNTA ALLEN

The shallow flats, coves, and tiny coastal islands of Sian Ka'an, Punta Allen, and Ascension Bay offer some of the best fly- and light-tackle fishing in the world. Popular catches include barracuda, bonefish, and the coveted permit, which range from two to twenty pounds. Many of the lodges host fly-tying sessions for anglers who want to tie their own flies. If you're not familiar with fly-fishing techniques, local guides can teach you how to do it. If that's not your thing, you can fish in many of the same spots using light tackle. Most fish are caught by sight-casting, where the guide or the angler stands on the boat and searches the water for signs of fish, and then makes pinpoint casts. At other times, anglers will wade into the waist-deep water and cast into the schools.

Led by a bilingual guide, the **Friends of Sian Ka'an Tour** (www.amigosdesiankaan .org) takes guests on a driving excursion through the reserve, a boat trip through the mangroves, and a visit to a freshwater spring.

If you have only one day to visit Sian Ka'an but want to fit in as much as possible, try **Jeep Safari Sian Ka'an** (www.siankaanjeepsafari.com), which includes a Jeep ride for four into the biosphere, an English-speaking guide, a boat tour to see dolphins, swimming, snorkeling, bird-watching, and beachcombing.

✳ Lodging

TULUM (HIGHWAY 307, KM 230)

Notable hotels and guesthouses can be found on the beachfront to the north and south of Tulum, as well as within the *pueblo*, or downtown area, of Tulum itself.

Quirky, grand, delightful, cheeky, and occasionally imposing, **Casa Malca** (4 miles south of Tulum's Cobá and QROO 15 crossroads, www.casamalca.com) is ideally suited for those seeking a touch of big-city chic in their Tulum experience. Eclectically curated by its owner, New York art gallery owner Lio Malca, the boutique resort is a bona fide curiosity. After entering its unmarked gates, visitors approach a grand white edifice, its entrance covered in tree bark and its frames adorned with massive, flowing white curtains which are rumored to have been poached from the wedding train in a British Royal wedding (they weren't). To either side, an old Victorian-style couch and a pair of comparably formal sitting chairs hang from chains, inviting guests to have a swing. The lobby space and (uncommon) common areas display works from contemporary artists, including a piece by New York pop favorite KAWS. Ample and spacious rooms are located in modern bungalows peppered along the beach, which are decorated with art from Malca's personal collection

and regionally sourced furniture. Comfy bedding, walk-in rain showers, air conditioning, and resort-wide Wi-Fi are additional amenities.

Like most of Tulum, the beach here is perfect. And while the hotel's pool is also quite nice, it contains a dark, inviting secret—a second, small subterranean pool tucked away off to the side, and beneath the beach. This second pool isn't a natural *cenote* but seems rather a tongue-in-cheek play on these natural wonders. Accessible by steps within the main pool or from a staircase outside of it, the round, blue-tile lined room is a fun, frivolous distraction (which also doubles as a sauna).

Just a stone's throw from the Tulum ruins, the Thai- and Mediterranean-influenced beachfront hotel, restaurant, and lounge **Mezzanine** (1 mile north of the crossroads from Tulum, www .mezzaninetulum.com) oozes style, with a provocative décor and deeply romantic appeal. A smallish *cenote*-like plunge pool and a cozy bar and lounge front its four hotel rooms. At night, tiki torches and red and orange candles bathe the whole of the pool deck and dining room in a sensual amber glow. The bar has become a trendy spot for traveling hipsters and locals alike. Every Friday, visiting DJs from Europe and around the world spin house and chill-out music for as many as 250 people.

Tucked away just north of the Sian Ka'an Biosphere Reserve, the five-suite

ONE OF THE SAND IN YOUR TOES OPTIONS AT CASA MALCA CHIP RANKIN

Casa de las Olas (southern limits of Tulum, www.casadelasolas.com) aims to differentiate itself through "great food, engaging conversation, discrete relaxation," and a general attentiveness to the local land and its people. Operating exclusively on solar power, the hotel's five richly appointed rooms offer a serene and sensory-laden escape from the everyday.

With clean, smooth beaches and an environmentally sustainable aesthetic, **Ahau Tulum** (Tulum beach road, km 7.8, www.ahautulum.com) is a solid embodiment of modern Tulum, where style meets eco-minded substance. Most of the twenty-three rooms feature high, triangular Polynesian-style thatched roofs, and all are air-conditioned, have Wi-Fi, and include romantic, but functional, mosquito netting. The hotel offers yoga classes and kite- and paddle surfing lessons.

Adults-only **Kore Tulum Retreat and Spa Resort** (at the Tulum crossroads and road to Cobá, www.koretulum.com) enjoys a prime position at the key intersection of Tulum's coastal hotel zone. The largest, most mainstream resort in the area, it is curiously one of the few lacking its own direct beach access. The only local large-scale property, it's a bit garish next to its neighbors, but if its size and slightly corporate feel aren't issues, it's a good option, especially for people who want to dip their toes into Tulum while holding onto the full-service resort comforts of Playa. The hotel facilities themselves have gone through several owners and concepts, including Zenserenity Wellness Resort, Blue Tulum, and a gay resort named Adonis. Due to a rocky waterfront and aggressive waves, ocean access is offered at the nearby beach club.

The adults-only resort **Azulik** (a half-mile south of Tulum *pueblo*, www.azulik.com) is a large village-style resort with fifteen beachside huts made from local hardwoods and other materials. Each sports a waterfront deck, a private bathroom with hot water, and a wooden bathtub situated smack dab in the middle of the room. Candles and matches are provided as the rooms do not have electricity, enhancing the far-away, escapist feel of the resort. The beach right behind the hotel is rocky with many sea fans that

THE LOW-KEY, STYLISH POOL AT CASA MALCA CHIP RANKIN

wash in with the tide, but there are sandy access points a short walk away.

Situated on a small, quiet beach, **Zamas Beach Cabañas** (3 miles south of the Tulum crossroads, www.zamas .com) takes its name from the Mayan word for "sunrise" and has *palapa* bungalows with eighteen rooms. Wind- and solar-generated power stays on until late at night. An open-air restaurant features Mayan-inspired dishes, Mexican specialties, wood-oven pizza, and fresh seafood, including lobster. Wi-Fi included.

With a self-styled jungle-chic vibe, **La Zebra Beachfront Cabanas & Cantina** (3.7 miles south of Tulum, www .lazebratulum.com) seems a landmark of an imagined and storied 1980s Tulum—even though there was nothing like it in Tulum's hippie heyday. Premium bed linens, ceiling fans, large beds, hole-free mosquito nets, wireless internet access, and local artwork ensure an air of casual luxury. Outdoor pit-roasts are featured on the giant charcoal grill each Sunday. Guests and visitors are invited.

The Ana y José Charming Hotel & Spa (5 miles south of Tulum, www .anayjose.com) offers twenty-three clean, comfortable, and well-designed rooms. Its beach club has developed a reputation for its party scene and frequently plays host to day-tripping revelers from Playa del Carmen and beyond, which can boost excitement in what is otherwise a fairly remote spot. Rooms are air-conditioned and have Wi-Fi.

Nearby, the ten serene beachfront casitas of **Shambala Petit Hotel** (www .shambalapetithotel.com) serve as a haven for couples and close friends seeking to disconnect from their regular lives and reconnect with each other, nature, and themselves. The hotel offers traditional Mayan-style rooms with *palapa* roofs and mosquito nets, plus yoga classes, Thai massage, scuba trips, wedding planning, and a pristine beach.

The nineteen beach cabins at **Alaya Tulum** (3 miles south of the crossroads, www.alayatulum.com) are simply appointed, but given the rich variety of textures and natural elements used in their making, they can feel quite decadent. Comfy beds and fantastic ocean views don't hurt either. You can also channel your inner Fred Flintstone and work out at the hotel's outdoor jungle gym, with weights and equipment constructed from natural local materials.

The tropical mod-styled **Mi Amor** (a half-mile north of the crossroads, www .tulumhotelmiamor.com) has seventeen airy, upscale rooms that would be equally at home in Bali or Saint Lucia. The ultra-sleek hotel sits on a rocky outcropping, but Zacil Beach Club next door presents a fine option for guests who want to run their toes through the sand. One of the more luxurious alternatives in Tulum, rooms are air-conditioned, including Wi-Fi, and some even offer private plunge pools.

Top-rated **Encantada Tulum** (3.5 miles south of the crossroads, www .encantadatulum.com) offers eight rooms in a handful of beachside bungalows. Half the rooms are air-conditioned, with the second story rooms cooled by ocean breezes.

If you're looking to stay in town, aka Tulum *pueblo*, you'll find a wealth of opportunities in the city's center. Best bets for longer stays can be found on the **Airbnb** and **HomeAway** websites.

Located one block off the main strip in Tulum *pueblo*, the small, stylish,

nine-room **Hotel Latino** (Andromeda Street at Colonia Centro, www .hotellatinotulum.com) has a hip vibe and a central location, if you're looking to base yourself in town. There is a small pool, and rates include free bicycle rental.

The best bet for low-budget info and activity in Tulum *pueblo*, **The Weary Traveler Hostel** (Tulum Avenue between Jupiter and Acuario Streets, www .wearytravelerhostel.rocks) provides a nice shaded courtyard and snack bar, a common refrigerator, and basic rooms with bunk beds. The hostel offers discounted tours, gear rental, and traveler camaraderie, and is known as a good place to party with other backpackers.

BEST PLACES TO STAY IN AND AROUND BOCA PAILA, SIAN KA'AN, & PUNTA ALLEN

Accommodations are eco-friendly "lodges," which means they are simple, offering few amenities—no air conditioning, bathtubs, or swimming pools. Travelers in these parts tend to be nature enthusiasts, backpacking adventurers,

A RUSTIC BEACH CABANA AT AZULIK IN TULUM

serious anglers, and others who are comfortable in tents, wooden *cabañas*, or other no-frills accommodations. For the hardy few who are up to the task, staying the night in the biosphere can reveal wondrous parts of the jungle rarely seen by others. The hotels in the area offer shuttle service from Cancún or the Riviera Maya, with advance notice required. Credit cards are not accepted, except for advance reservations in some cases, so plan ahead.

Now, in direct contrast to all those warnings, the **KanXuk Blue Maya Resort** (37 miles south of Tulum in www .kanxuk.com) offers simple but genuine luxury along a private beach about halfway to Punta Allen. The small, beachfront hotel features a pool, a spa, five rooms, and four ocean bungalows. The resort's well-appointed quarters are air-conditioned and provide Wi-Fi, room service, and flat screen TVs (if all the rustic nature gets to be too much for you). Stays include airport transfers by car and boat. This sort of indulgence doesn't come cheaply in Sian Ka'an, so expect to pay what you would for topnotch accommodations in the heart of Playa del Carmen or Cancún.

Just when you think you can't take the bumpy road through Sian Ka'an any more, you arrive at **Pesca Maya** (3 miles north of Punta Allen, www.pescamaya .com), on Mexico's Ascension Bay. The lodge is built on the grounds of the Chenchomac (Mayan for "land of the foxes") ranch, a former coconut plantation. It has a large, well-built *palapa* restaurant and bar, which also serves as a library, fly-tying station, and social center. Eight rooms, each with two double beds, are located in two seaside homes and a quadplex. These accommodations have air conditioning, walk-in showers, and Wi-Fi.

Owned and run by American husband and wife ex-pats, **The Palometa Club** (Punta Allen Road, www.palometaclub .com) sits on the beach in Punta Allen, close to the mouth of Ascension Bay's permit and bonefishing flats. The house has six air-conditioned rooms, each with two double beds, private bathrooms, 24-hour electricity, and Wi-Fi. The bar serves up complimentary margaritas, cold beer, and local rum drinks during happy hour.

Grand Slam Fishing Lodge (about a mile north of Punta Allen, www .grandslamfishinglodge.com) offers fishing aficionados and their traveling companions a mini-resort experience just north of town. Six villas contain twelve rooms, each with comfortable Balinese-style beds, air conditioning, and Wi-Fi. The thatched-roof lodge house contains a restaurant, bar, and social area.

With its tropical thatched awning and surfboard signs, **Fisherman Fly Fishing Lodge and Beach Club** (a half block north of the beachfront Punta Allen Road at the intersection of three unnamed roads, www.fishermanlodge.com) gives off a welcoming, Parrothead vibe. The facilities are much like those at some of the oldest beach hotels in Playa and feature air conditioning, Wi-Fi, and other creature comforts.

FIVE RESORTS FOR ECO-CONSCIOUS TRAVELERS

- **Mayakoba** (www.mayakoba.com, near Playa del Carmen): Any of the luxury resort destinations nestled in this planned community, including the Fairmont Mayakoba, Rosewood Mayakoba, Banyan Tree Mayakoba, and Andaz Mayakoba, reflect the beauty of the surrounding mangrove forests, canals, nature trails, and breathtaking wildlife.
- **Sandos Caracol Eco Resort** (www.sandos.com/sandos-caracol/sandos-caracol-eco-resort, Playa del Carmen): All-inclusive amenities like a waterpark and kids' club blend in with earnest environmental practices like water- and energy-saving programs, an on-site plant nursery, and organic gardens.
- **Hacienda Tres Ríos** (www.haciendatresrios.com, Playa del Carmen): An ecopark until 2008, the 326-acres of Tres Ríos is truly a private oasis. Guests can enjoy ten *cenotes*, kayaking on three freshwater rivers, and hundreds of species of native flora and fauna.
- **Azulik Eco Resort and Spa** (www.azulik.com, Tulum): Escape the urban bustle at this romantic, adults-only resort lit by candles and crafted from native materials.

Finally, if Punta Allen isn't far enough for you, you can always opt for **Casa Blanca** on Ascension Bay or **Playa Blanca** on Espiritu Santo Bay (www.casablancafishing.com) on the privately managed island Punta Pájaros, south of Ascension Bay. Set in stunning environs that recall Hollywood movie sets, accommodations here are rustic; the focus remains on the surrounding natural beauty. The rooms, however, do have air conditioning and Wi-Fi. You'll be hard-pressed to get there from Sian Ka'an. Transfers are provided by air from Cancún and are built into the pricey accommodation. A minimum five-day stay will run you more than $3,000 per person, assuming double occupancy.

MAHAHUAL

Hip, trendy, and right in the center of town on the beach, the ten-room **La Posada de los 40 Canones** or Forty Cannons Hotel (Malecón Mahahual, km 1.3, www.40canones.com) may seem bustling for the area but, relative to more touristy destinations up the coast, is still ultra-relaxed. It has twenty-six rooms with private bathrooms, including some swanky suites.

Sitting on downtown Mahahual's charming and colorful boardwalk, **Hotel El Caballo Blanco** (www.hotelelcaballoblanco.com) features seven air-conditioned rooms with Wi-Fi by the beach.

Almaplena Eco Resort and Beach Club (about 8 miles south of downtown on Huauchinango street, www.almaplenabeachresort.com) is a stylish little boutique with nine beachfront rooms, Wi-Fi, and a relaxed vibe.

LAGUNA BACALAR

A full-service hotel with thirty-three rooms and suites—some of them air-conditioned—and incomparable views of the lagoon, **Hotel Laguna Bacalar** (25 miles north of Chetumal, just off Highway 307, www.hotellagunabacalar.com) is an ideal, if simple, headquarters from which to explore the area. The crisp-white, turquoise, and pink hotel feels like a charming throwback to 1950s Baja California. A terrace restaurant overlooks the lagoon, and a sundeck offers direct access to it.

The thirty-two-room eco lodge **Rancho Encantado** (Highway 307, km 24, just north of the town of Bacalar, www.encantado.com) offers comfortably pleasant cabins with lagoon and garden views. Rooms have air conditioning and Wi-Fi.

✳ Where to Eat

The shining star in Tulum's dining scene, media darling **Hartwood** (2.8 miles south of the Tulum highway, www.hartwoodtulum.com) is an open-air, expat-owned establishment that, in line with its rustically hip atmosphere, eschews the grid. The restaurant serves up incredibly tasty and fresh dishes and its reputation is entirely earned. All cooking is naturally powered, with solar panels providing Hartwood's limited supply of electricity. Chef Eric Werner's farm-to-table concept features a constantly evolving menu reflecting the local meats and produce available on any given week. Tables are in high demand, and reservation policies change throughout the year, so check Hartwood's website for the latest instructions. When Hartwood says guests must line up at 3 PM for a same-day reservation, many, many people do. Walk-ins are still encouraged, but you may need to wait a while. All this drama exists for a reason. A meal at Hartwood's is easily the best you'll experience in the Riviera Maya, if not in all of Mexico. Open for dinner only Wednesday through Sunday, from early November through late August.

Philosophy, also known as Philosophia (4 miles south of Tulum's Cobá and QROO 15 crossroads, www.casamalca.com), at Casa Malca presents a mix of Mexican, Mayan, and international dishes in a quirky interior (think old wooden frames and marionette limbs) and on a perfect beachside patio. The bar has a tasty cocktail program as well.

The seaside dining at **Mezzanine** (1 mile north of the crossroads from Tulum, www.mezzaninetulum.com), in the hotel of the same name, features stunning views and tasty Thai and Asian fusion dishes. It's also an excellent place for a cocktail.

A few doors north of Hartwood, you'll find the hip and savvy soaking up the ambience at **Gitano** (2.9 miles from the crossroads, www.gitanotulum.com). The bohemian restaurant and mezcal bar serves up ceviches, tacos, seafood, and pork specialties. With spacious outdoor seating amid the vegetation, the venue is like a cool, modern outdoor living room in the jungle.

Nearby, the covered, open-air seating at **Casa Jaguar** (2.7 miles from the crossroads, www.casajaguartulum.com) spills out into its own, lush tropical garden, where guests toss back cocktails and dine on fresh seafood and other locally inspired dishes.

Argentinian steakhouse **Casa Banana** (3.1 miles south of the crossroads, www.casabananatulum.com) also serves homemade chorizo, fresh fish, and great drinks.

Traditional local cuisine is served up with innovative culinary style at the popular **El Tábano** (1.6 miles south of the crossroads). Seemingly squirreled away in the jungle growth, this rustic restaurant surprises with some seriously modern fare from the bustling kitchen.

In town, **La Coqueta** (Tulum Avenue and Cobá Avenue) delights locals and visitors with classic Mexican food in downtown Tulum. Expect live music, a casual atmosphere, good food served quickly, and a friendly environment—everything you would expect from a flirt (coqueta in Spanish).

A popular local spot, **El Camello Jr.** (Tulum and Kulkulkan) offers up fresh local seafood at a steal in a no-frills market setting.

If you're spending the day at the beach, most of the featured lodging options also have great little beachfront cafés. With your toes in the sand, it's hard to go wrong with tacos or fresh seafood.

THE RIVIERA MAYA: NORTH OF PLAYA DEL CARMEN

THE RIVIERA MAYA: NORTH OF PLAYA DEL CARMEN

Punta Bete to Puerto Morelos

Extending north of Playa del Carmen, the Riviera Maya is dotted by exclusive destination resorts, such as those in the grandiose and exotically modern Mayakobá development and the growing town of Puerto Morelos, which today resembles what Playa was back in 1995.

PUNTA BETE REGION

Marked by the large wood-and-stone entrance of the Mayakobá mega-development, Punta Bete is just 4 miles north of Playa del Carmen, at km 296–298, making it popular for visitors who want to stay somewhere out of the way but still be close to the action of town. Each fall, Mayakobá's El Cameleón Golf Course hosts the OHL Golf Classic, the only official PGA Tour event held outside of the US, which adds to the development's prestige and reputation.

PUNTA MAROMA (HIGHWAY 307, KM 308-312)

Quiet Punta Maroma has the kind of sugar-sand beach that's often featured on postcards and full-screen digital desktops. More than 100 feet wide in many parts and bordered by coconut palms and sea oats, the beach is caressed by light waves and has very few rocks, making it a great place for swimming and snorkeling. There are a few upscale resorts, villas, and private homes, but the town has an uncrowded, timeless, and faraway feel to it, ideal for a tropical escape.

PLAYA DEL SECRETO & PLAYA PARAÍSO (HIGHWAY 307, KM 308–312)

Playa del Secreto and Playa Paraíso combine to form one of the largest stretches of mostly undeveloped beach remaining in the area. Several spots along the shoreline are frequented by sea turtles, who lay their eggs during the balmy summer months. The area is dominated by the massive Iberostar resort complex, which includes five distinct but interconnected all-inclusive resorts, a convention center, and an 18-hole golf course.

PUERTO MORELOS (HIGHWAY 307, KM 320, TWENTY MILES NORTH OF PLAYA DEL CARMEN)

If you want to experience what Playa del Carmen was like 20 years ago, consider a stay in modern-day Puerto Morelos, the official northern edge of the Riviera Maya. The quiet town square is ringed by a few restaurants and shops, a natural beach, and the encroaching jungle. The route from the highway to town is a straight shot on a clean, modern road through 2 miles of scrub brush and mangrove swampland, ending at the town square. Most of the in-town development is within a mile of the square, which

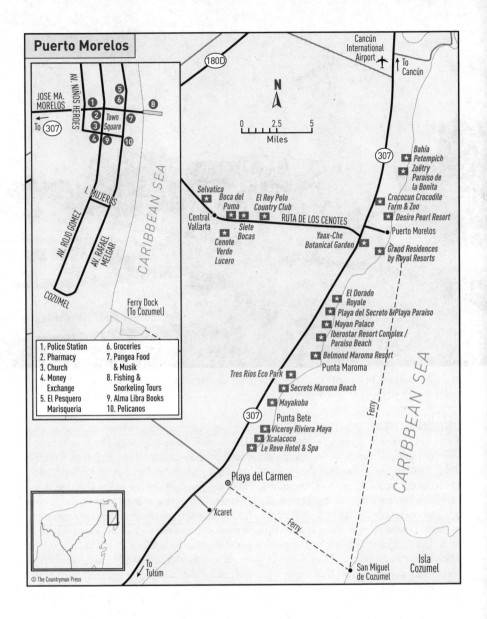

Puerto Morelos

JOSE MA. MORELOS

AV. NIÑOS HEROES

AV. ROJO GOMEZ

AV. RAFAEL MELGAR

I. MUJERES

COZUMEL

Town Square

To 307

CARIBBEAN SEA

Ferry Dock (To Cozumel)

1. Police Station
2. Pharmacy
3. Church
4. Money Exchange
5. El Pesquero Marisqueria
6. Groceries
7. Pangea Food & Musik
8. Fishing & Snorkeling Tours
9. Alma Libra Books
10. Pelicanos

Cancún International Airport

To Cancún

180D

N

0   2.5   5
Miles

307

Bahía Petempich
Zoëtry Paraiso de la Bonita
Crococun Crocodile Farm & Zoo
Desire Pearl Resort
Puerto Morelos
Grand Residences by Royal Resorts

Selvatica
Boca del Puma
El Rey Polo Country Club
RUTA DE LOS CENOTES
Central Vallarta
Siete Bocas
Cenote Verde Lucero
Yaax-Che Botanical Garden

El Dorado Royale
Playa del Secreto & Playa Paraíso
Mayan Palace
Iberostar Resort Complex / Paraiso Beach
Belmond Maroma Resort
Punta Maroma

Tres Ríos Eco Park

Secrets Maroma Beach

Mayakoba

307
Punta Bete
Viceroy Riviera Maya
Xcalacoco
Le Reve Hotel & Spa

CARIBBEAN SEA

Ferry

Playa del Carmen

Xcaret

Ferry

To Tulum

Ferry

San Miguel de Cozumel

Isla Cozumel

© The Countryman Press

has a couple of beachside restaurants, several open-air sidewalk restaurants, a couple of internet cafés, a coffee/pastry shop, and a few souvenir stores, pharmacies, money-exchange offices, and dive shops. Along the beach you'll see a leaning lighthouse and a fishing pier where the boats dock when they're not pulled up onto the beach.

Less than a half-mile offshore lies the barrier reef. The waves break where the coral meets the surface, indicating good spots for snorkeling when seas are calm. The paved road to the north and the unpaved one heading south from town both lead to some of the nicest natural beaches in the area. To the north are a collection of rental homes and small hotels, plus a few larger-scale resorts. To the south, the road curves behind an army base and then a shipping and industrial area before meeting the beach again near the entrance to a laid-back budget hotel.

THE INFAMOUS LEANING LIGHTHOUSE IN PUERTO MORELOS STILL ADDS LOCAL COLOR DESPITE THE PRESENCE OF ITS LARGER MODERN REPLACEMENT CHIP RANKIN

GETTING THERE Puerto Morelos is located at the midpoint between Cancún and Playa del Carmen. Only a few years ago, the turnoff from Highway 307 was marked with just a speed bump, but now it's a busy intersection with a raised highway, a traffic light, turning lanes, several shops in the growing *pueblo*, and plenty of traffic. There are frequent buses from the Cancún and Playa del Carmen stations that will drop you off at the crossroads, and from there it's a 2-mile hike to town or a $3 taxi ride. A new bus station was built in 2008 on Highway 307—just south of the main crossroads, next to the 7-Eleven convenience store—with regular departures to Tulum, Playa del Carmen, and Cancún. Though it may not be generally encouraged, it's also fairly easy to hitch a ride along the road that leads to town. Since the road basically goes to only one place, it's a pretty fair bet that anyone headed down that road is going somewhere close to where you are.

✳ To See & Do

PLAYA DEL SECRETO & PLAYA PARAÍSO (HIGHWAY 307, KM 308–312)

In another first for the ever-growing tourist region, the internationally acclaimed Cirque du Soleil has set up shop in the Riviera Maya. **Cirque du Soleil *JOYÀ*** is inspired by Cirque's touring stage spectacles and Vegas productions, and it is the company's first resident theater in all of Latin America. The purpose-built theater honors the region's natural environment, elements of which are reflected in the creative food presentations and overall storyline of the show. Tickets include round-trip transportation (either to and from Cancún or Playa del Carmen) and optional food and drinks. Prices start at $97 per person.

Some modest Mayan ruins and a coconut grove mark the small, secluded beach of **Xcalacoco**, which is just south of Punta Bete. There are a couple of *palapa* restaurants that serve seafood and Mexican dishes, and campers can set up their temporary home at the Xcalacoco campsite, which has solar power and public showers.

PUERTO MORELOS (HIGHWAY 307, KM 320, TWENTY MILES NORTH OF PLAYA DEL CARMEN)

Part traditional polo field, part real estate development, **El Rey Polo Country Club** (8 miles down the Ruta de Cenotes Road in Puerto Morelos, www.elreypolocountryclub .net) hosts regular, first-rate polo tournaments that draw players and spectators from around the country. The larger development encompasses seventy-three rustic home lots, a clubhouse, dressing rooms, golf driving range, horse stables, and a children's play area. Deep in the Mayan jungle, this subdivision-cum-polo-haven seems wildly out of place, making it a curious spot to visit and ponder what might lie ahead if the region keeps growing so rapidly.

The largest new-and-used English bookstore in the Yucatán, **Alma Libra Books** (south side of the town square on Tulum Avenue, between Rojo Gomez and Rafael Melgar Streets, www.almalibrebooks.com) is a great place to dig up some new reading material and a good source for arranging local day trips and even vacation rentals.

The friendly folks at **Fishing & Snorkeling Tours** (northeastern corner of the town square, next to the beach) can arrange fishing and diving trips along the Puerto Morelos coastline. With their own fleet of 25-foot covered boats and a roster of local guides, they can custom-create a trip that suits your fancy. Making reservations a day or more ahead is preferred and will ensure that staff can obtain all necessary equipment and supplies, though impromptu trips can be arranged too, so long as you're willing to be flexible.

The humble **Puerto Morelos Church** (west side of the town square) may not have any historical significance, but its Spanish-only services are open to visitors and offer an authentic glimpse into daily life for the locals.

Selvatica (Ruta de Cenotes, km 19, www.selvatica.com.mx) also runs adventure tours through a 300-acre nature preserve (see *Diving, Snorkeling & Cenotes* on page 195).

✳ Lodging

PUNTA BETE REGION

This area is dominated by the 1,600-acre master-planned luxury resort development **Mayakobá** (Highway 307, km 297, www.mayakoba.com), whose name translates roughly to "Village of Water" in Mayan. The complex features a mile-long white sand beach; the 18-hole, Greg Norman–designed **El Cameleón Golf Course**; and three exclusive resorts, each with its own custom spa, distinct design, and luxurious atmosphere. All Mayakobá guests and residents are encouraged to travel among the three resorts via a series of pristine jungle-lined waterways and sample the wider variety of spa and dining options.

To build the resort and its waterways, developers collapsed the land's limestone crust in strategic spots throughout the property, which created basins for lakes and canals and produced the limestone material that makes up most of Mayakobá's buildings. Although the resorts all have private beach access, beachfront accommodations are limited, as most of the development rests in the jungle behind a natural mangrove buffer. These jungle reserves were preserved to maintain the natural defenses that originally made the Riviera Maya resilient to hurricanes but which have since been largely stripped out with development up and down the coast.

Situated at the very heart of the complex is the warm and family-friendly, 401-room **Fairmont Mayakobá** (www.fairmont.com), which features a grand, home-style Mexican décor characterized by dark woods, light stone, and a palette of gold, soft reds, and oranges throughout. The cool, comfortably elegant, open-air lobby overlooks a stunning lagoon one story below. A wide and arching bridge extends across the far side of the lagoon, connecting to a green island concealing many of the resort's amenities.

The canals winding through the Fairmont sit lower than most of the resort itself, revealing rocky and porous limestone walls, topped off by thick and lush jungle vegetation. The effect is sublime, offering both a direct connection to nature and an uncommonly exposed, but still pristine, visual.

The resort itself sits on expansive grounds, allowing for dense vegetation between many structures. Open-air motorized shuttles whisk guests from the lobby to their rooms, the resort's three pools, a fitness center, or the private beach and adjacent beachfront restaurant.

Guest rooms offer private marble bathrooms with a rain shower and bathtub beneath a large window shielded from public view. Rooms come with all the luxurious, modern amenities you might expect, including ample pillows, high-thread-count sheets, plush bathrobes, and slippers.

In addition to a large, family swimming pool, a more serene adult pool, beach diversions, and golf prospects at

THE MAIN BUILDING AT THE FAIRMONT MAYAKOBA OVERLOOKS A PICTURESQUE SUNKEN LAGOON FAIRMONT MAYAKOBA

the adjacent El Cameleón course, the Fairmont offers a 40-minute boat ride through Mayakobá's canal system. The shaded motor launch takes passengers beyond the resort's grounds into the untouched and natural habitat that surrounds it. It's a fun, captivating, and intimate exchange with nature. And the wildlife around you makes the trip pleasantly unpredictable as well.

The Fairmont is the only Mayakobá resort operating primarily on the European plan. Some all-inclusive packages are available, but you must specifically select these packages to receive the extras, which are limited to select hotel restaurants and facilities. There are several excellent restaurants and bars on site, which are not included in any all-inclusive offers. If you want to experience all of the Fairmont's dining options, plan to pay for those meals in addition to your stay.

Nearby, the 107-room **Banyan Tree Mayakobá** (www.banyantree.com/en) has a stark, modern Asian-meets-Mayan motif and aspires to connect guests to the elements. The hotel and most of the villas are set back, inland from the beach, along a series of canals and waterways winding through the hotel and connecting it to the larger resort. All rooms are stand-alone villas, each complete with a private garden, pool, and outdoor bathtub.

The unusual 128-room **Rosewood Mayakobá** (www.rosewoodmayakoba.com) features a contemporary design in high contrast with its natural setting. The property's ties to the jungle are apparent, however, in its use of local materials, integration of tropical flourishes, and easy proximity to Mayakobá's network of canals. Rooms on and near the beach tend to be crowded together, while accommodations set further back—especially the adults only island suites are almost entirely secluded.

The new **Andaz Mayakobá** (www.andazmayakoba.com) is a crisp, modern addition to the complex, with 214 rooms overlooking the mangroves, gardens,

golf course, ponds, and ocean. Rooms feature an artisanal décor, and the resort boasts two pools, four restaurants, and two spas.

Families love the options at the 571-suite **Azul Fives Hotel by Karisma Resorts** (Fraccionamiento El Limonar, Xcalacoco, www.karismahotels.com), including the Azulitos Playhouse, pristine white sand beaches, and endless activities. One, two, and three-bedroom residences include separate living rooms and full-size kitchens, some featuring swim-up access and Jacuzzis on the patio. Thirteen restaurants, six bars, six pools (connected by a series of winding lazy rivers), and amenities galore round out the options at this large all-inclusive resort, which is especially popular for its luxury wedding services and breathtaking ceremony venues, including an elegant rooftop terrace, a tropical garden gazebo, and a gorgeous beach.

Small and very upscale, **Viceroy Riviera Maya** (Highway 307, km 294, Playa Xcalacoco, just south of Punta Bete, www.viceroyhotelsandresorts.com) is one of the more likely places to spot a vacationing celebrity or tycoon. It dispenses with the grandeur of Mayakobá, offering a private, intimate experience not found at any other hotel or resort in the region. Far from pretentious, the lush resort strives to provide a warm and sophisticated environment that harmonizes with nature. A thatched-palm pavilion at the hotel entrance serves as the lobby, and the forty-one villas are modernized replicas of Mayan-style huts, freestanding and scattered along a winding sand trail that leads from the powdery white beach to the jungle. The villas and their furnishings are made from local stones and hardwoods, and all feature a comprehensive list of amenities and comforts, plus a few big extras such as large private plunge pools, private outdoor moon showers, and soap carved for you personally when you check in.

Most villas are set back in the jungle, and entrances are designed to carefully

VISUALLY STUNNING ROOFTOP POOLS ARE COMMON THROUGHOUT THE REGION, INCLUDING THIS DECK AT AZUL FIVES HOTEL IN PLAYA DEL CARMEN KARISMA HOTELS

conceal all views of the private outdoor space. A few select villas are situated near the pool, offering clear views of the beach and providing external views of these villas' outdoor pool areas in return. Most hotel guests are couples, whether straight or gay, and children are permitted only when the entire resort is rented out for a private event.

Wandering along the Viceroy's winding pathways, you'll come across outdoor living rooms composed of colonial furniture arranged in a jungle clearing, a large and undulating infinity pool, one of the region's most sought-after spas, a beachside restaurant, a modern fitness center, and more.

With a barefoot-chic décor, the stylish twenty-five-room boutique **Le Reve Hotel & Spa** (www.hotellereve.com) mixes modern design elements with tropical flourishes. The restaurant showcases an evolving, chef-prepared menu utilizing many fresh ingredients, local products, and international flavors. There is a fitness center on site, and yoga classes are available on the beach. Packages are available for those who wish to rent the entire hotel for private celebrations, including weddings, retreats, and family reunions.

The 128-room, adults-only **Blue Diamond Riviera Maya** (Highway 307, km 298, www.bluediamond-rivieramaya .com) sits squarely in the ultra-luxurious, all-inclusive category. Formerly the Mandarin Oriental Riviera Maya, the hotel projects a thoroughly modern aesthetic with gravitation toward smooth, architectural lines and cool colors. Interiors utilize native hardwoods, stone, and other local accents.

PUNTA MAROMA (HIGHWAY 307, KM 308-312)

El Dorado Royale Maroma by Karisma (Highway 307, km 312, Playa Paraíso, www.karismahotels.com) was voted the fourth-best beach resort in the world by *Condé Nast Traveler* readers in 2016. The intimate, 157-room, low-rise resort stretches along a perfect beach peppered with countless palms. Taking a cue from Tahiti, the resort's **The Palafitos Overwater Bungalows** jut out from the beach and offer glass-bottomed floors, private infinity pools, and other special amenities. A small marina and a Dolphin Discovery park are located immediately to the north of the resort.

Recognized as one of the top hotels in the world, the sixty-five-room **Belmond Maroma Resort & Spa** (Highway 307, km 305; enter through the Venta Club entrance, www.maromahotel.com) deserves its stellar reputation, with returning guests making up a large percentage of its monthly reservations. The resort occupies some twenty-five acres of land, giving it an uncluttered and private feeling hard to find in the region. Unlike many Riviera Maya resorts, the Belmond is not the kind of place where visitors hang out in their cutoffs and tank tops, swilling margaritas and playing volleyball in the pool. Guests are typically more subdued, and there's a dress code at the restaurant for dinner. Don't assume it's stuffy, though. The atmosphere is definitely relaxed, just upscale.

The resort is closed for upgrades each August. The four-bedroom **Villa Pisces** has its own private pool and feels much

MAROMA'S LOMI-LOMI MASSAGE

The Lomi-Lomi massage is one of the oldest and most powerful forms of healing. It works gently yet deeply into the muscles with continuous, flowing strokes, offering a complete nurturing of the body and gifting the recipient with a sense of repose and well-being. This flowing massage allows for a close bond between the energies and bodies of therapist and client, as the therapist uses long, slow movements and a loving touch to relax you to the inner core, helping you to let go of old beliefs, patterns, and behaviors. Some people cry, others laugh, and others have a near out-of-body experience as they descend into a very deep state of relaxation.

more like a beach house than part of a hotel.

A lavish resort complex on 71 acres of pristine beach just south of Playa Maroma, the 285-room Secrets Maroma

EACH ROOM AT THE LUXURIOUS VICEROY RIVIERA MAYA IS A STANDALONE JUNGLE BUNGALOW WITH A PRIVATE PLUNGE POOL AND MOON SHOWER VICEROY RIVIERA MAYA

THE FIRST OVERWATER BUNGALOWS IN MEXICO ARE AT THE EL DORADO MAROMA EL DORADO SPA RESORTS

Beach (Highway 307, km 298, www .secretsresorts.com) is adults-only and all-inclusive and appeals to active couples wanting to experience a broad range of recreational options while submerged in the comforts of a high-end resort. The architecture presents a blend of Mediterranean and colonial Mexican characteristics, featuring graceful arches, tile work, and tropical plants throughout. Guests are welcomed into the lobby with a glass of champagne and a chilled towel before they descend a grand staircase to the pool deck area. This is a popular spot for weddings and honeymoons, and the resort offers an on-site wedding planner.

BEST PLACES TO STAY IN PLAYA DEL SECRETO, PLAYA PARAÍSO, & PUNTA MAROMA

The 478-room, all-inclusive, adults-only **El Dorado Royale—A Spa Resort by Karisma** (Highway 307, km 312, Playa Paraíso, www.karismahotels.com) bills itself as "laid-back luxury," and that description seems appropriate for a resort best known for its in-room hot tubs and patio hammocks. Spanning 450 acres of prime beachfront land, the hotel has a mile-long beach (called Punta Brava) marked by white sand, a few rocks, and hundreds of palm trees. The on-site day spa offers a variety of traditional European and Mayan treatments. For an additional level of exclusivity and amenities, opt for the adjacent El Dorado Casitas Royale's private pools and swim-up bars, concierge services, aromatherapy and pillow menus, and more.

Five resorts share amenities at the massive all-inclusive **Iberostar Playa Paraíso Complex** (Highway 307, km 309, www.iberostar.com), which provides more than 1,900 rooms among Iberostar's Paraíso Beach, Del Mar, Lindo, and Maya hotels. Varied architectural themes are on display across the resorts, with rooms varying in price, décor, and amenities. Guests at all properties are encouraged to visit the shared beach, which is almost a mile long, and to visit select pools, restaurants, and bars located throughout the property. Also on-site, the Iberostar Playa Paraíso Golf Club features eighteen holes of golf designed by P. B. Dye, son of renowned course designer Pete Dye. In addition to the facilities offered at each individual hotel, a central shopping and entertainment center contains a nightclub, a sports bar, a spa, and a variety of stores. Guests of the most luxurious and adults-only Iberostar Grand Hotel Paraíso have access to all complex features but also enjoy additional benefits and amenities not found in its hotels.

Home to one of the largest and most impressive hotel entryways in the region, **Vidanta Riviera Maya** (Highway 307, km 310, Playa Paraíso, www.vidanta.com) is equally splendid inside. The complex is actually a collection of five resort hotels, including the family-oriented Mayan Palace and Grand Mayan, the modern Bliss and Grand Bliss boutiques, and the more exclusive Grand Luxxe.

Though much of the architecture is inspired by traditional Mayan construction—thatched-palm roofs, low-rise buildings, large stones, and locally sourced materials—the standards of luxury remain decidedly modern. The beach is beautiful but rocky, so be prepared to pick your way through the rough terrain if you want to go swimming. The on-site Vidanta Theater is home to *JOYÀ*, an original dinner show by Cirque du Soleil. You'll also find the 18-hole, Nicklaus Design **Golf Course El Manglar**, tennis courts, and a kids' club that provides complimentary childcare in a fun environment. Since the property is so large, some guests complain about the walking distances from one attraction to another, but the landscaping and the natural beauty seem to keep most happy.

BAHIA PETEMPICH

With fewer than one-hundred rooms and suites, the very high-end, all-suite **Zoëtry Paraiso de la Bonita Resort & Thalasso Spa** (Highway 307, km 330, www.zoetryresorts.com/paraiso) has 1,100-square-foot standard rooms with ocean views. The recipient of the AAA Five Diamond award, the hotel's service

THE IBEROSTAR COMPLEX IS ONE OF THE AREA'S LARGEST RESORTS IBEROSTAR RESORTS

is impeccable, and the staff does an excellent job of making guests feel special. The architecture and décor are unusual, combining African, Asian, Balinese, Caribbean, European, and Mayan influences. The beach is raked clean, but the tides are full of seaweed, making swimming less than pleasant.

The very feng shui, 148-room **Azul Beach Hotel by Karisma** (Highway 307, km 330, www.karismahotels.com) is an up-market, family-friendly, all-inclusive boutique resort located on an idyllic beach just a few miles north of Puerto Morelos, past the gated entrance to Bahia Petempich. The hotel lobby is memorable for its marble floors and blue-and-white minimalist décor, and unlike many all-inclusives, the resort's restaurants feature gourmet menu options and its bars serve premium liquors. For wellness-oriented travelers, the on-site Vassa Spa offers spa, beauty, and hydro-therapy treatments, and a fitness center, while families will appreciate the hotel's Nickelodeon-themed kids program which offers activities based on characters like SpongeBob SquarePants, Dora the Explorer, and the Teenage Mutant Ninja Turtles.

PUERTO MORELOS PROPER

If you'd like to stay in the heart of Puerto Morelos, where you can easily walk to the beach, local bars, and restaurants, then you'll be best off with a private vacation rental. There are more than twenty properties near the town square on **HomeAway** (www.homeaway.com) and **Airbnb** (www.airbnb.com).

THE SWINGS AT UNICO BEACH IN PUERTO MORELOS ARE PERFECT FOR PASSING THE TIME CHIP RANKIN

If you're set on a hotel, the simple and inexpensive **Hotel Ojo de Agua** (Highway 307, km 321, Avenue Javier Rojo Gómez at the beach, www.ojo-de-agua.com) serves as somewhat of a home base for local beachfront activity and lies between Bahia Petempich and the town square. Each of the hotel's thirty-six rooms, decorated in contemporary Mexican style, have either air conditioning or a fan and include a kitchenette.

SOUTH OF PUERTO MORELOS

Rancho Sak Ol (Highway 307, km 318, southern end of Puerto Morelos, past the Army base and shipping facility, www.ranchosakol.com), formerly known as Rancho Libertad, offers an alternative to the large, corporate-owned hotels that will appeal to travelers seeking simplicity and serenity over luxury and indulgence. Fourteen minimalist rooms feature suspended beds, air conditioning (downstairs units), and purified drinking water. All quarters face a rocky, natural beach—calm and practically deserted—a good spot for more hotels. If you look to the north, you'll see a half-sunken barge that's been there for years.

Located south of Puerto Morelos' town square, **Grand Residences by Royal Resorts** (El Cid Boulevard, www.grandresidencesrivieracancun.com) is an ideal spot for families, offering 103 spacious luxury suites along the beach, an infinity pool overlooking the ocean, a kid's club, and plenty of activities to keep all ages entertained.

✳ Where to Eat

PUERTO MORELOS (HIGHWAY 307, KM 320, TWENTY MILES NORTH OF PLAYA DEL CARMEN)

Although notable standbys and old favorites remain, Puerto Morelos is starting to grow and has accumulated a number of hip new restaurants, bars, and beach clubs.

In the town square, the second-story, air-conditioned **La Casa del Pescador** (north side of the town square) offers fresh lobster, hogfish in butter, grouper, and other seafood dishes, as well as good *chiles rellenos* and grilled steaks and chicken. The waiters are longtime local residents who can give you advice on tours and activities.

South of the square, overlooking the beach, is the charming, open-air **Punta Corcho** (southeastern corner, www.puntacorcho.com.mx). It takes its name from Morelos' nineteenth-century moniker, when the port was a trading hub for wood and forest products. The menu features wood-grilled seafood and local meats, plus specialty cocktails, mezcal, and regional beer selections. You'll spot the second-story restaurant quickly, but the entrance below is easy to miss, tucked away behind vendors who crowd the sidewalk with their wares. From the square, turn right and skirt the building. The door is aligned with the back end of the restaurant, which is visible above you.

Across the street, the most prominent restaurant near the town square, **Pelicanos** (southeastern corner), is also the largest, offering a selection of Mexican and American breakfasts for less than $5. For lunch and dinner, it's seafood or nothing. Try the fried whole fish, shrimp ceviche, or grilled shrimp, and you won't go wrong.

Also on the beach—to your left when facing the pier, with the road into Morelos behind you—is **Pangea Food and Musik** (Jose Maria Morelos and Rafael Melgar Streets). The restaurant serves traditional Mexican and seafood dishes in an open atmosphere. Dancers and musicians perform most nights.

Continuing north on the beachfront Rafael Melgar street, you'll find more of Morelos' new drinking and dining destinations, including **El Pesquero Marisqueria** (half a block north of the town square on Rafael Melgar Street). This spot is drawing repeat visitors with its freshly-caught seafood preparations, friendly staff, and lively tropical atmosphere.

Cancún Billy's Beach Club (just north of the square on Rafael Melgar Street, www.cancunbillys.com) features barbecue brisket, pork ribs, and chicken wings, along with tacos, salads, and more. The full bar offers drinks until 2 AM, with great beach views just steps from the square.

Spilling out of a beachfront home built in 1979 is the colorful **Merkadito del Mar** (400 feet north of the square on Rafael Melgar Street, www.elmerkadito.mx), also known as El Merkadito. The place is an amalgamation of thatched *palapas*, bamboo, and all the trappings one would expect from a Mexican seaside restaurant perched at the edge of a jungle. The menu boasts tasty takes on tostadas, tacos, and ceviches, with an overall focus on seafood.

The slick and stylish **Bianco** (450 feet north of the square on Rafael Melgar Street, www.restaurantesbianco.com) brings a touch of Miami Beach to Morelos' playa. The open-air, beachfront lounge serves up modern seafood dishes that fuse Italian and Mexican flavors.

Further north from the heart of Morelos, you'll find **Unico Beach** (a little over a half-mile north of the square on Javier Rojo Gomez Avenue, www.unicobeach.mx). In addition to the beach club's main attraction—its beautiful white sand—Unico's kitchen serves up gourmet ceviches, salads, stuffed avocados, and other dishes. You'll also find a full bar, massage therapists, snorkel tours, and more. Live music and special events are held regularly.

Traditional Mexican dishes are the specialty of **Dona Triny's** (south side of the town square on Tulum Avenue between Rojo Gomez and Rafael Melgar Streets), while just down the street near the square's southwestern corner, the small and inexpensive **Le Café D'Amancia** serves sandwiches, fresh breads, cheesecake, fruit, and coffee drinks for early risers.

Well-known for its once popular, now-shuttered location in Playa del Carmen, **John Gray's Kitchen** (Niños Heroes Avenue, north of the town square) is still going strong in uber-relaxed Morelos, serving up steaks, seafood, and Mexican fare. Even though this is likely one of the more upscale independent restaurants in Puerto Morelos, things remain flip-flop casual.

OTHER DESTINATIONS NEAR PLAYA DEL CARMEN

OTHER DESTINATIONS NEAR PLAYA DEL CARMEN

Cozumel, Cancún, Isla Mujeres,
Isla Holbox & More

Mexico's entire Caribbean coast is marked by both popular and lesser-known tourist destinations. The diving mecca of Isla Cozumel, the exploding resort city of Cancún, the bohemian island town of Isla Mujeres, the remote, authentic Isla Holbox, the unpopulated Isla Contoy, and the adventurous Mayan Coast all make noteworthy overnight side- or day-trip destinations.

Most travelers to the Riviera Maya arrive via Cancún, which is one of the world's most popular mega-resorts. The small islands to the north of Cancún offer an abundance of relaxation, sunshine, and pristine beaches minus the crowds. Cozumel, meanwhile, is a scuba diver's dream, where shore, wall, and night dives can all be done in a single day.

Destinations featured here are listed in order of their proximity to Playa del Carmen and the Riviera Maya, from closest to furthest away.

ISLA COZUMEL (11 MILES FROM PLAYA DEL CARMEN BY BOAT)

Measuring 28 by 10 miles, Cozumel is only 5 percent developed and consists mostly of open land ripe for exploration by Jeep, on horseback, or with a moped. Once considered the sacred home of Ix-Chel, the Mayan goddess of fertility and childbirth, Isla Cozumel is today a mecca for scuba divers and snorkelers, who revel in the amazingly clear waters, easily accessible reefs, and first-class dive operators.

The ferry from Playa lands on Cozumel's western shore at the town square of San Miguel, the island's only town. From nearly every beach hotel on this side of the island, guests have a spectacular view of the sunset as it slowly dips into the Caribbean. Dozens of shops, restaurants, bars, and other attractions are within easy walking distance of the ferry dock. A few hotels are located downtown, but the majority sit along the beaches to the north and south of the square. The far-less-developed eastern side of the island faces the open ocean, and the water here is much rougher, with less reef. Visitors can drive around it to the south side of the island, hugging the shoreline almost the entire way. It's a great way to get away from the crowds and feel like a real explorer, even though you'll never be more than 15 minutes away from a cold beer and a tasty plate of food.

CANCÚN (45 MILES NORTH OF PLAYA DEL CARMEN)

Though officially too far north to be considered part of the Riviera Maya, many visitors choose to stay a night in Cancún for a taste of its world-class shopping, great restaurants, powdery beaches, and over-the-top nightlife. The hotel zone is about 14 miles long, with dozens of options and every tourist service imaginable. Once a sleepy suburb, Cancún's downtown area has since morphed into a dense metropolitan city and offers great local restaurants, many shops and nightspots, ferry ports, and a large

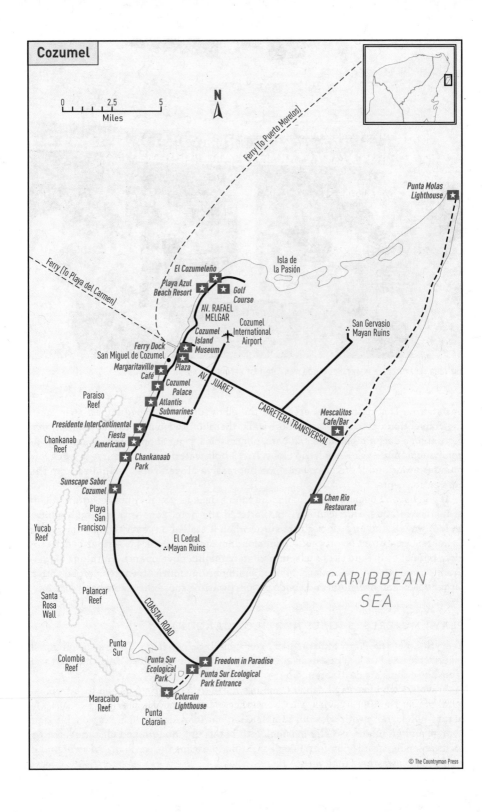

BUY YOUR FERRY TICKETS IN ADVANCE IF YOU WANT, OR JUST BEFORE YOU BOARD

bus station. The main tourist area is at the elbow of the 7-shaped tourist strip, near the convention center. Within a short walk, there are two malls, twenty restaurants, more than a dozen nightclubs and bars, pharmacies, cigar shops, grocery stores, souvenir shops, and—yes—even strip clubs. An 18-hole waterfront golf course is just a few minutes away, and there are even some impressive Mayan ruins just miles from the convention center.

If you haven't been to Cancún in more than a decade, you may not recognize much of it. In late 2005, Hurricane Wilma battered the hotel zone with 150-mph winds, 25-foot waves, and an 11-foot storm surge when it stalled out over the city for nearly 12 hours. Oceanfront resorts suffered major damage, and there was serious beach erosion. But not only were the hotels immediately rebuilt, developers built things bigger, grander, and even more modern. Mexico's number-one tourist town reemerged with a larger beach and new hotel and condo towers dwarfing those that came before them.

PLAYA MUJERES (9 MILES NORTH OF CANCÚN)

Everything at the Playa Mujeres has been done big, by design. The master-planned resort welcomed its first guests in 2007, and though near Cancún, it's also isolated and feels like a separate destination.

Travelers who journey beyond Cancún's northern outskirts will find lush tropical landscaping framing a lavish grand entrance. Within the complex are two upscale luxury hotels, both with spas, an 18-hole Greg Norman–designed championship golf course, and an inland 176-slip marina. Both hotels are modern and elaborate, with a focus on opulence and comfort. People wanting to escape the world in style will find it easy to hide away here for a week.

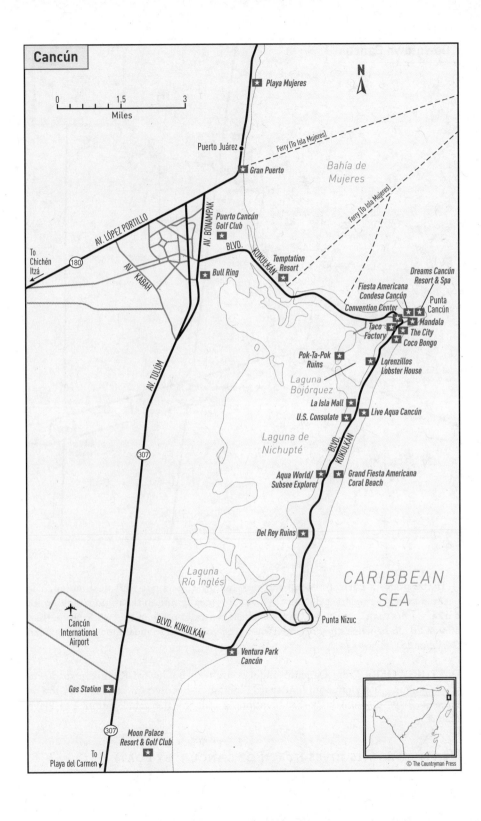

Cancún

0   1.5   3
Miles

N

Playa Mujeres

Puerto Juárez

Ferry (To Isla Mujeres)

Gran Puerto

Bahía de Mujeres

AV. LÓPEZ PORTILLO

AV. BONAMPAK

Puerto Cancún Golf Club

BLVD.

KUKULKÁN

Ferry (To Isla Mujeres)

Temptation Resort

To Chichén Itzá

180

AV. KABAH

Bull Ring

Dreams Cancún Resort & Spa

Fiesta Americana Condesa Cancún

Punta Cancún

Convention Center

Taco Factory

Mandala

The City

Coco Bongo

Pok-Ta-Pok Ruins

Laguna Bojórquez

Lorenzillos Lobster House

AV. TULÚM

La Isla Mall

U.S. Consulate

Live Aqua Cancún

BLVD. KUKULKÁN

Laguna de Nichupté

307

Aqua World/ Subsee Explorer

Grand Fiesta Americana Coral Beach

Del Rey Ruins

Laguna Río Inglés

CARIBBEAN SEA

Punta Nizuc

Cancún International Airport

BLVD. KUKULKÁN

Ventura Park Cancún

Gas Station

307

Moon Palace Resort & Golf Club

To Playa del Carmen

© The Countryman Press

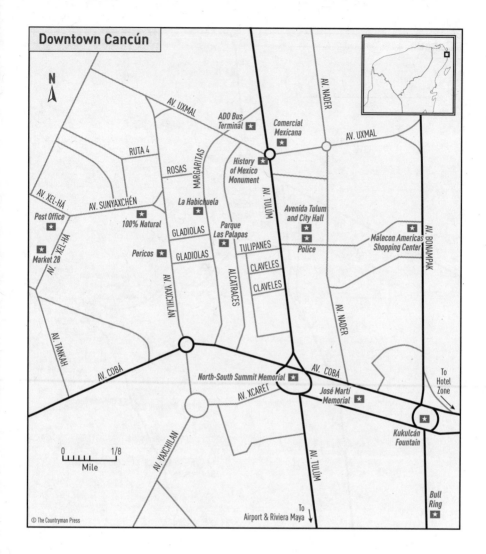

Downtown Cancún

If you prefer a perfect beach over pure luxury, this is not your destination. The ocean beyond the resort is deeper than you'll typically find in the region, making for darker waters than some may expect. The beaches are kept clean, and while better than almost all US beaches, they're underwhelming compared to most along the Mexican Caribbean.

GETTING THERE From Cancún's hotel zone, take Boulevard Kukulkan to downtown Cancún. Turn right onto Boulevard Bonampak, heading toward the ferry to Isla Mujeres. From downtown Cancún, continue 9 miles to the gated entrance to Playa Mujeres.

ISLA MUJERES (15 MILES NORTH OF CANCÚN, BY BOAT)

Once a sacred pilgrimage site for Mayan natives, the 5-mile-long Isla Mujeres is now a top spot for travelers seeking sunny days, pristine beaches, good food, tropical bars,

PARTS OF ISLA MUJERES ARE STILL REMOTE AND LARGELY UNPOPULATED   CHIP RANKIN

yoga classes, and a casual lifestyle not found on the mainland. Spanish conquistador Francisco Hernandez de Cordoba named the island when he visited in 1517 looking for gold and other riches. He didn't find precious metals but did discover a large number of Mayan statuettes of women, once used in religious ceremonies. He named the spot Isla Mujeres, meaning "Island of Women." Later visitors included pirates like Jean Lafitte, followed more recently by hippies and bohemians seeking a place to get away from civilization and commune with nature. Today, the island's narrow roads are best explored in golf carts, which are available for rent by the hour or by the day. Draws include tranquil beaches, charming restaurants and bars, local shopping, snorkeling, fishing, and diving.

GETTING THERE   Sleek modern ferries depart every 30 minutes to Isla Mujeres from **Gran Puerto** (www.ultramarferry.com/en), located in the neighborhood of Puerto Juárez (and not far from the eponymously named older port). Start times and evening schedules vary.

The shiny new port complex—complete with a parking garage, a convenience store, and a McDonald's—is located 5 miles north of Cancún, while the older terminal is a few blocks beyond it. Unless you want to indulge in nostalgia for the old route, Gran Puerto is the simpler bet.

And if you're interested in a little local color during your trip, bypass the air-conditioned cabin and head to the rooftop deck seating. Most days, once the boat gets going, you'll be treated to the sounds of a local musician covering tropical and popular classics—often in unintentionally entertaining ways. Be sure to have a few dollars (or 10 to 20 pesos) on hand for when the hat is passed.

HURRICANE WILMA—MEXICO'S MOST COSTLY NATURAL DISASTER EVER

Three months after Hurricane Emily tore through the Riviera Maya in July 2005, Tropical Storm Wilma formed in the Atlantic Basin, churning and sputtering for a few days without much strengthening or fanfare. On Wednesday, October 19, however, things rapidly changed. Within hours, the storm had developed into a massive Category 5 hurricane, reaching a minimum central pressure of 882 millibars and sustained winds of 175 mph, making it the most intense hurricane on record in this part of the world. The US State Department issued an urgent evacuation notice for all US citizens in the region. By the morning of Thursday, October 20, the MTV Latin Music Video Awards in Xcaret had been canceled, and music performers and celebrities crowded the Cancún airport with thousands of tourists, all trying to get a flight back home. Meanwhile, the storm was poised offshore, forecast to veer to the east and spare the region—not yet showing signs of the turn to come.

By late afternoon, winds from the outer bands of Hurricane Wilma began lashing the coast of Cancún and the Riviera Maya. Palm trees were bending and waves were crashing, despite the fact that the storm was still 150 miles offshore. At dawn on Saturday, October 21, 10-foot waves were pounding into the seawall on the western shore of Cozumel, shooting sprays of water 30 feet up into the air. The outer bands of the storm were tearing at trees and rooftops, and some signs had already blown down. Up and down the Riviera Maya and Cancún, hotels prepared for the worst, and visitors and residents were bussed to shelters while the military patrolled the streets, ensuring everyone had a place to ride out the storm. As the hurricane's eye neared the coast, the area braced for a direct hit, with landfall predicted to take place somewhere between Playa del Carmen and Cancún.

At 10 AM on Friday, Cancún police reported the city's first death. A local woman was on her roof, cleaning debris, and a power line fell and electrocuted her. At 2 PM, the wall of the eye passed over the northern tip of Cozumel, while all across the region, the situation deteriorated rapidly. Gary Walten, an Akumal resident and owner of LocoGringo.com, was seeking shelter in his home while talking on the phone to CNN, which broadcast the conversation to the world. Wolf Blitzer asked him to hold his phone near the window so the audience could hear the sound. The noise was howling at a near-deafening volume, described by one survivor as "one thousand cats, screaming in pain." Water was washing across the main street through the Cancún hotel zone, and Quinta Avenida in downtown Playa del Carmen was a shallow river, with whitecaps cresting between storefronts. Most of the windows were boarded up; those that weren't were shattered. Cars were washing down the street in downtown Cancún and in the back streets of Playa and Puerto Morelos.

By sundown, the eye had stalled over the Cancún hotel zone, creating the worst-case scenario for the region, as the rainfall continued relentlessly. The wind created a 50-mile-long wall the strength of an f2 tornado, and the storm surge inched higher and higher. Reports of an exploded gas tank and associated injuries made their way across the internet, with

ISLA HOLBOX (105 MILES NORTHWEST OF CANCÚN)

Holbox (*hol-bosh*), a narrow island 7 miles off the Yucatán Peninsula's northern shore, is one of the region's lesser-known and more underappreciated destinations. It's also about to be discovered by that niche of American travelers who are actively looking for the next great authentic travel getaway.

Named after the Mayan for "black hole," Holbox has a year-round population of fewer than two thousand, including descendants of the island's original eight families. Stories claim pirates settled it—using it as a hideout—then mingled with the locals and decided to stay.

observers praying for the safety of loved ones stranded in shelters across the area. Water was waist-deep along the Cancún hotel zone and had completely washed out the road leading from Tulum to Punta Allen. Through the night, things only got worse. Witnesses in Playa del Carmen reported seeing 200-gallon water tanks, stoplights, plate glass, and even automobiles flying through the air. Water had completely washed over Kukulcán Boulevard in Cancún, connecting the ocean and the lagoon to make one solid sea of water.

At sunrise on Saturday, October 22, weary-eyed residents and tourists, many kept awake by the screeching winds and rising waters, peeked out the windows and were horrified by what they saw. The devastation was worse than anyone had imagined. Mexico's President Vincente Fox had already declared the entire region a disaster zone. To make matters worse, the storm was still stalled, meaning the misery would last at least another 12 hours. Nearly every hotel in Cancún had lost dozens, if not hundreds, of windows, while the ocean in Playa del Carmen had risen to meet Quinta Avenida, forming a 3-foot deep sea along the town's main tourist district. By 3 PM, the winds had receded below hurricane strength for the first time in 24 hours, though the conditions were still too severe for anyone to leave the shelters. Food and water were running scarce, and reports of looters being arrested in Cancún did little to calm any fears. Across the entire region, waves of up to 25 feet continued to crash ashore, ripping apart everything in their path.

By Sunday, rumors of "total devastation" swept across the internet, as Hurricane Wilma left the Yucatán and made a beeline for the Florida coast, where it went on to cause $11 billion in insured damages. Back in the Riviera Maya, thousands of travelers were stranded, with no way to get home. The Cancún airport was damaged, and some tourists paid up to $400 for a taxi to Mérida to catch a plane out. Tour operators scrambled to take care of their passengers and get them home. Some stranded survivors waited in line for 2 hours to use a payphone to tell loved ones they were alright. Over the next week, the Mexican government passed out roofing materials for rebuilding houses and thousands of bottles of water, also clearing the streets. Generous locals prepared food for hungry tourists. Residents and visitors banded together to start cleaning up.

Within weeks, most of the damaged buildings had been cleared or were in the process of being rebuilt. The Capitan Lafitte, just north of Playa del Carmen, was declared a total loss. Cozumel's beachfront and Cancún's hotel zone took the brunt of the storm, with some hotels forced to replace hundreds of windows as well as soft goods in all of their rooms. But over the following months, the beaches regained their natural splendor. Restaurants along Quinta in Playa put on fresh coats of paint and rebuilt their *palapas*. The large all-inclusive resorts along the Riviera Maya were rebuilt, bigger and better than ever.

Thankfully, Hurricane Wilma claimed only five lives in all of Mexico. Once again, the region proved itself incredibly resilient in the face of great challenges. By 2006, the crowds were returning in droves, evidence that the Riviera Maya—a place full of history—would remain a world-class travel destination with unlimited drive for the future.

The island is a come-as-you-are hideaway for ultra-casual vacationing. If the Riviera Maya is the land of *mañana* (tomorrow), then Holbox would be that of sometime *la próxima semana* (next week). It's doubtful anyone has ever worn a tie here, unless it was a joke. Most locals don't even wear shoes, given the powdery sand roads. In fact, the mayor led an effort to pave the streets several years back, but locals voted it down.

Most visitors to the island come from Italy, Europe's Nordic and Scandinavian countries, or from Mexico itself. So aside from Spanish, you're more likely to hear Italian, Norwegian, Finnish, Swedish, or even Russian than English. Most Europeans come for the warmth, a low and reasonable cost, and proximity to nature, and they often stay for a couple of weeks.

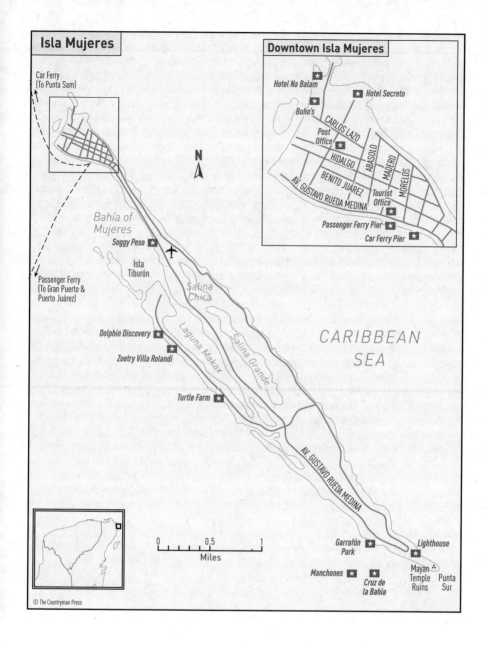

Isla Mujeres

Car Ferry (To Punta Sam)

Bahía of Mujeres

Soggy Peso

Isla Tiburón

Salina Chica

Passenger Ferry (To Gran Puerto & Puerto Juárez)

Dolphin Discovery

Zoetry Villa Rolandi

Laguna Makax

Salina Grande

Turtle Farm

CARIBBEAN SEA

Av. Gustavo Rueda Medina

Garrafón Park

Lighthouse

Manchones

Cruz de la Bahia

Mayan Temple Ruins

Punta Sur

0   0.5   1
Miles

© The Countryman Press

Downtown Isla Mujeres

Hotel Na Balam

Hotel Secreto

Buho's

CARLOS LAZO

Post Office

HIDALGO

ABASOLO

MADERO

MORELOS

BENITO JUÁREZ

AV. GUSTAVO RUEDA MEDINA

Tourist Office

Passenger Ferry Pier

Car Ferry Pier

Since the island faces the Gulf of Mexico, it doesn't have quite the same turquoise water common in the Riviera Maya. It's blue with a murky, greenish hue. Some areas are clear enough for snorkeling. Due to currents and the island's location, thousands of shells wash on shore at each high tide. Usually still whole and without cracks, the shells are highly prized by gatherers.

From November to January, the waves also wash heaps of seagrass onto the shores of most northern-facing beaches. The locals don't sweep it up because this grass is integral to holding the island together. Over the course of the year, waves push sand over the grass, forming new beaches and protecting the island. Without the grass, the ocean would eat away at the beaches and then the island itself. Understanding this environmental benefit, the local government has made it illegal to remove the grasses and disturb the natural process. However, you can still find beautiful beaches that are largely grass-free, particularly along the shore immediately northwest of the town square, where the island's shore continues to curve away from true north.

Yalahao Lagoon, on the sheltered side of the island, features a mangrove swamp, flamingos, schools of dolphins, and a freshwater spring just up from the beach. It's a popular gathering spot for locals and tourists alike. In the times of the Mayans, it was believed to have curative properties, and natives would come from miles away to rejuvenate and refresh.

For people, life on the island is not an elaborate affair. There are no cars, just motorized and electric carts, bikes, and mopeds. Locals operate the handful of restaurants, bars, and inns. But most go fishing and lobstering and sell their catches each day at the beach and to dis-

ISLA HOLBOX IS STILL A BEACH TOWN THAT KNOWS HOW TO AVOID THE STRESS AND SOUNDS OF CITY LIFE
CHIP RANKIN

tributors on the mainland. Today, it's fairly easy to find ATMs in town, but they often run out of bills, and many businesses still accept only cash. Tourists while away the day on the beach, explore mangrove canals in kayaks, go windsurfing, or head out on the water to sail, fish, and occasionally even dive.

The town of Holbox has an unusual and compelling energy about it, as locals live their day-to-day lives among the tourists. Visitors are welcome enough, but the locals don't show a great deal of interest in them. Although many of the islanders live simply, few would consider themselves poor. As one restauranteur suggested, even the family living in a simple dirt floor shack typically has a small fleet of four or more fishing boats, a truck on the mainland, and cash at its disposal. On Holbox, there's not a great deal for the locals to spend money on, so they forget about it, according to some. Regardless of the veracity of this observation, visitors will quickly note that children on Holbox don't ask for handouts, no one appears to be homeless, locals seem genuinely content, and few local shopkeepers try to hustle you into their shop to buy souvenirs. There's a live-and-let-live attitude set on island time.

At present, Isla Holbox finds itself at a rare, and usually temporary, equilibrium where its charms have manifested, tourism infrastructure exists but is contained, and the visitors themselves present just a small percentage of the island's income, activity, and importance. If you like authenticity with a tropical twist, this is a place worth seeing. But that might also pose an eventual problem for the very character that makes the island so interesting.

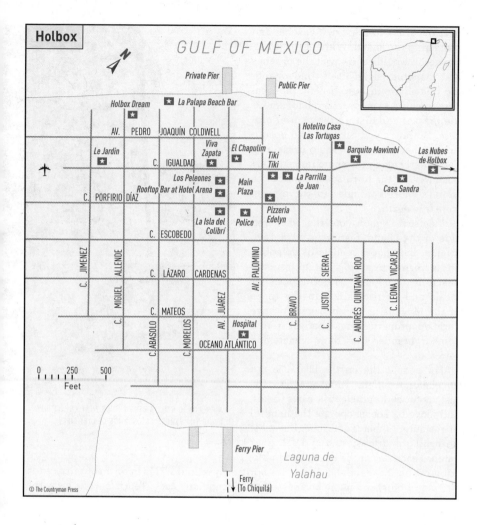

Unfortunately, Holbox's current magnetism probably foreshadows the dramatic growth that tends to transform once-sleepy villages into something wholly different—not unlike Cancún or Playa del Carmen itself. Already, the Mexican government has stated that hundreds of acres of untouched Holbox scrub will be given over to the development of large resorts. The introduction of carnivorous creatures to the island, such as the badger-like, egg-eating coati, has also led to a dramatic decrease in Holbox's bird population.

However, all is not lost. Holbox is clearly on the move. And given its leadership's apparent understanding of infrastructure preservation, such as the beach-replenishing seagrass and lessons learned elsewhere in the region, Holbox may manage to preserve its own unique personality as it grows and matures as a tourist destination.

GETTING THERE With the opening of a new connector road from Puerto Morelos, the ferry to Isla Holbox is a 2.5-hour drive from Playa del Carmen and a three-hour drive from Cancún. The island is 7 miles offshore from the dock in the quiet town of Chiquila. The 30-minute, air-conditioned ferry ride costs $7.30 for tourists and $4 for locals. If you're reading this book, expect to pay full price with no debate.

THE PERFECT SELFIE SPOT ON ISLA HOLBOX CHIP RANKIN

Most of the small boutique hotels listed in this book include transportation from the Cancún airport. If you drive, parking is available at small, private lots across the street from the ferry, typically at $2.60 per day.

If you take a chartered flight, the airstrip is just a few blocks from the town plaza. The company **Aerosaab** (Playa del Carmen, www.aerosaab.com) offers plane charters starting at around $325.

ISLA CONTOY (25 MILES NORTH OF CANCÚN, BY BOAT)

This bird sanctuary and wildlife refuge is offshore from the northeastern tip of the Yucatán Peninsula. There are no bars or restaurants, no hotels, no roads, and very few facilities. A small group of Mexican marines runs a lighthouse, museum, lookout tower, and outpost, but there are no other full-time inhabitants. The island is a popular nesting ground for sea turtles, and occasionally naturalists will camp out and care for them and watch for poachers, backed by the marines. There are a few rolling hills and a long-deserted beach, ideal for strolling and snorkeling.

GETTING THERE Visitors can arrive by private boat or with a tour group, but proper authorization is required. The island (www.islacontoy.org) is managed jointly by the local NGO Amigos de Isla Contoy A.C. and by the Secretary of Environment, Natural Resources, and Fishing (SEMARNAT), who limit island visitors to two hundred per day. If traveling with a tour group, your permit is likely included, but visitors traveling by private watercraft must apply for permits at the park offices in Cancún or Isla Mujeres.

✳ To See & Do

ISLA COZUMEL (11 MILES FROM PLAYA DEL CARMEN BY BOAT)

Situated on Playa San Francisco, long considered Cozumel's best beach, **San Francisco Beach Club** (Southern Coastal Road, km 15) is still its most popular. It's been the site of thousands of weddings and remains a favorite place for water sports, seafood, and cold beers.

At **Mr. Sancho's Beach Club** (Southern Coastal Road, km 13, www.mrsanchos .com)—a lively beach club on a picture-perfect, white-sand beach south of town—visitors can swim, snorkel, ride ATVs or motorcycles into the jungle, or partake in other playful activities. The beach is public property, but facilities have a fee.

The well-established **Playa Mia Grand Beach Park** (Southern Coastal Road, km 15.5, www.playamia.com) is a tropical recreation paradise. Visitors pass the day kayaking, sailing, parasailing, sunning, swimming, and applying sunblock. The park is notable for its small zoo, floating climbing wall, and underwater replica of Mayan relics submerged for snorkelers' enjoyment.

Created in 1980 to protect the region's marine life and flora and fauna along the shoreline, **Chankanaab Park** (Southern Coastal Road, km 9.5, www.cozumelparks .com/eng) is Cozumel's main beach and nature park. Crystal-clear water, with more than 100 feet of visibility on most days, makes for excellent snorkeling and scuba diving, and the beach offers easy water access, slow currents, and exciting shore dives, where statues of Jesus and the Virgin Mary beckon from the shallows. The park boasts a lush botanical garden, a reproduction of a Mayan village, and a dolphin and sea lion discovery lagoon.

Punta Sur Lighthouse Park (Southern Coastal Road, km 27, www.cozumelparks .com/eng), a one-hundred-hectare ecology reserve and beach park, features white-sand beaches, mangrove swamps, lagoons, and a thick jungle.

The San Gervasio Mayan Ruins (Cross-Island Road, km 7.5, www.cozumelparks .com/eng), Cozumel's primary Mayan site, were an important destination for Mayan women seeking to honor Ix-Chel, the goddess of fertility. Spanning a couple miles, the ruins include several different temples and small pyramids, and are home to many tropical birds and iguanas (see *Activities & Tours* on page 167).

Cozumel Island Museum (Rafael Melgar and 4th Street, www.cozumelparks.com/ eng) documents the island's history through a series of re-creations, drawings, and artifacts. Exhibitions cover the Mayan era, sixteenth-century discoveries made by Juan de Grijalva and Hernan Cortez, the island's pirate years, the War of the Castes, present-day Cozumel, and more.

Rancho Buenavista (Southern Coastal Road, Km 32.5, www.buenavistaranch.com) offers 2-hour horseback tours through some of the island's most rugged and picturesque landscapes.

ISLA MUJERES (15 MILES NORTH OF CANCÚN, BY BOAT)

Situated on the southeastern tip of Isla Mujeres, **Garrafon Park** (Punta Sur, km 6, www .garrafon.com) is home to the Yucatán Peninsula's highest cliff and marks Mexico's easternmost point. Each New Year's Day, locals flock to this spot to be the first people in their country to see the sun in the new year. The park gets its name from the Spanish word for "canister," either because the site used to be a fuel depot or because the bay is shaped like a water bottle's curved neck, depending on whom you believe. Inside

WAY SOUTH: THE EXPLOREAN KOHUNLICH

Set almost at the border of Belize, The Explorean Kohunlich by Fiesta Americana (Carretera Chetumal Escarcega, km 5.65, Ruinas Kohunlich, www.explorean.com) is a remote all-inclusive jungle retreat for guests looking to escape and truly connect with nature. The low-rise hotel utilizes stone, thatched roofs, and native materials to blend in with its jungle surroundings. The resort is located adjacent to the Kohunlich Mayan ruins, 30 miles from the Chetumal International Airport, and approximately 200 miles from the Cancún airport. It emphasizes adventurous activities—jungle treks, hiking, Mayan ruin tours, kayaking in the nearby lagoon, cycling, rappelling, and bird-watching—with one excursion per day included in its rates.

Meals are taken at the hotel restaurant, La Palapa, which features a thatched-roof dining room and open terrace perched above the swimming pool and jungle canopy. The forty-room hotel offers a modern take on jungle chic and is interspersed with Mayan artifacts, handcrafted furnishings, and terraces outfitted with sofas and hammocks where guests can sit and enjoy the natural landscape. Rooms don't have TVs or telephones, but do have air conditioning and provide an authentic escape from the stress and bustle of modern life. If you're still not relaxed, the Ki'Ol Spa will design a custom spa treatment tailored to your needs, or choose from their menu of traditional mineral treatments, massages, or wraps.

The hotel is popular with sophisticated and adventurous adults, who generally stay for a few days while visiting Mayan ruins and taking eco-friendly tours. With no nightlife in the area, most guests retire fairly early after an evening of star-gazing and listening to the nighttime fauna.

EXPLORE ALL OF THE WILD AND UNTAMED SURROUNDINGS AT THE EXPLOREAN KOHUNLICH EXPLOREAN KOHUNLICH BY FIESTA AMERICANA

are several restaurants, souvenir shops, an ice-cream parlor, a swimming pool, a sundeck, a hammock area, and a protected snorkeling area. There is also a museum and an ancient Mayan lighthouse relic. Visitors can rent snorkeling equipment, clear-bottom kayaks, as well as Snuba or Sea Trek suits to experience the underwater realm.

ISLA HOLBOX (105 MILES NORTHWEST OF CANCÚN)

Beyond its reputation as a haven for beach-loungers and foodies, Holbox is also known as the home of the whale sharks, the largest species of shark in the world—often growing as long as a standard seventy-two-seat school bus. Fortunately, the fish are gentle giants, slow and docile, and prefer to passively feed on plankton.

Whale shark sightings primarily happen from mid-July to September. Many tour operators will still guarantee that they'll find the sharks or refund your money. Others warn that this might mean a 2.5-hour boat trip to reach more fertile waters. When making your arrangements, be sure you understand exactly what's being promised and how long the excursion might be expected to take.

On successful trips, the captain typically zeros in on a shark and slowly pulls the boat within several feet. Two at a time, snorkelers swim alongside for about 10 minutes. The shark continues to move, so there's a fair amount of swimming involved to keep up, though most people are so engrossed in the experience that they don't notice how tired they're getting. Boats carry about ten people, so after an hour or so on deck, you'll have another turn to jump back into the water and continue the interaction.

Some boat captains and tour operators offer private charters. Tours are available that include transportation from Cancún, Playa del Carmen, or even Cozumel. A top operator is **Holbox Tours & Travel** (www.whalesharktours.com).

Tours and private charters can also be arranged to visit the **Island of the Birds**, a natural habitat a few miles away where you can go on sportfishing and fly-fishing excursions, visit the **Yalahau Cenote** (www.en-holbox.com.mx/yalahau), and go horseback riding.

✳ Lodging

ISLA COZUMEL (ELEVEN MILES FROM PLAYA DEL CARMEN BY BOAT)

The all-inclusive 175-room dive resort **Cozumel Palace** (southern hotel zone, km 2.5, www.palaceresorts.com) features modern contemporary design with Mexican flourishes. Though right on the water, its shoreline is exposed reef, so a small beach was constructed above the rocks. Snorkeling is excellent right at the hotel, where you'll encounter barracuda, parrot fish, colored coral, sea anemone, sea urchin, lobster, and other marine life.

At the southern end of the island, the casual 224-room **Fiesta Americana Cozumel All Inclusive** (Southern Coastal Road, km 7.5, www.fiestamericana.com) is popular with families, serious scuba divers, and other guests who value ready access to the best dive sites over proximity to downtown (which is still only 20 minutes away by car). The hotel's beach club lies across the street from the main building. Refurbished in early 2014, the hotel's rooms have been completely updated, and its restaurants have been expanded to complement the all-inclusive operation.

One of Cozumel's original hotels, the 251-room **El Cozumeleño** (northern hotel zone, km 4.5, Santa Pilar Beach, www.elcozumeleno.com) remains one of the most popular spots for families and others looking for affordable, all-inclusive beach vacations.

SNORKELING, DIVING, AND OTHER WATER SPORTS AWAIT AT THE ALL-INCLUSIVE FIESTA AMERICANA IN COZUMEL FIESTA AMERICANA

With comfortable modern rooms and facilities, the **Presidente InterContinental Cozumel Resort & Spa** (www.ihg.com) places its focus on location. Situated on Cozumel's western shore, the hotel offers premium access to dive locations and sunset views.

CANCÚN (FORTY-FIVE MILES NORTH OF PLAYA DEL CARMEN)

Most Cancún hotels (and all listed below) are located in the aptly named hotel zone. Scores of resorts across different price categories offer something to suit almost every type of traveler.

Fiesta Americana Coral Beach Resort & Spa (Boulevard Kukulcán, km 9.5, www.fiestamericana.com) sits on Cancún's most prime stretch of crystal-white beach. It's so noteworthy that it bears repeating: this resort spills out onto an utterly spotless, perfect beach. With 602 rooms, it's regularly rated at the top of Mexico's resorts. It's modern, tropical, and decadent.

Known for its near perfect location—on the beach and in walking distance to the convention center and main tourism entertainment district—**Dreams Cancún Resort & Spa** (Boulevard Kukulcán, km 10, Punta Cancún, www.dreamsresorts.com) offers the best beach in this part of Cancún—and it's even hidden in a sheltered cove. The lack of easy public access makes this beach especially safe and relaxing. Though the resort is all-inclusive, guests are not required to wear wristbands and instead sign all meals and drinks to their room, and staff go out of their way to provide great service, even though tips are included in the room price.

For something a few miles removed from the central tourist area, **Live Aqua Cancún** (Boulevard Kukulcán, km 13, www.liveaqua.com) is set on an optimal beach across from a new shopping center. Thoroughly contemporary in every way, the all-inclusive hotel focuses on sensory experience, offering

The Sunscape Sabor Cozumel (Coastal Highway Sur, km 12.9, www.sunscaperesorts.com/sabor) features family-friendly amenities, and the nearby **Aura Cozumel Grand Resort** (www.auraresorts.com) has a loyal base of returning guests.

The fifty-room, hacienda-style **Playa Azul Beach Resort** (northern hotel zone, km 4, San Juan Beach, www.playa-azul.com) offers its guests unlimited play at the Cozumel Country Club golf course, created by Nicklaus Design Group, just a few minutes away.

aromatherapy kits in each room, 24-hour lounge music, and phosphorescent pillows at the beachside lounge. On-site restaurants feature celebrity chefs and have become the hip spots in town for the see-and-be-seen crowd. Guests, however, get preferential reservations. Other highlights include an upscale spa, a "garden of secrets" nature walk, a wine and mezcal bar, and a poolside lounge area with sun *cabañas*.

For those who complain that Cancún has no charm, the all-inclusive **Grand Fiesta Americana Condesa Cancún** (Boulevard Kukulcán, km 15.5, www.fiestamericana.com) may change their mind. With the tallest *palapa* in all of Cancún, the resort evokes a grand re-imagination of a Mexican village. Inside, a slick mix of traditional Mexican-hacienda décor is accented by local touches and modern upgrades. The lobby is cooled by ocean breezes, and the beach is composed of flour-like sand.

Although there's not a W Hotel Cancún (yet), you can find Starwood Hotels' swanky W offshoot **Aloft Cancún** (Boulevard Kukulcán, km 3.5, www.starwoodhotels.com) nestled against a revitalized convention center and shopping district. With sleek lines, bright accents, and playful designs, the hotel is exactly what you would expect and fits in nicely among the bright blues, vivid pinks, and smooth white lines of Cancún's hotel zone.

PLAYA MUJERES (9 MILES NORTH OF CANCÚN)

Three resort hotels make up the accommodations within Playa Mujeres. The 450-room, all-inclusive **Excellence Playa Mujeres** (Prolongación Bonampak, Punta Sam, www.excellenceresorts.com) puts tropical grandeur and playful pomp on display in its ornate lobby with massive chandeliers and a promenade staircase leading down to the resort grounds. A modern, tropically chic pool and bar set the tone for this upscale, adults-only resort. Set right alongside the resort's seven winding pools, all ground-floor rooms feature swim-up access, and some suites feature rooftop Jacuzzis.

With its crisp lobby showcasing plush textures and shades of white, **The Beloved Hotel** (Prolongación Bonampak, Punta Sam, www.belovedhotels.com) makes no bones about its designer leanings. At The Beloved, originally known by its Spanish translation *"La Amada,"* palm trees and local vegetation offset the bright white building and sands of the landscaped grounds. Honeymooners, couples, and guests docked at the adjacent V&V Marina (www.marinavv.com/en) make use of the hotel's restaurants and bars.

Finest Playa Mujeres (Prolongación Bonampak, Punta Sam, www.finestresorts.com), the resort area's most recent addition, is a modern, family-friendly all-inclusive. A section with a private pool and other amenities is reserved for adults.

ISLA MUJERES (15 MILES NORTH OF CANCÚN, BY BOAT)

Accommodation options range from backpacker to boutique and include several unique spots that make Isla Mujeres an appealing stop for any budget.

Set on a flawless white sandy beach, the elaborate **Hotel Na Balam** (Calle Zazil-Ha, H118, Playa Norte, www.nabalam.com) is adorned with Mayan décor, lush jungle foliage, and hammocks ideal for napping in the warm breeze. The hotel specializes in hosting weddings, yoga retreats, and other group rendezvous.

Straight out of a trendy magazine photo shoot, the minimalist twelve-room **Hotel Secreto** (Punta Norte, www.hotelsecreto.com) overlooks a secluded cove of Halfmoon Beach and grants its guests a sense of privacy and exclusivity hard to obtain elsewhere on the island. A great spot for a romantic hideaway, the hotel regularly picks up visitors who've

HOTEL SECRETO IN ISLA MUJERES IS A HIP GETAWAY FOR COUPLES CHIP RANKIN

found their original Isla accommodations to be more rustic than charming. Gay and lesbian travelers will find themselves welcomed here without any eyes batted.

Ideal for budget travelers, the friendly **Hotel Bucaneros** (downtown, www .bucaneros.com) exudes a genuinely local vibe. The inn's sixteen rooms are simple but attractive and clean, and some have air conditioning. Restaurants and bars are within easy walking distance, and the beach is a 10-minute walk away.

Guests arrive at the opulent, thirty-five-room **Zoetry Villa Rolandi** (East Beach, www.zoetryresorts.com/mujeres) via a deluxe yacht that picks them up in Cancún. The hotel's sincere and insightful staff, quirky yet luxurious rooms, elegant restaurant jutting over the sea, and private beach all ensure supreme satisfaction.

Formerly known as Villa las Brisas, the six-room, seaside bed-and-breakfast

Villa la Bella (2.5 miles from Playa Norte, www.villalabella.com) offers a relaxing respite from the hurried world, with no phones, TVs, or alarm clocks. From May to July, sea turtles nest on the hotel beach.

Exclusive and indulgent, **Casa de los Sueños** (on the road to Garrafon, www .casasuenos.com) is more like a grand private villa than a hotel. It offers ten rooms and suites with ocean views, premium bedding, and unique décor.

ISLA HOLBOX (105 MILES NORTHWEST OF CANCÚN)

Not long ago, overnight visitors to Holbox had to be content with sleeping on hammocks and taking quick showers before the water ran cold. While barebones lodging of this sort is still available, you can also obtain rooms with cold air conditioning, warm water, comfortable beds, and an artistic tropical style with a little panache. All hotels in this book fall into the latter category. If you need Jacuzzi bathtubs and four-star dining come nightfall, you're best off visiting the island on a day trip and returning to your upscale hotel in Cancún or the Riviera Maya.

BOUTIQUE HOTELS & LOCAL LODGING Guests at the ultra-relaxing, rustic-chic **Hotelito Casa Las Tortugas** (Playa Blanca, www .holboxcasalastortugas.com) can swing in hammocks outside the hotel's twenty-four eclectically designed suites and bungalows or retreat inside to curl up in Egyptian cotton sheets. The boutique hotel has winding staircases, twisting pathways, colorful walls and tiles, and a private pool. It's home to a *mezcaleria* and *cevicheria*, a yoga studio, and a kite-surfing school. The picturesque beachside restaurant and bar is sometimes open to the public, but at times is limited to hotel guests, depending on the provisions it has on hand. The hotel is both on the beach and just a couple of short blocks from town. It's quite easy to get to it on foot or bicycle.

If you're looking for less town square and more Swiss Family Robinson in your getaway, then **Hotel Villas Flamingos** (toward the end of Paseo Kuká, www .villasflamingos.com/en) is your spot. Situated a mile up the beach from Downtown, the twenty-nine-room boutique hotel is a destination unto itself. Most rooms and suites are tucked away in tropical white bungalows topped with thatched *palapa* roofs. The property feels like a perfect little village, with space to roam and greet your neighbor as you pass. There's a deep blue pool on the beach, next to the outdoor seaside restaurant. In addition to seagulls, expect to see small, harmless iguanas sunning themselves on the pool steps and the tiny seawall that runs alongside the restaurant.

Rooms range from rustic to fairly modern, and some are better suited to couples than families, but all have sea views and central air conditioning and island-inspired touches, like conch shell shower heads, wood accents, and other details. Select bungalows feature private pools or enclosed third-floor Jacuzzis that overlook the sea. Guests are welcome to borrow courtesy bikes and kayaks, and although the hotel feels remote, downtown is just a 5-minute bike ride or 20-minute walk away, down the carless beachfront road.

Slightly further removed from downtown and bordering the island's reserve, **Las Nubes de Holbox** (at the end of Paseo Kuká before it dissolves into the reserve, www.lasnubesdeholbox.com) offers twenty-eight peaceful rooms and suites tucked away inside thatch-roofed bungalows. An older property, views of the sea are more concealed or hard to come by for many rooms, but the overall effect is charming. *Palapa* roofs and traditional white stucco walls conceal upscale air-conditioned interiors. Guests are welcome to make use of courtesy bikes and kayaks, and a small private yacht is available to rent for an additional charge. In addition to three swimming pools, the hotel offers relaxing massage and facial treatments at Orquídea Spa, located on-site. Like its neighbor Villa Flamingos, Las Nubes is one of the few properties in Holbox's hotel zone that has direct beach frontage.

Designed and owned by a once-traveling artist who decided to stay, the romantic eighteen-room **CasaSandra** (Calle de la Igualdad, www.casasandra .com) showcases hand-made décor reflecting Holbox's back-to-nature ambiance. Original art is on display throughout the charming boutique hotel, which sits northeast of downtown Holbox, across from the beach on a sandy road.

Set on idyllic little stretch of beach with palm trees and hammocks, **La Palapa** (Esmedregal Street and the beach, www.hotellapalapa.com) carries the tropical theme into its twenty-five rooms, most of which boast an ocean view. All have seashell showerheads and faucets in the bathroom. Guests will have fun exploring the small hotel, with its winding stairwells, rooftop patio, and more. An open-air third-floor living room provides sea views, comfy chairs, and a small library.

The twenty-room **Holbox Dream** (Pedro Joaquin Codwel Avenue at the beach, www.holboxdream.com) is small, simple, and charming. The hotel offers air-conditioned rooms with comfortable beds at a very reasonable price. Downtown is a short walk but also sufficiently removed that travelers will feel far away from its modest bustle. The hotel is an ideal pick for travelers wanting a boutique experience at a lower price.

You can also find home and room rentals online at **Airbnb** (www.airbnb.com), which has over fifteen listings, and on **VRBO** (www.vrbo.com) and HomeAway (www.homeaway.com), each with more than ten Holbox listings.

✳ Where to Eat

ISLA COZUMEL (11 MILES FROM PLAYA DEL CARMEN BY BOAT)

Most of your meal options can be found downtown, either on or within walking distance of the town square.

Facing the ferry dock on the west side of the town square, **Las Palmeras** (along the *malecón*, facing the ferry dock, www.restaurantepalmeras.com) is a fun spot to pass time waiting for the boat to Playa del Carmen. Famous for its fishbowl margaritas (served ice-cold, potent, and delicious), it offers breakfast, lunch, and dinner, as well as covered seating with open windows and walls that allow in the ocean breezes.

Since 1945, inexpensive **Casa Denis** (www.casadenis.com) has served some of the best food in town and is especially popular for its fish, tacos, enchiladas, shrimp, and steak. The restaurant also prepares *sopes*, a traditional dish from Acapulco served on thick, soft corn tortillas with lettuce, cheese, refried beans, and meat toppings.

One of the fancier and pricier restaurants on the island, **Pepe's Grill** (one block south of the town square, www.pepescozumel.com/eng/) is the traditional spot for a first or last meal on Cozumel. The chef prepares tender steaks, fresh seafood, Mexican specialties, fresh salads, and pastas. It may be best known, however, for its Mayan coffee, containing *Xtabentun*, a local orange schnapps. Waiters make the after-dinner drinks tableside, and as they're prepared, the whole restaurant watches as the liquor is set aflame and poured into the coffee. The popular restaurant refreshed both its menu and its décor in 2013, bringing a more relaxed, upscale flavor to the already warm and friendly spot.

The casual outdoor café **Plaza Leza** (south side of town square) specializes in inexpensive fajitas and steak, and the fragrance from its grills will catch your attention as you walk by. After dinner, linger over a cup of coffee or a tropical drink while enjoying prime views of the sidewalk parade. On Sunday nights, it's a great place to watch the music and festivities that take place at the plaza's gazebo.

The popular **Kinta Mexican Bistro** (a block and a half north of the square on North 5th Avenue, www.kintarestaurante.com) serves up contemporary Latin dishes on a lush, shaded outdoor patio.

Guido's (on the seaside Rafael E. Melgar Avenue between 6th and 8th Streets) offers Italian dishes, seafood, and pizza in a pleasant, low-key courtyard setting.

Owned by a winning mother-daughter duo, **Chocolateria Isla Bella** (next door to Kinta, a block and a half north of the square on North 5th Avenue) delights with fresh artisanal chocolates prepared daily.

There are also several good choices when you leave downtown and explore the island. A great place for a lunchtime stop, **Chen Rio Restaurant & Beach Bar** (7 miles up the coast on the island's east side) has a limited menu—fried whole fish is its main specialty—served beside a superlative beach with calm waters on Cozumel's east coast. No credit cards.

Local favorite **Mezcalitos** (at the intersection of the cross-island road and the northern end of the road that traverses the eastern shoreline, www.mezcalitos .com) serves Mexican dishes and snacks and has a full bar. Everyone here is doing the same thing—cruising around the island—so it's easy to meet other travelers and pick up tips on hidden beaches and good places to go.

CANCÚN (45 MILES NORTH OF PLAYA DEL CARMEN)

Restaurants are plentiful in the hotel zone and on the main strips in downtown Cancún, making it easy to find options in or near your hotel. However, there are several destinations worth a special trip.

Though the air-conditioned original dining room of **La Habichuela** (25 Margarita Street, www.lahabichuela.com) in downtown Cancún is quite pleasant and sufficiently upscale to impress any date, the true joy of this place is its back patio, where trees, tropical plants, Mayan replicas, and twinkling lights create a majestic setting well-suited for a long, slow meal. The specialty of the house is the *Cocobichuela*, a coconut stuffed with lobster in a cream sauce. The dish has a unique flavor and goes great with ice-cold beer.

Though hardly an authentic cantina, **Pericos** (Yaxchilán 61, in the downtown area of Cancún) throws a fun nightly fiesta. There are folkloric dancers, funny skits, conga lines, and a live mariachi

THE SPRAWLING GROUNDS OF THE ALL-INCLUSIVE FIESTA AMERICANA GRAND CONDESA FIESTA AMERICANA GRAND CONDESA CANCUN

BUY LOCAL FOR LOCAL

Taking its singularity seriously, Isla Mujeres frowns on international chains. Aside from a few small hotel groups, the only international brands permitted on island to date are the 7-Eleven convenience store and Grupo Anderson's Official Multi-Brand outlet, both across from the ferry dock. Even the Multi-Brand store is a concession to local policy. The corporation that owns Carlos 'n Charlie's and Señor Frog's may get to sell official souvenirs, but it hasn't been allowed to use either brand name on its public signage nor open a restaurant or bar on the island.

band. The menu features a selection of Mexican standards, including fajitas, tacos, enchiladas, and grilled steak or shrimp.

Built on stilts over the Nichupté lagoon and across the main road from the beach in the hotel zone, **Lorenzillos Lobster House** (Boulevard Kukulcán, km 13, www.lorenzillos.com.mx) advertises its lobster all over town and lives up to its hype. The experience is like being on a luxury cruise ship in days gone by. Choose from tails or whole live lobster, and pick your meal from the tank. The restaurant is a great place to watch the sun set, and at night you can see the city lights and the stars at the same time. The dining room fills up nearly every night, so go early or call ahead if you want one of the coveted waterside tables on the outer deck.

Right next door to Lorenzillos, **Trattoria Limoncello** (Boulevard Kukulcán, km 13, www.limoncellotrattoria.com) offers a more buttoned-up approach to seafood and the over-the-water dining experience.

Enjoy a touristy take on Mexican food served by a lively wait staff at **Carlos 'n Charlies** (Boulevard Kukulcán, km 8.5, www.carlosandcharlies.com). Sure, it's packaged, but the entertainment is non-stop and everyone stays engaged.

Find cheap, delicious tacos with great sauces and no frills at the always-busy **Taco Factory** (Fiesta Plaza at Boulevard Kukulcán, km 9, www.tacofactory.mx). The choice is inexpensive, delicious, and efficient.

ISLA MUJERES (15 MILES NORTH OF CANCÚN, BY BOAT)

Plenty of quality restaurants and cafés can be found in downtown Isla. **Chi-Chi & Charlie's** (Playa Norte, www.chichisandcharlies.com) serves inexpensive burgers, cocktails, and sunset views, while the romantic **Oceanus** (Calle Zazil-Ha, #118, Playa Norte, www.nabalam.com) at the Na Balam hotel offers delicious vegetarian and regional specialties under a large *palapa* roof by the beach.

Removed from town and set on a dock behind the hotel of the same name, the gourmet restaurant **Casa Rolandi** (www.zoetryresorts.com/mujeres) is known to draw the Cancún elite who boat over for the restaurant's seafood, steak, shrimp, Mexican specialties, and an excellent wine list. The owners also have a delicious, and more casual, outpost downtown—**Rolandi's Pizzería** (Calle Hildalgo), which, while equally popular, doesn't offer the same romance or seaside views.

ISLA HOLBOX (105 MILES NORTHWEST OF CANCÚN)

Primarily centered around the town square, Holbox restaurants welcome locals and visitors as they mingle and compare menus. Several restaurants display samples of their fresh fish and other dishes. Select shops along the square proffer fresh fruit smoothies and ice cream treats.

The tropical, French-inspired café **Le Jardín Panaderia** (on Lisa Street between Damero and Pedro Joaquin Cordel) is a popular stop for pastries, panini sandwiches, quiches, omelets, and other tasty goodness. The casual open-air dining room sits beneath a thatched roof and feels like a living room, complete with a couple of couches, plenty of magazines, and a kids' play corner. It's one of the most popular stops on Holbox for locals and travelers. Be sure to put a pin in the world map there to show where you're visiting from, if you can find room for it.

Perched above the southwestern side of the plaza, **Restaurant Los Peleones** (Juárez Avenue across from the town square) celebrates Mexico's love of the *luchador* (masked wrestler) with a witty atmosphere and delicious food and drink. Owned by an Argentinian chef turned local, the small and charming restaurant serves fresh seafood, Argentinian-grilled meats, and a unique selection of pastas. Save room for Los Peleones' original and curiously tasty dessert creation: dark chocolate crumbles and nuts on a thin layer of fresh olive oil, topped with fresh vanilla ice cream.

During the day, **La Casa de la Tortilleria de Española** (Juárez Avenue across from the town square, directly beneath Los Peleones) pours coffee, tea, and

TOURISTS AND LOCALS STOP IN FOR FRESH FAVORITES AT LA ISLA DE COLIBRI, AT THE SOUTHERN CORNER OF HOLBOX'S MAIN SQUARE CHIP RANKIN

lemonade and serves up healthy vegetarian lunches. Their most popular dish is the Spanish tortilla, which is really an omelet prepared with potatoes and cheese.

Located on the south side of the town square, across from the large Isla Holbox band shell, **La Isla de Colibri** (Juárez and Porfirio Diaz Avenues) resembles an old Caribbean homestead whose town sprung up beyond its doorstep. The simple local restaurant serves fresh seafood, Mexican dishes, and basic international fare for the faint of heart. Beneath its tin roof, the edifice boasts bright colors as well as Mexican and Caribbean art. On a nice day or evening, take a street-side table, order a large, fresh margarita, and watch locals and tourists drift by. Visa and MasterCard accepted.

On a third-floor patio overlooking the ocean, **La Parrilla de Juan** (Igualdad Street between Palomino Avenue and Bravo Street, one block northeast of the town square) is an Argentinian steakhouse with a decent assortment of wine. As with most restaurants on Holbox, freshly caught seafood is on the menu as well. The food is of good quality, but since there is no local beef on the island and Holbox is quite remote, expect to pay premium prices for steak.

There is no set menu at **El Chapulím Mexican Bistro & Artisan Beer House** (Juárez Avenue, just northwest of the main plaza). Instead, the owner prepares an original four-course meal each day based on what he finds fresh and available during his morning market run. Closed most Sundays, Mondays, and throughout October.

Básico Cocina de Playa (between the square and the beach on Tiburon Ballena Street) serves up tasty breakfast, lunch, dinner, and drinks in a hip, stylish spot that could easily be at home in Playa or Tulum.

Although *vino* is highlighted in its name, **Papalotes Wine Bar** (a block and a half southeast of the square at Damero Street) serves food all day, from breakfast to dinner. Specialties include pizza, Mexican dishes, and seafood. The smart-looking patio is a great, soothing spot to curl up and sip a coffee, juice, or the bar's eponymous wine.

Other popular stops include **Pizzería Edelyn** (eastern corner of the town square)—offering up amazing lobster pizzas, ice-cold beers, and a lively atmosphere on a second-story terrace overlooking the town—and the inexpensive, open-air **Viva Zapata** (a half-block west of the main plaza), which features lobster, whole fish, shrimp, and traditional Mexican fare under a *palapa* roof and along the longest wooden bar in Holbox. The no-frills, outdoor **Las Panchas** (Morelos Street between Pedro Joaquin Codwell Street and the beach) is a favorite breakfast stop among locals. Tourists are welcome too.

✳ Bars & Nightlife

ISLA COZUMEL (11 MILES FROM PLAYA DEL CARMEN BY BOAT)

While restaurants welcome patrons to linger over drinks, most nightlife takes place in chain establishments located on Rafael Melgar Avenue between the town square and the cruise-ship dock.

Built on the water, Jimmy Buffet's **Margaritaville Café** (Rafael Melgar Avenue by the cruise-ship dock, www.margaritaville.com) is a Parrothead paradise, with an oceanfront tiki bar, beach music (including plenty of Buffett hits), burgers, seafood, and an open-air dance floor. Patrons tend to be passionate about their beach-bum hero, and impromptu sing-alongs are commonplace.

The Mexican mainstay tourist bar by the cruise-ship dock, **Señor Frog's** (www.senorfrogs.com), is conveniently steps away from **Carlos 'n Charlie's** (www.carlosandcharlies.com). Frog's is the more nightlife-oriented of the two, featuring a stage, dancing waiters, and a full-time party, while Charlie's offers instead a lively restaurant atmosphere. Depending on the day and how many cruise ships are in town, these tourist havens might be packed or entirely empty.

Located away from downtown, the come-as-you-are daytime beach bar **Freedom in Paradise** (Southern Coastal Road at the southern tip of the island, www.bobmarleybar.com) has no electricity, doesn't accept credit cards, and is rather ramshackle, but it's a must-see waypoint for travelers circumnavigating the island.

CANCÚN (45 MILES NORTH OF PLAYA DEL CARMEN)

One of the city's top nightspots sits across from the convention center. But to call **Coco Bongo** (Boulevard Kukulcán, km 10.5, www.cocobongo.com) a bar would be woefully inadequate—even to refer to it as a nightclub is somewhat of a joke. It's more like an entertainment center where travelers congregate to celebrate life and go a bit crazy. There's often a line wrapping around the corner, but it moves fast, and you can start making friends before you get inside. There you'll find a central bar area ringed by stadium-like seating, an upper deck with

THE SHOW AT COCO BONGO LASTS UNTIL SUNRISE   COCO BONGO

another bar and more seating, and an elevated stage where most of the club's nonstop action happens. From celebrity impersonators and high-flying acrobats to live rock music, there's always something happening on stage or someone hanging from the rafters above the main bar. The atmosphere is very convivial, with a strong spirit of communal fun.

A big-sister club to Playa's own popular hotspot, **Mandala Nightclub** (Boulevard Kukulcán, km 9, www.mandalanightclub.com) sits next to Coco Bongo but is entirely its opposite. The plush, vivid, red interior is open to the street, allowing all the world to see the bright lights and table-dancers at this all-you-can-drink establishment. This nightclub is ideally suited for mingling and making new friends.

Megaclub The City Cancún (Punta Cancún, Boulevard Kukulcán, km 10.5, www.thecitycancun.com) features a swanky Miami Beach–style *cabaña* bar and a massive indoor discotheque complete with laser light shows, smoke machines, and live performances. There are nine bars, big-name DJs, and a four-level dance floor. The whole place can accommodate more than four thousand partiers, making it one of the largest nightspots in all of Latin America.

ISLA MUJERES (15 MILES NORTH OF CANCÚN BY BOAT)

Popular with both locals and tourists, **Buho's** (Avenue Carlos Laza, Playa Norte, by the Maria del Mar hotel, www.cabanasdelmar.com) is Isla's de-facto happy-hour, offering cocktails made with tropical fruit and a hybrid playlist of reggae and American rock. Downtown's **La Adelita Tequileria** (Avenue Hidalgo) features a selection of 150 tequilas and often has a two-for-one tequila special.

For some daytime drinking and a change of pace from downtown, head to the **Soggy Peso Bar & Grill** (Avenue Rueda Medina, south of the naval base on the bay side of the island, www.thesoggypeso.com). This ultra-casual Jimmy Buffett–friendly *palapa* bar is open from noon until around 8:30 PM, offering ceviche and other special treats. Marked only by a small handmade sign, the bar is hidden behind a house on the right, a few miles south of downtown. From downtown, you'll need a golf cart or a taxi, but finding your way there is part of the adventure. Do yourself a favor and try the bloody Mary.

ISLA HOLBOX (105 MILES NORTHWEST OF CANCÚN)

When the sun goes down, the island grows noticeably quiet. Visitors stroll the square and the main streets and tend to linger over dinner with a few extra drinks. Many lights are dimmed, and candlelight provides much of the atmosphere. A few places on and around the square tend to be livelier, but only by comparison to the overall hushed town.

There are few dedicated bars on the island. However, most restaurants that remain open past the dinner hour are happy to serve drinks.

Across from Las Tortugas, you'll find **LUUMA** (Damera Avenue and Sierra Street), a hip bar, gathering place, and social haven. The sandy, stone-enclosed patio is dotted with palm trees. This glowy, hybrid destination also features a boutique fashion and dress shop (suitable for Tulum), a kitchen serving tapas, and an art gallery.

Habana Nights (on Damera Avenue, a half-block toward the airstrip from the main plaza, next to Viva Zapata) is the most popular hangout in town, thanks to its laid-back Caribbean atmosphere and big-screen TVs, which are especially in demand during key soccer matches and other sporting events.

Under new management, the **Rooftop Bar at Hotel Arena** (Juárez Avenue across from the southeastern side of the town square, www.hotelarenaholbox

.com) invites revelers in with a solid bar, comfy chairs, a rooftop plunge pool, and the highest perch around, with a view of the main plaza below.

Barquito Mawimbi (on the beach at the Wawimbi Hotel on Damero Street northwest of Sierra Street, www.mawimbi.net) isn't open late, but it's a favorite stop for tourists exploring the island who are looking for a beach bar away from their own hotel.

Mingle with friends, or maybe even make some new ones, at **Ukulele Grill** (Igualdad Street between Palomino Avenue and Bravo Street, one block northeast of the town square). The second-story terrace overlooks the town square, and you can usually catch a *fútbol* match or other sports game on one of the televisions if you ask.

ACTIVITIES & TOURS

Adventure abounds in the Riviera Maya, and wherever you are, most activities are no more than an hour away from any hotel in the area. Nearly every hotel tour desk can sell you tickets that include round-trip transportation. Attractions are also easy to get to by rental car or even bus, which additionally make for good self-guided outings. Note: secondary and local attractions are discussed in other chapters in this book, based on location.

✶ Nature Parks, Amusement Parks & Aquariums

Once a sacred Mayan site, the Mayan-themed **Xcaret** recreational park (Highway 307, km 287, 3 miles south of Playa del Carmen, www.xcaret.com) is hands-down the top attraction in the area. It's part water park, animal adventure, museum, cultural experience, and archeology lesson rolled into one amazing day! True to its roots, Xcaret has several native ruins on site, and each evening performers put on an incredible two-hour show of Mexican dances and rituals called Mexico Espectacular.

Visitors can go tubing or snorkeling through an underground river, marvel at macaws in the aviary, see native fish and coral in a saltwater aquarium, watch butterflies in their natural habitat, go scuba diving, lounge on the beach, swim with dolphins, and even visit a re-creation of a native Mayan village (the cemetery is a must-see). Tour buses from Cancún come in hourly, so it's best to arrive early to experience the park before it gets too crowded. Arrive after 4 PM, to visit the park at night and receive a somewhat discounted admission.

Next door, Xcaret's **Xplor** (Highway 307, km 282, www.xplor.travel) caters to the active adventure set, letting them explore its grounds by air, water, and land. Guests can enjoy 2.5 miles of zip lines that include water landings, tour through the jungle on amphibious ATVs that they drive themselves, and swim or hand-paddle a personal raft through an underground river surrounded by striking stalactites and stalagmites. Book through a local tour agency, or just show up at the ticket office. The Xplor Fuego offers nighttime thrills in the park until 11:30 PM. All-inclusive available.

The perfect family-friendly activity for a rainy day is found deep underground at **Río Secreto** (Highway 307, km 283.5, www.riosecreto.com) just a few minutes from Xplor Park. Marvel at the subterranean beauty of stalactites and stalagmites as you traverse caves carved out by an underground river. A tour of this unique nature reserve includes a guided exploration of the natural cave formations and a short swim (wetsuits and lifejackets provided). The park's commitment to preserving the native environment is evident in all aspects of the tour. Recommended for ages 4 and up and persons physically able to participate in light climbing.

Nature park **Xel-Ha** (Highway 307, km 245, 8 miles from Tulum, www.xelha.com) was once a Mayan seaport and later a popular snorkeling cove frequented by an adventurous few. Today it's part of Xcaret's family of attractions. Xel-Ha (meaning "where the waters are born" in Mayan) features underground rivers where fresh- and saltwater meet, an animal nursery, cliff jumping, a tubing area, a dolphin discovery

AN AFTERNOON SAIL THROUGH AKUMAL BAY RIVIERA MAYA DESTINATION MARKETING OFFICE

SWIMMING WITH DOLPHINS AT XCARET

Ancient Mayans saw the dolphin as a sacred animal and a source of inspiration for the creation of myths and legends. Today, dolphins contribute to aquatic therapies and research in several humanities disciplines, and experience has shown that they lack merely the ability to speak.

At Xcaret, dolphins are treated with care and respect, and their well-being is always the main priority. Biologists and veterinarians on-site meet all the needs of the park's dolphins. They monitor their health, weight, and food intake, and conduct research on their behavior. In fact, biologists claim that the forty-year life expectancy of a dolphin can increase for those living in captivity or semi-captivity (in expansive areas of its natural habitat). Dolphins have actually been born in captivity at Xcaret, and the way in which the baby mammals arrive into this world is quite a sight. They come out of their mother's womb tail first, so as not to drown, and they emerge like torpedoes at the surface as they take in their first breath. Their first year is a delicate time because dolphins are born without antibodies; however, their mothers feed them for one to two years, helping to build up these defenses.

Qualified dolphin trainers, who are constantly learning new skills, spend long hours with the dolphins and form extremely strong, family-like bonds and communication abilities. Every single approach of the trainer receives an answer from the dolphin: a jump that soars more than two meters up in the air, a tail dance, a flipper greeting, a friendly sound, or an underwater trick.

Due to their high cognitive ability, dolphins understand every instruction their trainers give them. Dolphins have the ability to associate, and this allows them to translate signs and develop a series of perfectly synchronized movements. With a "target pole," which functions as an extension of their trainer's hand, dolphins learn to identify instructions until they develop a language that establishes a sophisticated communication with their trainer.

center, massage huts, ocean snorkeling, mountain bike trails, and hiking. All-inclusive available.

Mayan for "underground river cave," **Aktun Chen** (Highway 307, km 107, between Akumal and Xel-Ha, www.aktun-chen.com) is a 1,000-acre nature park with a large cavern and jungle tour. The main, 600-yard-long cave is said to have been a natural bunker for the native Mayans, who sought its protection during serious storms. An hour-long guided walk through the park reveals badgers, iguanas, spider monkeys, tropical birds, and wild turkeys. There's also a motorized ATV tour, if you'd rather ride than walk. Along the way, you'll see many tropical flowers, coconut palms, and a gum tree called the *chicozapote*. The cave itself has amazing formations of stalactites and stalagmites, as well as a fantastic underground *cenote* more than 35-feet deep. Though the cave winds its way several hundred yards through the ground, there are frequent openings and areas where fresh air and the sun shine through, so the experience is not as claustrophobic as it may sound.

If you prefer fauna over flora, you'll enjoy **Crococun Crocodile Farm & Zoo** (Highway 307, km 323, near Puerto Morelos, www.crococunzoo.com). Formed in 1985 as a commercial croc farm where animals were raised for their skins and skulls, it's since been transformed into a preserve, where visitors' admission fees go toward rescuing the crocs rather than killing them. The park is now home to dozens of other animals, including white-tailed deer, spider monkeys, snakes, spiders, and birds. Excluding the 300 crocodiles, many of the animals are tame enough for kids to pet.

If you're not into snorkeling or diving, **L'Aquarium** (Plaza Corazón between 12th and 14th Street just off Quinta) offers up-close views of more than two hundred species of

SNORKEL IN AN UNDERGROUND RIVER (AMONG OTHER THINGS) AT XCARET XCARET

marine life, including coral, sharks, fish, jellyfish, and other non-aquatic animals like frogs and lizards. Each of the three floors in the aquarium offers something new to see and explore, and the attraction makes for a great rainy day or non-beach activity for families. The aquarium hopes to promote ocean conservation and the preservation of endangered species, including many which have been threatened by heavy tourism in the area.

A fun little stop-off between Cancún and Playa del Carmen is the 150-acre **Yaax-Che Jardín Botánico** (Highway 307, km 33, just south of Puerto Morelos). Set up like a museum, with everything clearly marked and explained, this botanical garden and nature preserve has hundreds of species of plants, trees, and flowers. From a hilltop overlook you can observe the jungle canopy and the ocean beyond, as well as a small Mayan ruin called *El Altar* that dates from the 1400s. There's also a mock-up of an ancient Mayan homestead and a *chicle* camp, where farmers worked to process the rubber gum from the *chicle* tree. Look for the native tree called the

LEARN ABOUT SHARKS AND OTHER AQUATIC WILDLIFE AT XCARET RIVIERA MAYA DESTINATION MARKETING OFFICE

IT RAINS IN THE JUNGLE

June through September is typically rainy season, but in the jungle, the occasional rainy afternoon should be expected. The rain usually clears, but don't let a bit of precipitation ruin one of your precious vacation days.

At the Hotel: While away a few hours at the pool's swim-up bar which is likely *palapa* covered. If you're already in a bathing suit, it doesn't matter if you get a little wet. Larger all-inclusive resorts also have amazing kids' clubs to help wear off some energy, or check out the arts and crafts or activities hosted by the events staff.

Go Exploring: Plan on visiting an underground *cenote* if rain is in the forecast. Since a handful of *cenotes* in the area are underground (like Dos Ojos and Rio Secreto) and naturally covered, you won't even be aware of the rain above ground.

Learn Something: Playa del Carmen has amazing museums for a variety of interests, and any one of them is perfect for a rainy day. The aquarium highlights all of the amazing sea life of the area, and is fun for ocean lovers of all ages. The **Sayab Planetarium** (Central Avenue between 115th and 125th Avenues, www.planetariodeplayadelcarmen.org) features exhibits on Mayan history, *cenotes*, and other geological features of the area. You'll also find telescopes and movies played in the planetarium dome. On weekends, kid-friendly matinees help young scientists learn about our fragile planet and the wonders of space.

Express Yourself: Although inside voices are still required at the **Museum of 3D Wonders** (Plaza Pelicanos between 8th and 10th Street, www.3dmuseumofwonders.com), kids are encouraged to interact with the art at this museum dedicated to the cultivation of creativity. A theater also shows 3D movies, so a rainy afternoon will fly by as you give your selfie stick a workout.

ceiba, which the Mayans called *yaax chen*. Considered a spiritual totem, it was said to connect the three levels of the universe.

Popular with families and nature buffs, the privately run **Xaman Ha Aviary** (Paseo Xaman Ha, behind Plaza Playacar, Playacar) exhibits more than fifty species of tropical birds, including flamingos, toucans, macaws, and others native to the region. Some are caged, while others roam free in their natural habitat. There are also iguanas, butterflies, turtles, brown squirrels, and freshwater fish. It's best to go in the morning when the animals are more likely to be moving about.

A small replica of a Mayan temple marks the entrance to **Kantun Chi** (Highway 307, km 266.5, 14 miles south of Playa, 1 mile south of Puerto Aventuras, www.kantunchi .com), an ecology and adventure park, located across from the Barcelo Maya Hotel. Meaning "yellow stone mouth" in Mayan, Kantun Chi has nature trails, swimming holes, caves, and an animal sanctuary. Fauna include raccoons, spider monkeys, and white-tailed deer, along with several endangered local species, which the park is helping to bring back. There are four *cenotes* large enough for swimming and snorkeling, including one called Uchil Ha, or "ancient water," said to have been an ancient Mayan religious site. The Grutaventura underground cave offers stunning stalactite and stalagmite formations and two connected *cenotes* traversable via kayak.

Just across the highway from the Cancún airport, as you head to the Cancún hotel zone, you'll find the eighteen-acre amusement and water park **Ventura Park** (Boulevard Kukulcán, km 25, Cancún, www.venturapark.com). Six wildly different experiences (or worlds) are offered, including a high-tech gaming center with virtual reality, a go-kart track, an amusement park complete with a roller coaster, a lazy-river zipline adventure, and a Wet 'n Wild waterpark with a white-sand beach, wave pools, and water slides. Dolphin-swim programs are provided through Dolphinaris, where

FIRST AID KIT MUST-HAVES

Especially important for families traveling together, a well-packed first aid kit can help keep minor scrapes and illness from ruining a vacation. Playa does indeed have plenty of drug stores, so not to worry if you forget a few items, but it's best to have everything you might need from day one.

- **Anti-nausea medication:** Once you're off the airplane, there's still plenty of car, bus, and boat travel ahead if you plan on exploring. Sea-Bands also make a great drug-free option for alleviating motion sickness.
- **Antihistamines:** If anyone in your family suffers from seasonal allergies or food allergies, have some Claritin or Benadryl on hand to deal with any itching or sneezing that springs up.
- **Electrolyte tablets:** All-natural and portable electrolyte tablets help replenish fluid losses in case of diarrhea or illness. Trioral, Nunn, and Hydralyte are a few brands to try.
- **Hand sanitizer:** One of the most important means of preventing illness is to clean hands frequently and especially before meals. Look for alcohol-based hand sanitizer.
- **Thermometer:** Hopefully nobody gets a fever on vacation, but it's especially important to have a thermometer when traveling with smaller children.
- **Pain reliever & fever reducer:** Travel with children's Tylenol or Motrin and an adult version too.
- **Bandaids:** You'll do a lot of walking, and plenty of adventuring, so make sure to have at least a handful in various sizes.
- **Antibiotic cream:** Neosporin with pain reliever is always great to have when you need to fix a boo-boo.
- **Anti-itch cream:** Mosquito bites in the jungle are inevitable, so pack some Cortizone-10 or Benadryl Itch Cream. Handy for helping soothe mild sunburns too!

featured activities include swimming with the dolphins while holding their dorsal fin, or becoming a dolphin trainer for a day.

For some free family fun, explore **Parque La Ceiba** (South 1st Street at 60th Avenue, Playa del Carmen, www.florafaunaycultura.org), which supplies walking trails, a kid-friendly playground, shaded picnic areas, and a small community café with drinks, snacks, and free Wi-Fi. On weekends, this treasured community space also hosts Friday-night movies in the park and an open-air market called a *tianguis* held the third Saturday of the month.

COOKING CLASSES One of the best ways to experience the region is to add some of its signature dishes to your cooking repertoire. These courses are ideal for solo travelers or anyone wanting a more immersive cultural experience.

In Playa, **Cocina Cosmopolita Culinary School** (La Gloria Avenue and Highway 307, www.cookinplaya.com) offers hands-on instruction in preparing a three-course meal using local ingredients. Chef Coty wraps up the 4- to 5-hour class with a mezcal and tequila tasting. Friday nights also feature a three-hour cocktail and appetizer class perfect for a fun night out.

Chef Alexandra of **Food Motion Cooking Workshop** (20th Street at 20th Avenue, www.foodmotionmexico.com) will bring her 3-hour cooking class to you, or if you prefer the class can be held in her kitchen, seven days a week. In addition to flexible scheduling, menus can be customized to suit a variety of tastes and dietary preferences. Personal chef service is also an option.

HORSEBACK RIDING Many horseback riding excursions can be booked through your hotel's concierge, and local tour companies often combine a ride with other activities like a *cenote* or beach outing.

Tucked away by Maroma Beach, 20 minutes north of Playa del Carmen, **Rancho Baaxal** (along Highway 307, km 51, by Maroma Beach, www.ranchobaaxal.com) is a small ranch with just twelve horses. Prioritizing the health and well-being of its horses above all else, the ranch offers a very personalized tour, which takes riders into the jungle and along a beach that the Travel Channel has rated as one of the world's "top ten most beautiful" for four years in a row. Moonlight rides are also available.

BIKE RIDING Bike rental is available in all urban areas, and you'll likely find a bike-rental operation near the heart of most towns in the area. Many all-inclusive resorts provide complimentary bikes for guest use, so double check with your hotel before you rent from a third party.

In Playa, **Playa Rida** (8th Street at 10th Avenue, www.playarida.com) offers some attractive bike-rental options, as does **Hola Bike Rental** (www.holabike.com).

SKYDIVING & PLANE TOURS Certified by the US Parachute Association, **Skydive Playa** (Plaza Marina, Playa del Carmen, www.skydive.com.mx) offers tandem and solo jumps. Its rectangular parachutes have ram-air canopies, allowing for a very stable and controlled descent. Dives include instruction and about 45 seconds of freefall, plus a 6- to 7-minute parachute descent. Landings are on Playa's main beach.

Offering sightseeing tours, private transportation, and air-taxi service, **Aerosaab** (www.aerosaab.com) services Playa del Carmen, Cozumel, Holbox, and Chichén Itzá.

FISHING Fishing options range from a do-it-yourself, wade-fishing expedition to a full-day excursion trolling on a luxury yacht—complete with meals, drinks, guides,

FISHING BOATS ALONG THE ISLA MUJERES WATERFRONT

TEN WAYS TO SAVE MONEY ON YOUR NEXT RIVIERA MAYA VACATION

By Kay Walten of Loco Gringo (www.locogringo.com)

Who doesn't love to save money? We all do, and there are some surefire ways to get that vacation for less!

After living here for over 20 years, we know the ins and outs of how to economize in the Riviera Maya. If you want a cheaper vacation, read on. If you want to spend more on your accommodations and less on your day-to-day stuff, read on. If you want to spend all your vacation money on food and save on accommodations, read on!

1. **Get Your Own Kitchen.** Rent a condo or house with a kitchen, and save money cooking two out of three meals a day. Fruits and vegetables are much cheaper here than in the US and Canada, and they are really fresh. Plus, you'll get to try new foods right in the comfort of your own rental. We typically go out for a meal once a day, and prepare the rest. Happy hour at your condo is also always cheaper than paying retail.

2. **Take Public Transportation.** Yes, it can be intimidating to try out new public transportation, but the Riviera Maya makes it easy, affordable, and comfortable. Large buses are fully air conditioned, have on-board movies and Wi-Fi, and deliver you seamlessly from city to city. *Colectivos* or shared vans are found in cities and also from city to city. These passenger vans stop where you ask them to instead of only at bus terminals. Prices range from twenty cents to $3 for local travel. If you are going to other states, $20 will have you traveling up to 5 hours into another region.

3. **Eat Locally.** Local food in Mexico outside the popular tourist streets is a great way to try fresh, regional cuisine and save a ton of money! The food is great, the flavors are authentic, and you will likely get some recipe tips from any family-run restaurant. Look for *cocinas economicas*, street food carts, food trucks, or a little hole in the wall. In the Riviera Maya's smaller beach towns, cross over the highway and start investigating. If you stumble upon a local market, go eat there.

4. **Check Out Cultural Activities.** Whether you visit a town's main square or venture into a museum, theater, or *casa de cultura* (community center), there are always fun free things to do—you just have to know which ones to pick. In Playa del Carmen, the planetarium, city theater, and the main *zocalos* (town squares) all have free activities. Digging into these local attractions can provide some of the most memorable experiences of your stay.

5. **Shop at the Grocery Store or Corner Fruit Market.** I have to admit, whenever I travel I love going to the grocery store. I find I learn more about a culture by strolling the aisles of a grocery store than I do walking through some cities' streets. I also love buying items at local prices. Picking up the basics for your condo or vacation rental can save a ton of cash.

gear, and a video recording of all the action. From your hotel in the Riviera Maya, several distinct fishing spots are within easy reach. From the deep waters off Cancún to the north, to the reefs of Puerto Morelos, to the shallows of Cozumel, to the drop-offs near Playa, to the bays of Akumal and Puerto Aventuras, and all the way down to the flats of Sian Ka'an—each area holds something unique and exciting for fishing. And whether you're a novice who enjoys just being out on the water and reeling one in, a regular enthusiast in search of your first marlin, or an old pro going for a coveted grand slam, you can find what you're looking for in the Riviera Maya.

Fishing is great year-round, but if you're looking for a specific type of fish, then you'll need to take note of the seasons to make sure your target is around when you plan to visit. Many visitors come to Playa seeking the majestic billfish, a catch which produces a thrill like no other when it takes the bait and then jumps in the air for all to

In Mexico, you will find modest, family-run fruit stores with great prices. As small as they are, these are fantastic places to buy local fruits and vegetables.

6. **Beach It Away From the Beach Clubs.** If you just want to chill on the beach, either rent a beachfront condo or villa, or put your towel down with your cooler by your side, far away from the beach clubs. If your condo is not on the beach, ask if the rental has portable beach chairs. These are easy to carry and common on the coast.

7. **Pay in the Local Currency.** Once you land in Mexico, get yourself some pesos and take advantage of better exchange rates through your bank or a *casa de cambio* (exchange house). Do not rely on local stores and restaurants to provide a fair or friendly exchange rate. Bartering is also better in pesos if you want a better deal. CI Banco has the best ATM fee on the coast. These ATM's are located in Puerto Morelos, Playa del Carmen, and Tulum.

8. **See Attractions on Your Own.** We love visiting local hot spots on our own without the assistance of a tour company. Chichén Itzá, Cobá, Tulum, and local *cenotes* can all be explored via local transportation or by renting a car. If you are traveling in a group, you will save a lot of money doing a DIY tour. If you are not confident driving internationally and would prefer the convenience of a vehicle, renting a private van with friends or a large group will still save you quite a bit. Oh, and when you are on the road, opt for a cheap and tasty roadside meal.

9. **Buy Travel Insurance.** This is an infallible way to have security and save money if anything happens on your trip. Premiums are low, headaches are fewer, and you will have peace of mind if anything goes wrong. We have heard hundreds of stories from people who are thankful for having purchased trip insurance. This applies to travel anywhere in the world, not just the Riviera Maya.

10. **Travel After Peak Season.** A good time to save money on Riviera Maya accommodations is from May 1 to November 1, and I have to admit I love the summer here. Sure it's a bit hot, but if you plan your day right, you'll have a dreamy vacation. If you work out, do so before 8 AM. With sea breezes and refreshing water, the beach provides an ideal place to spend the day. Evenings are glorious and offer a good opportunity to walk around and see the city. If you want to see local attractions, go early and leave early. There is something spectacular about seeing the ruins when they open and leaving as the tour buses arrive.

Kay Walten moved to the Yucatán in '92 to explore underwater caves and started the Loco Gringo site in 1996. An all-encompassing guide to the area, Loco Gringo (www.locogringo .com) features concierge tours and insider info for the region in addition to a curated selection of rental accommodations available for online booking. After exploring the region for more than 20 years, Loco Gringo is able to offer vacationers a bevy of insights pertaining to the Riviera Maya.

see. These beautiful creatures, weighing up to five-hundred pounds, are seen throughout the year, but the prime time is from March to July, when they ply the deep waters between Cozumel and the Yucatán mainland in abundant numbers. Each year, there are several billfish grand slams recorded, when a single group manages to boat a blue marlin, a white marlin, and a sailfish on the same trip. When fishing for these beauties, a strict catch-and-release policy is followed, so make sure to capture the moment for bragging rights.

Tuna, mahi-mahi, bonito, bonefish, and wahoo prefer the warmer waters and generally are more active from March to August or September, though catches of each have been recorded in every month of the year. Due to the varied underwater terrain and year-round temperate climate, however, many fish species can be caught throughout the year, including barracuda, grouper, kingfish, shark, skipjack, snapper, and other

TOP FISHING DESTINATIONS

Recognized as the best place in the world for a permit, tarpon, and bonefish grand slam, Ascension Bay and Boca Pila are also prime spots for snook, barracuda, and Spanish mackerel. The bay has various inlets, ensuring that your boat captain can find fishing no matter the wind direction. Anglers can visit on a day trip from the Riviera Maya or stay overnight at one of the many lodges found between Boca Paila and Punta Allen.

Excursions from Cancún promise day- and night-fishing expeditions to the reefs not far from shore, between the coastline and Isla Mujeres. Common catches include grouper, hogfish, mackerel, and snapper.

The lagoons, jagged shorelines, and flats of Cozumel Island offer up excellent bonefishing, which is most often done using fly-fishing tackle or a lightweight spinning reel. There's good bottom fishing along the northern coast near Passion Island and on the island's east coast, where the coral reef is not part of the federal reserve. Further from shore, in the Cozumel channel, anglers troll for marlin, sailfish, and other large game.

The fishing mecca of Puerto Aventuras is the southernmost deep-water marina in the Riviera Maya, with many sportfishing and deep-sea fishing charters available. A walk around the marina reveals dozens of well-equipped boats awaiting their next expedition.

reef and bottom fish. They're so abundant, in fact, that many chartered boats promise to prepare a meal on the boat or on a hidden beach, relying exclusively on the day's catch to supply the main course. Though certainly bad luck occasionally strikes and the group is left to dine on crackers, salsa, and sides, the trips almost always end with a bounteous feast of ultra-fresh ceviche or fried fish.

A Mexican fishing license is required for boat fishing, and fees go toward worthwhile conservation and regulation programs. Reputable tour operators, such as those listed in this guide, include all required licensing in the cost of their tours.

GOLF Though the Mayans never used the wheel, they did have the ball, and it is believed that they took great pleasure in playing various games. Their most famous ball game was called *pok-ta-pok*, and it was serious business. The ball was about the size of a kickball, and the game was played on a large field about the size of a basketball court. Similar to basketball, the game's object was to shoot the ball through a hoop mounted above the playing surface. Considering that players weren't allowed to use their hands, though, scoring was quite rare and considered a tremendous feat. Large numbers of villagers turned out to watch the

EL CAMELEÓN IS THE PGA TOUR SITE FOR THE OHL CLASSIC AT MAYAKOBA MAYAKOBA

games, which had great religious and ceremonial importance.

Today, the open fields, beachfronts, and carved-away jungles of the Riviera Maya make a perfect backdrop for a more modern, popular ball game—golf. There are fifteen courses within the Riviera Maya, spanning Cancún, Cozumel, and the town of Bacalar (south of the Riviera Maya). Beautiful views of the ocean and tropical jungle abound, and several of the courses have actual Mayan ruins next to the fairways.

Most courses have clubs for rent, and unless you're a real pro or planning on playing multiple rounds, the loaners are normally sufficient. Balls can be expensive (and the loss ratio can be high), so it's usually best to bring some of your own, since they're cheap back home and fairly easy to pack. The larger courses have full-service pro shops with name-brand equipment and apparel, club repair, and instruction.

PACK THE PERFECT PICNIC

Many of the organized tours will include meals as part of the package, but when the outing or day trip requires more than a protein bar, putting together a quick and classy picnic just takes a few steps and a quick trip to the grocery store.

- Pack items that don't require refrigeration. Skip anything that has raw eggs, mayonnaise, or soft cheeses.
- Cured meats like chorizo and hard cheeses are perfect for picnic lunches if you have a small pocketknife or if the deli can cut slices for you.
- Pack oranges, apples, and bananas, or pre-sliced fruit.
- *Bolillo* (small rolls) are great for stacking with meat and cheese, or pick a few *pan dulce* for dessert.
- Don't forget dried fruit, nuts, and bottled water.

ARRANGE A FISHING TRIP WITH THE BOAT CAPTAINS AT VARIOUS SPOTS ALONG THE BEACH IN PLAYA

TOP FIVE MOST BREATHTAKING GOLF COURSES

Known for their amazing beauty and world class design, these five golf courses in the Riviera Maya are not especially budget-friendly but are all worth a visit.

El Cameleón Golf Club at Mayakobá (Highway 307, km 297, north of Playa del Carmen, www.mayakobagolf.com) is the first course in Mexico to be designed by Greg Norman. It curls around the Fairmont Mayakobá hotel and along the beach of the 1,600-acre tourism development. Players enjoy unusual hazards such as *cenotes*, mangrove swamps, and other tropical features. Two of the holes are right along the beach, while fifteen of them have some sort of water hazard. This course is the site of the yearly OHL Golf Classic pro tournament, first played in 2007, marking the first PGA event in Mexico.

The 27-hole Riviera Maya Golf Club (Highway 307, km 250, www.bahia-principe.com), designed by Robert Trent Jones II, is part of a massive real estate development with condos, private residences, and resorts. It's about an hour from the Cancún airport and 30 minutes

Some of the courses operate with an all-inclusive concept, where the greens fee includes a cart, range balls, and all the food and drink you care to consume during your round. To keep the costs down, consider playing in the afternoon to take advantage of discounted twilight rates. Just make sure to bring a hat, sunscreen, and plenty of water.

The Riviera Maya is becoming more of a golf destination with each passing decade. For information on all area golf courses, check with the **Mexican Caribbean Golf Association** (www.cancungolf.org).

ORGANIZED TOURS Just a handful of group tour and travel-providers service the Riviera Maya, and they own the vehicles, employ the guides, set the itineraries, negotiate rates, and provide the actual tours. Sometimes they sell directly to the public, but primarily they rely on tour resellers to market their tours and book the majority of reservations. Nearly every hotel has a tour desk, and there are tour offices on nearly every block of Quinta in Playa del Carmen. Some restaurants have tour kiosks at their entrances, and tour representatives even walk the beaches carrying a notebook describing the trips they can sell. Authorized agencies and individuals have licenses and ID cards, and it's recommended that you verify tour representatives' credentials before giving them any money. Most sellers have the same catalog of twenty or so tours, though there can be some variation in the selection. Prices are generally fixed and do not vary much from one operator to another.

Most tours require advance reservations so that transportation and meals can be planned accordingly. If you're interested in a spur-of-the-moment trip, your choices may be limited, but there's usually something available. When a tour is reserved, a deposit or even full payment is normally required, and you'll receive a voucher that proves you have paid and tells you when and where to go for the trip. Most major tours include hotel pickup and drop-off, while others begin at a predetermined location. If you have only put down a deposit, the balance is typically paid at the start of the tour.

Many tours and adventures can be purchased well in advance, through your local travel agent, the web site where you booked your flight, or directly from the tour operator. This can be a good way to guarantee availability and set your itinerary before your trip even begins, but prices are generally the same whether you book in advance or not.

TOUR OPERATORS **Alltournative Expeditions** (various locations along Quinta, Playa del Carmen, www.alltournative.com) specializes in natural and cultural tours, eco-adventure, and alternative adrenaline-rush activities, and trips can be

south of Playa del Carmen. More than two-hundred acres of Mayan jungle and limestone form the backdrop for lakes and *cenotes* throughout the course.

Inaugurated in 2008 in a large-scale development just north of Cancún, the 808-acre, 18-hole, par 72 **Puerto Cancún Golf Course** (east of Bonampak Avenue, near where Kulkulcán Avenue meets downtown Cancún, www.puertocancun.com.mx/golf), designed by Tom Wesikopf, features 185 acres of water features, sand traps, and manicured greens.

Designed by Greg Norman, the 18-hole, 7250 yards, par 72 **Playa Mujeres Golf Club** (Bonampak Avenue, Punta Sam, www.playamujeresgolf.com.mx) snakes through tropical mangroves, the beachfront, and a saltwater lagoon.

The Jack Nicklaus Signature Course, **Moon Palace Spa & Golf Club** (Highway 307, km 340, Cancún, www.moonpalacecancun.com) includes three separate courses, each with distinct environments (jungle, lake, and dune), totaling twenty-seven holes and a par of 108. Total length is 10,798 yards. The layout requires golfers to navigate through native vegetation, wetlands, and a plethora of sand traps.

custom-designed for large groups. Many tours stop at the company's crafts shop, where profits are shared with the indigenous communities who offer their land to be used for the adventure trip. Tours are adventurous, educational, and a great way to meet other travelers. Most of the activities require participants to be in relatively good physical shape, and children need to be at least six years of age to participate. Many of the featured tour locations are on private land and cannot be visited any other way. Current offerings also include a customizable traditional Mayan wedding and native adventure camps for school-aged kids.

EcoColors (www.ecotravelmexico.com) appeals to environmentally conscious travelers who want to experience the Riviera Maya but don't want to alter it. Adventures include boat trips through Sian Ka'an, bird-watching, biking, kayaking, *cenote* swimming, and jaguar discovery trips. The company also offers guided trips to Chichén Itzá, Cobá, and a *temazcal* experience.

Popular for their ATV adventure combos, the team behind **Aventuras Mayas** (www.aventurasmayas.com) makes sure the whole family packs some fun into their jungle excursion, whether by flying high on a zip line or through snorkeling in sacred waters.

Yucatán Explorer (south of Playacar, www.yucatanexplorer.com.mx) offers expeditions by land and sea that tend to be a bit more extreme than those of other operators—but in a good way. The ATV tours take about 2 hours and guide participants deep into the Mayan jungle to swim and snorkel in a hidden *cenote*. The tour company also offers unique access to a wild sea turtle reserve, secret snorkeling spots, and some of the best fishing spots via their 'Cool Runnings' catamaran.

Boasting a catalog of "tours for people who don't take tours," **YucaTreks Far Out Adventures** (www.yucatreks.com) features intensive excursions to some of the area's top historical Mayan sites, *cenote*, and zip-line experiences. The company also leads trips to some lesser-known attractions most travelers will never have even heard of.

Riviera Maya Adventures (www.rivieramaya-adventures.com) offers a mix of adventure, culture, and nature excursions sure to create some lasting memories. Easy online bookings and professional, safety-focused staff make this a great option for families looking for group or private outings. One popular tour is a day trip to Cozumel on a luxury yacht followed by snorkeling in Palancar Reef.

For a genuine exploration of culture in the Yucatán, **Ojos Mayas** (www.ojosmayas.com) promotes sustainable tourism through their locally staffed and ecologically focused tour company. Truly appreciate the ancient cultures of the region with their intimate (twelve people max) daylong tour featuring Mayan medicinal plants and history (as relayed by actual Mayans), lagoon swimming, and a traditional meal.

POPULAR TOURS & EXPERIENCES

Unless otherwise specified, these tours can be reserved through the aforementioned tour operators or through local agencies. Availability, times, and prices can vary.

ADVENTURE

Maroma Adventures (www.maromaadventures.com) offers a variety of exciting tours for adventure seekers, including combinations of ATV/speedboat trips, parasailing and snorkeling at Paradise Reef, and horseback riding. If a horse ride on the beach is too tame, try exploring the mangrove forest on a camel.

Four adventures rolled into one makes for a crazy and amazing day full of memories. For adventure-seeking families with kids ages 8 and older, **Riviera Maya Adventures' Outdoor Adventure Tour** fits off-road driving in the jungle, rappelling into an underground *cenote*, snorkeling, and zip-lining all into a single day.

CULTURAL

Chichén Itzá Deluxe (departs from Playa del Carmen and hotels along the Riviera Maya, www.cancunadventure.net) is a good bet for a first-class visit to the legendary ruins. In addition to the ruins tour, the trip includes entrance to Ik-Kil nature park and a chance to swim in the world's most photographed *cenote* of the same name.

Mixing Mayan history and modern adventure, the **Cobá, Tulum, & Maya Encounter** (www.alltournative.com) trip includes a two-hour guided tour to the Cobá ruins, 2.5 hours in Tulum, an authentic Mayan lunch buffet, and some jungle exploration for a *cenote* swim. The cultural experience is rounded out with a visit to the traditional village of Esmeralda, a lagoon-side town whose inhabitants are living much as their ancestors did centuries ago.

WILDLIFE & NATURE

The Rio Lagarto and Ek Balam Tour (www.playadelcarmentours.com) lasts a full day, taking travelers to the traditional town of Tizimin and to the Ek Balam ruins in the northern part of Yucatán State. The highlight is a visit to Rio Lagarto, a remote river where hundreds of flamingos make their home.

You don't have to spend the night in a sweaty, un-air-conditioned lodge to experience the incredible fly-fishing or light-tackle fishing in Ascension Bay. **Fly Fishing Tulum's** (www.flyfishingtulum.com) all-day trips start with a pickup from your hotel at 5 AM for the adventurous drive through the Sian Ka'an biosphere. Spend the day fishing for bonefish, permit, tarpon, snook, barracuda, and other game fish, plus have lunch on the boat. You'll be back at your hotel by 8 PM.

Holbox Adventures coordinates the seasonal **Whale Shark Tour** (www.holboxadventure.com) for travelers staying throughout the region. The tour offers the chance to swim and snorkel with the docile 50-foot-long whale sharks at Isla Holbox, north of Cancún. Tour price covers transportation to a dock north of Cancún and then the boat ride to Holbox. Not available year-round, this tour must be scheduled in advance. Based on availability and presence of the whale sharks.

ROMANCE

Catamaran Sailing Adventures (Puerto Aventuras, www.fatcatsail.com) offers you the chance to sail through the Caribbean aboard a 41-foot catamaran: the *Fat Cat*. Launching at 9 AM, the first stop is the hidden beach of Xaac, where you can go snorkeling, climb the Mayan ruins, play on the beach, and grab a bite to eat before undertaking some more open-water sailing.

CATAMARAN CRUISING IN PUERTO AVENTURAS PHILIP GAMON

Private charters can accommodate up to forty people or book a romantic sunset sail for just the two of you.

At the new evening dinner and entertainment option Xoximilco (Cancún, www.xoximilco.com), visitors board colorfully decorated canal boats known as *trajineras* for a three-hour dinner cruise through a dedicated system of canals. Along the journey, boats will stop at docks where musicians will play mariachi, *grupo jarocho*, marimba, bolero, and other traditional and regional Mexican music. The meal is all-inclusive and includes an open bar of tequila, beer, soft drinks, and *aguas frescas*.

FAMILY FUN

Though there's no pillaging and plundering on the Jolly Roger Pirate Dinner Cruise, (Cancún, www.pirateshowcancun.com), there is plenty of eating, drinking, and laughter on this swashbuckling adventure. Board a 93-foot Spanish galleon replica and sail the waters of Cancún while enjoying a pirate-themed show and dinner. Though there's an open bar, the show and dinner menu are very kid-friendly.

Mayan Canopy Expedition (www.playadelcarmentours.com) provides an all-day trip combining water fun and jungle adventure—featuring a bumpy ride on a safari truck, zip-lining, and a visit to the Yaxmuul *cenote* for a relaxing swim and some chill time in the hammocks. In the Kantenah Nature Park, you can experience the healing powers of a Mayan cleansing ceremony and a traditional Mayan lunch. Kids ages 6 and up are welcome.

The combo trip of Tulum and Xel-Ha (www.cancunadventure.net) offers something for travelers who want to see the ruins but also want to do something active. First stop is Tulum, where visitors will have a chance to see the cliffside ruins and the ocean below. Next is Xel-Ha water park, where you can play in the water, snorkel, or lie on the beach.

ADD A ROMANTIC SUNSET CRUISE TO YOUR VACATION PLANS IN PLAYA BRIAN E. MILLER PHOTOGRAPHY/ WWW.LOMIMONK.COM

A MAYAN LEGEND

Following the great flood, the world was dark and full of chaos. Nothing moved and nothing existed. The sea and the sky were empty. On the second day, the gods became tired of dancing over cold waters, so they created a thin layer of solid land where they could rest while they finished their work. "Let there be land," they said, and a beautiful layer of earth rose from the ocean. On the third day, the gods called upon Chaac, the god of rain, who poured rich water into the cracks of the land, giving life to the plants, flowers, and trees.

As the rain continued on the fourth day, water filled all the cracks and basins, producing amazing lagoons and *cenotes*. On the fifth day, Kukulcán, the god of wind, flapped his wings, blowing warm breezes over the land, giving all living things a gentle dance. On the sixth day, Kukulcán turned his winds toward the sea, creating waves and forming Ixchel, the goddess of the moon and womanhood. Ixchel rose to heaven and gave birth to Itzámna, the lord of the skies, who created the day and the night and then painted the night with thousands of stars. "Let the trees have their own guardians," the gods ordered on the eighth day, and birds were created in astonishing varieties, including Mo, the scarlet macaw, who became the guardian angel of the skies. On the ninth day, Hunab-Ku buried a white knife in the land, and from it flowed all sorts of animals, including reptiles, jaguars, monkeys, and Huh, the iguana and guardian of the land.

Like a falling star, Ixchel descended from the night sky on the tenth day. She dove naked into a *cenote*, and the waters came alive with millions of fish, of all colors and sizes. The gods then picked the parrotfish, or Kay-Op, as the guardian of the waters. The gods rested on the eleventh day, but they were feeling cold, so they asked the sun god to help them. He came from the skies with his magic fire and heated the waters of the sea, the lagoons, and the *cenotes*, thus creating a warm and gentle climate.

On the twelfth day the gods created humans, the most perfect of living creatures. With their intelligence, speech, sight, smell, taste, hearing, and touch, they were the ones gifted with the right to enjoy all the magic the gods had made for them. The gods danced and sang, full of joy for what they had created, and then they returned to the heavens. Pleased with what they saw and the world they had created, they decided to name it Xel-Ha, or "the place where the water is born."

Living Dreams Mexico (www.livingdreamsmexico.com) also breaks the mold of the bigger, more commercial tour companies by providing a personalized experience with highly specialized guides. By paying their tour guides a living wage and focusing on the unique character of the region, each of their packages provides a more intimate way to explore *cenotes*, jungles, and local culture, whether you're seeking adventure or selfies with howler monkeys.

MAYAN RUINS

I f you could travel back in time and see the Riviera Maya as it was centuries ago, you'd see a thriving civilization with a complex social, political, and religious life. From the Cancún hotel zone to the Playa del Carmen shoreline to the beaches and jungles of the Riviera Maya, there were hundreds of structures—religious temples, dwellings, stone roads, and even recreational facilities. When the Mayans abandoned their cities, the jungle reclaimed their buildings and many deteriorated. Some sites retained their spiritual significance and were occasionally used as ceremonial sites by the local population until not long ago.

Archaeologists began uncovering these sites in the early 1900s, and little by little, more sites were rediscovered, studied, and, in some cases, restored to their original splendor. Many have been declared federal property by the Mexican archaeological institution and turned into public parks where locals and tourists can visit to learn about Mayan culture and history and experience firsthand the places where the ancient Mayans lived, worked, prayed, and played. Many other sites remain buried, shrouded by jungle, sometimes just out of view. Some are too remote to be easily explored, but new sites continue to be uncovered.

If you're investing the time to visit these sites, it's also worth reading up on the Mayans. Many tour guides seem to want to stimulate the crowd with tales of human sacrifice (which did indeed occur) at the expense of broader aspects of Mayan culture.

If you can't make time to visit any of the area's major sites, you can always peek through the fence on the east side of Quinta Avenida at 14th Street in Playa del Carmen to see an authentic, though quite unassuming, bit of Mayan history. Surrounded by a chain-link fence and official-looking signs declaring it a federal archaeological site is a small temple built at the base of a tree. It's not labeled, but it's rumored to be a small ceremonial site or possibly an ancient dwelling.

Make sure you bring some water and a hat when you visit any of the other ruins. The humidity and the sun will get to you faster than you think.

CHICHÉN ITZÁ

Mexico's best-known Mayan ruin site, Chichén Itzá, is about 112 miles southwest of Cancún, a 2.5-hour drive from Playa via Highways 305D and 180D. Cutting a more direct trail through the Yucatán, the newly built Highway 305D also takes great efforts to protect the animal inhabitants of the jungle, offering wildlife underground tunnels, protective fencing, and aerial netting. The drive makes for a fun "I Spy" diversion of hunting for monkey families climbing overhead. The route through the jungle is interesting with many picturesque places at which to stop along the way, such as the beautiful town square in the colonial city of Valladolid (just 45 minutes from Chichén Itzá), worth a quick detour.

Chichén Itzá is the jewel of the Mayan sites, easily reachable from the Caribbean coast, and its grandeur makes it the obvious choice if you have time to visit only one of the ancient cities. This breathtaking site is visited by 1.4 million tourists annually and is an obvious pick for one of the new Seven Wonders of the World.

EK BALAM IS MUCH LESS FREQUENTED THAN OTHER SITES DR. JOHN ANDERSON

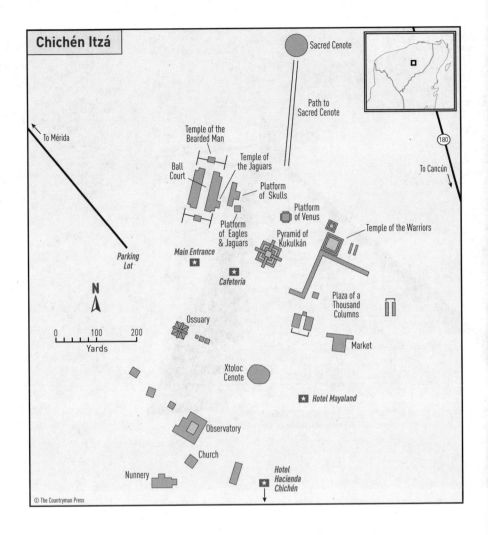

The area covers more than 6 square miles and is divided into two very distinct parts, and you can observe classic Mayan as well as later Toltec-influenced structures. Be sure to check out a map and see both—many tours cover only the later structures that are typically seen on postcards, like the Pyramid of Kukulcán (better known as El Castillo) and the *pok-ta-pok* ball court. These two structures are the largest here, and the ball court (270 feet long and one of twenty-two on the entire site) is the largest in Mesoamerica. El Castillo, the iconic pyramid of the feathered serpent deity, is notable not only for its size, but for its astronomical significance: the pyramid's four sides and the temple platform add up to 365 steps, equal to a calendar year. During the spring and summer equinox, feathered serpents appear to crawl down the sides of the northwestern corner of the pyramid as the sun dips in the horizon. It's quite a "bucket list" spectacle and draws some of the largest numbers of tourists, both national and otherwise, twice a year.

The large size of the newer city means you could easily miss the old city if you were unaware of it. These older structures also include examples of the softer *pu'uc* architecture (the church and its annex in particular) and display beautiful carvings not seen on

THE AWESOME SIZE OF CHICHÉN ITZÀ HAS MADE THE SITE FAMOUS AROUND THE WORLD DR. JOHN ANDERSON

later structures—they are not to be missed. A good plan is to head over to the older area first and work your way back to where you started.

The Pyramid of Kukulcán and the Nunnery (where an explosion was employed in the nineteenth century to access one side of the structure) are the two places where it's most obvious that the Mayans built these structures in two different time periods. The temple interior is interesting so long as you're not claustrophobic, but don't spend your time standing in line for it if you haven't seen the rest of the site. The exterior features are more impressive.

Not mentioned on many tours, a museum on the grounds displays some of the smaller artifacts that weren't taken to other museums around the world. If you're visiting on your own, it's worth seeing, but if you're on an organized tour, your limited time is likely better spent outdoors.

There are nightly shows here with light and sound, but these are impractical for the traveler from the coast, given the long drive back after dark.

The entrance fee is $13 per person, and tours (including transportation, snacks, and drinks) can be arranged through any local travel agency or tour desk.

BRING YOUR SWIMSUIT

Another experience offered by Xcaret is the Xichén Clásico Tour (www.xichen.com.mx) which offers an immersive twelve-hour experience that includes meals and transportation to and from Chichén Itzá. In addition to a guided tour of the Mayan ruins, the day also includes a stop at one of the most famous and photographed *cenotes* in the world, Cenote Ik Kil (Highway 180, km 122). This iconic *cenote* is famous for its striking beauty, and at 85 feet below ground level, it has been home to some epic cave dives. Without a dome, or roof, typical of most underground *cenotes*, this vegetation-draped swimming hole also has vertical vines that drop down into the deep blue water, creating an amazing visual experience. The ecological park also has a restaurant and changing area with lockers.

Book your tour in advance online to save up to fifty percent on tickets.

TULUM

Given its proximity to the hotels of the Riviera Maya, Tulum (2 miles east of Highway 307, 40 miles south of Playa del Carmen) is one of the most frequently visited Mayan sites.

Tulum is unlike any of the other major Mayan ruins in Mexico in that it is right on the coast. Originally called Zama, meaning "sunrise" in Mayan, it faces due east. The beauty of the Caribbean Sea enhances the structures, and many people say this is what

TAKE YOUR BATHING SUIT IF YOU VISIT THE RUINS IN TULUM DR. JOHN ANDERSON

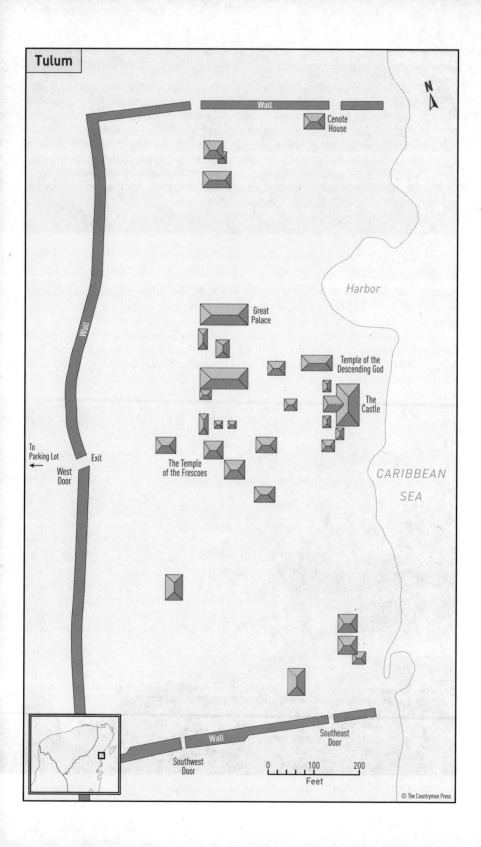

ANCIENT MEETS MODERN

If you're staying in Cancún and have neither the time nor inclination for a day-long archaeological excursion, you're in luck! Check out El Rey in the Cancún hotel zone (across from Playa Delfines) for a glimpse of some centuries-old Mayan Ruins. While nowhere near as grand as some of the more notable sites in the area, El Rey allows visitors to get up close to these awe-inspiring structures, which include stone walls, platforms, and a few larger and more complete buildings. You'll get to explore without the crowds and be poised to take some serious iguana close-ups (remember not to touch) to show everyone at home. For a glimpse of the king himself (which is not a reference to the huge iguanas but the namesake sculpture recovered here), visit the Museo Maya de Cancún (Kukulcan Boulevard at km 16.5), where you'll experience a more in-depth history and artifacts of the Mayans in the region.

The entrance fee is $3. Open daily.

makes Tulum so appealing. The site, known as the Walled City, rose to prominence during the post-Classic period (AD 1000–1500), and it is the polar opposite of Chichén Itzá in terms of what makes it beautiful.

While Chichén Itzá has a sense of isolation about it, given its distance and the thick jungle surrounding it, Tulum has a sense of openness and airiness, and the ocean views are amazing. At the same time, its proximity to the ocean leads to a great deal of erosion, and between this and the many hurricanes that hit the Caribbean, most of the detail of Tulum's structures has been lost. Some restoration work has been done, but the structures do not at all bear the crisp lines of those at Chichén Itzá. Instead, you'll find well-rounded, bleached limestone, and the few remaining detailed carvings are protected by woven structures to keep the rain off. As such, you won't get an accurate picture of the Mayans if this is the only ruin you see.

Since Tulum is so close to the population centers, there are many more tourists for the size of the area than you would find elsewhere (this is also in part because it's a small area and thus more difficult to find a place to retreat from large groups). The convenient access also means that many of the tourists are not particularly interested in the Mayans and come because it's close and "worth seeing." This can make for an atmosphere that's somewhat less sacred than what you would encounter elsewhere.

But as a relatively small site, there is no problem finding time to see all the major elements of the Tulum ruins, which makes it a good first stop if you're visiting several ruins, as well as an option to consider if you are traveling with small children or anyone with limited mobility. If you have your own vehicle, you can easily start off at Tulum early and go to Cobá the same day. In fact, most commercial tours combine visits with other activities in the area. If you would rather go it on your own but haven't rented a car, consider the **ADO** bus which goes to Tulum regularly throughout the day. Just be sure to verify the bus schedule for your return trip on their site (www.ado.com.mx).

For around $7, parking is available at Tulum's back gate, from which it's a half-mile walk to the entrance booth. For a dollar more, you can catch a ride on a primitive train to save your energy for the actual ruins. The entrance fee is typically less than $5, and a well-informed guide service is available at the gates for an additional fee.

EK BALAM

The ancient Mayan city of Ek Balam is one of the Yucatán's most extraordinary sites, but incredibly, it's also one of the least visited. Excavation began in 1987 and has uncovered a long stretch of perfectly preserved sculpture-work on part of the main

A HISTORICAL WALKING TOUR IN PLAYA DEL CARMEN

Start at the very center of the Riviera Maya, at **Parque Fundadores** in the town square where Quinta Avenida (5th Avenue) meets Juárez Avenue. Stand in the center of the gazebo and gaze out at the bustling plaza with its pirate-ship playground, shade trees (notice the painted white trunks), and the massive 50-foot-high **Portal Maya** sculpture arch in front of the beach. Walk toward the water and consider buying a cup of fresh fruit (cantaloupe, watermelon, mandarins, mangos, cucumbers, and coconuts), topped with chili and lime for $2.

Keep going south to the ferry dock, which was first built in 1969–70 and has regular departures for Cozumel Island, 11 miles offshore. Head uphill and cut left a half-block up, at an arched passageway between two shops, and then walk toward the Playacar Palace hotel. This was the first "large" hotel in town and was called the Continental Plaza when it opened. You'll see a small Mayan shrine on a little ridge to your right, but keep walking parallel to the creek and a block or so past the hotel to where the road takes a sharp left

THIS TRADITIONAL MAYAN CEREMONY CALLED DANCE OF THE FLYERS IS DEFINITELY IMPRESSIVE TO WATCH MIKE STONE

temple, which shows how elaborate the exterior of these ruins once was. In addition to perimeter walls, the structures consist of two main palaces, numerous temples, and a larger pyramid called **El Torre** (The Tower). Roads leading into the Central Plaza mark the four cardinal directions of north, south, east, and west, further indicating the Mayans' proclivity for astronomy. The entrance arch to the tower is believed to have had a ceremonial purpose.

El Torre's massive size (500 feet long by 200 feet wide) and numerous preserved glyphs and drawings shaded by *palapa* roofs make these ruins unique in the Yucatán and more than worthy of a side trip during your visit to Chichén Itzá. Consider hiring a guide for this lesser-known site to learn its many secrets. Halfway up El Torre, the enormous toothed mouth of the Witz Monster, symbolizing the entry to the underworld, is surrounded by elaborate Mayan figures that in 2000 were discovered to be guarding a royal tomb. After a long morning of exploring, the pristine and meditative Cenote Maya Park is just a short bike ride away.

The entrance fee to the site is $10.

COBÁ

In its heyday, Cobá encompassed 44 miles of urban sprawl, making it one of the largest cities in the Mayan civilization. It is located an hour inland from Tulum, on the road that

toward the beach. There you'll see an even bigger one.

This is the **Xaman-Ha** ("Waters from the north") structure, an important ceremonial shrine discovered in 1528 by Francisco de Montejo (the same Montejo whose name was given to a local beer from Merida that's sold around town). Mayan women would pray here before heading across the straits to Cozumel in their dugout canoes to worship Ixchel, the goddess of fertility. A placard at its base tells more of the story. Keep your eyes open for some native fauna of the area, a large rodent called an agouti. They look like small beavers or very large rats, and are completely harmless. And fast. So, have your camera ready.

ANCIENT RUINS ARE SCATTERED THROUGHOUT THE REGION, LIKE THIS ONE IN PLAYACAR

starts at Tulum *pueblo* and passes several popular *cenotes*, such as Grand Cenote and the Carwash (see *Diving, Snorkeling and Cenotes* on page 195), before yielding to the jungle.

The city of Cobá flourished during the Classic period (300–1000 AD) and was once home to more than fifty thousand inhabitants. It's the least excavated of the region's major ruins. Thick jungle encroaches onto the site and near the structures themselves, creating an atmosphere of discovery. (Chichén Itzá is also surrounded by jungle, but the area around the structures themselves has been largely cleared.) A number of the ruins at Cobá are partially reconstructed, but not in the finished way that one sees at Chichén Itzá. Unlike other sites, the ruins here look like ancient, unrestored buildings. Because of this, things appear much as they would have looked when European explorers first arrived.

Since the city of Cobá was very large, the excavated ruins are spread across the jungle in groups. Bicycles come included with many commercial tours (or can be rented for $2.50; tricycle taxis for two go for $8.50) and are advisable. If you're on an organized tour, you'll have limited time here, and more of it can be spent exploring the ruins if you can move between the groups of sites more quickly. However, if you have the time, the jungle walk is pleasant and relaxing.

The highlight of Cobá is **Nohoc Mul**, the largest pyramid in southern Mexico (138 feet tall), and it's considerably larger than the Pyramid of Kukulcán at Chichén Itzá. The fact that it's surrounded by jungle rather than open space further magnifies the size difference. Unlike the majority of other Mayan ruins in the area (Ek Balam is the only other), this structure can be climbed, but take great care: while the stone steps are stable, they are very irregular. A thick rope hung from top to bottom can help with the climb, and the view from the top is worth a selfie or two. Standing at the summit of the temple of Nohoc Mul, you can see the tops of many other structures, the lake (rare in the Yucatán) on which Cobá sits, and also a vast canopy of surrounding jungle. The ball court here, one of the smallest in the Mayan world, is also an interesting counterpoint to Chichén Itzá's massive court.

There are several other significant structures, including **Xaibe** (the Crossroads Pyramid), a rounded, tiered structure very different from any others on this side of the Yucatán and more reminiscent of Uxmal. There are also many *stelae* (standing stone markers) here noting important events in Mayan history, and many are still detailed enough to see the forms carved onto them.

Tours to Cobá are still less common than to other ruins, and so the area is often less crowded than others. If you are looking for a place with fewer tourists, this is likely your best choice. A number of commercial tours combine a visit to Cobá with a tour of a local Mayan village, intending to both show the ancient architecture and expose the visitor to the Mayans in their modern lifestyle.

A LARGE IGUANA CATCHES SOME RAYS AT TULUM   DR. JOHN ANDERSON

PLAN A SIDE TRIP FURTHER SOUTH

Archaeology buffs and aspirational Indiana Joneses should consider planning a trip to the Costa Maya (Mayan Coast) further south. The trip requires at least a couple of days to properly visit all of the other big sites in the area, or research your favorite and go for an amazing overnight trip.

Consider visiting:

- **Dzibanche:** Peaceful and out of the way, with a howler monkey soundtrack.
- **Kohunlich:** The 8-foot-tall masks at their namesake temple are inspiring and humbling at the same time.
- **Oxtankah:** Just 10 minutes from Chetumal, the remains include the oldest Spanish church in the area.
- **Chacchoben:** "The Place of Red Corn" is about 100 miles from Tulum and a popular spot for cruise ship excursions.

Entrance costs less than $5, and guide service is available. Open 8–5 daily. Parking is $3.

CHUNYAXCHE/MUYIL

Fifteen miles south of Tulum on Highway 307 and 7 miles from the coastline, the ruins of Chunyaxche/Muyil are located within the Sian Ka'an biosphere and are significantly less visited than the better-known temples of the Caribbean coast. Some researchers believe, however, that the site will someday rival Tulum in scale and importance to the historical record. Inhabited from 300 BC until the Spanish conquest, the site has some seventy-five individual structures believed to be still hidden beneath the jungle vegetation. Archaeological evidence indicates the site was built to honor Ix-Chel, the Mayan goddess of fertility.

Built on La Laguna freshwater lake, the site is traversed by narrow canals that lead to the ocean and once served as passageways for seafaring adventurers and traders. Explore the ruins and the well-maintained, wooden boardwalk trail through the peaceful woods, then climb to the top of the four-story observation tower for endless views of the turquoise lagoon.

Entrance fee is $5, and guide service is available.

SAN GERVASIO

The center of Cozumel's Mayan World, San Gervasio was inhabited from 200 AD until the arrival of the Spaniards and was of great spiritual importance to many Mayan women who traveled to the island to make offerings and pay homage to the fertility goddess Ix-Chel.

Although there are no grand pyramids, the site features about forty structures, including smaller temples, pyramids, and dwellings. The structures are congregated around a central plaza, much like a traditional Roman forum. Experts theorize that these structures were once larger due to additions and extensions made from wood and thatched leaves. Tiny red handprints still visible on an interior wall of one home named Manitas have prompted jokes that it was probably a village day care for visiting mothers.

BEWARE THE BEWITCHING CALL OF X'TABAI

According to Mayan legend, X'tabai (Ish-TAH-buy) was a beautiful woman and ensnarer of men, known to live in the Yucatán jungle. Much like the mythological sirens of Greece, she reportedly drew unsuspecting men to her with her beauty—after which they were never seen again. But rather than entrancing men through song, she is said to have possessed them as soon as they first spied her physical splendor and flowing black hair.

Modern accounts contradict themselves as to whether she was a singular spirit or belonged to a race of women, but most stories claim X'tabai is connected to the beautiful *ceiba* tree found throughout tropical Latin America.

Known for its winding, tall, and wall-like roots, the *ceiba* tree has often been used in Mayan ceremonial art. From the roots, which depict the underworld, the tree connects itself to the terrestrial world via its trunk and ultimately reaches up in every direction to the heavens through its branches.

Stories suggest that X'tabai removed men from the terrestrial world, though some speculate that she provided passage to the heavens, rather than to the underworld.

Today in the Riviera Maya, warnings of X'tabai still persist, though often with a knowing wink. Given that some reports question whether it was her deep eyes, her lustrous hair, or simply her willingness to expose her breasts that stunned the men, it seems as though she might also easily conceal herself in plain sight on the beaches of Playa del Carmen.

Set in relative isolation, amid the Cozumel rainforest, the ruins remain overgrown today and are home to many tropical birds and large iguanas. Visitors can easily walk around the 2-square-mile site.

The entrance is located on Cross-Island Road at km 7.5.

Entrance is $5 (free for children under 10), and guide service is available. Open 8 AM–3:45 PM daily.

DIVING, SNORKELING & *CENOTES*

The Riviera Maya is home to some of the most immaculate dive sites in the world. It's one of the few places where you can swim with a green moray eel on a 100-foot wall dive in the morning, go free-diving and snorkeling with dolphins after lunch, explore virgin caverns on a freshwater cave dive in the afternoon, and then pet sleeping sharks on a shallow-water dive that same night.

The Great Mayan Reef is the second longest living barrier reef in the world—only Australia's Great Barrier Reef is larger. It starts in Cancún and extends just offshore along the eastern tip of the Yucatán Peninsula and all the way down to Honduras. From many towns, the reef is only a short swim from the beach, making for excellent snorkeling without the need for a boat or special equipment. You can usually see the water breaking over the reef, which helps to pinpoint its location.

The reef itself is razor sharp and extremely delicate, so touching it, bumping it with your equipment, or even kicking sand onto it can cause serious damage from which it will take the reef years to recover. It is home to hundreds of species of live coral, fish, anemones, eels, rays, and other life forms, small and large.

The water itself is gin-clear, with horizontal visibility up to 150 feet in some areas. The prevailing current is north to south, though it varies widely depending on the weather and local geographic conditions. Water temperature ranges from a low of 75 in the winter months up to the mid-80s in the height of the summer. Many divers choose to dive without a wetsuit, which reduces the weight they are required to carry, making for a less-encumbered dive and more bottom time. Other divers opt for a spring suit, shorty, or Farmer John–style wetsuit, which provides a good layer of warmth while still allowing for freedom of movement.

There are a variety of open-water dives available. Divers in Cozumel and Akumal frequently go on shore dives, either in small independent groups or with a dive master. In these locations, the reef comes within 100 yards of the shore, enabling divers to reach excellent dive spots with a short underwater or surface swim. Cozumel is also known for its wall dives and drift dives, where the dive boat will stop at one end of a reef and let the divers out, follow their bubbles as they drift along with the current, and then be waiting to pick them up when they surface at the end of the dive. This type of diving can be very relaxing for the divers, who hardly need to swim, as they're swiftly drawn along with the current, which travels up to 5 mph.

On other dives, where there isn't as much current, such as off the coast of Puerto Aventuras, Isla Mujeres, or Playa del Carmen, the boat will anchor, the dive master will lead the group on a dive, and then all divers will return to the entry point. Diving this way requires all divers to stay in sight of one another, ensuring that nobody gets lost underwater. If you don't have a dive buddy, you'll be assigned one on the boat before the dive begins.

OPEN-WATER DIVES Experienced divers can go on self-guided dives right from the shore at many hotels, particularly in Cozumel and Akumal. You can bring your own gear or rent it at the hotel dive shop. Most shops have tanks available for around $10, allowing you to custom-create the dive profile that you want and then go for it. On these dives, the maximum depth is usually around 50 feet, but divers can see just as much variety and just as much beautiful underwater scenery as on boat dives.

Organized boat trips are another way to go. These trips are normally booked at least one day in advance so that the boat captain can prepare all gear and ensure there will be enough assistants on the boat to handle the group. These trips offer either one or two dives and can take place in the morning, afternoon, or even night. Most boat rides will run 30 minutes to an hour long, giving you plenty of time to prepare your gear, document the trip in your log book, socialize with other divers, and even do some sightseeing along the way. The boats range from 14-foot, open-hull *pangas* carrying just a couple of divers all the way up to 40-foot yachts that can accommodate more than a dozen divers and typically offer air conditioning, a galley, a shower, and other luxuries. Divers can choose to go on a private trip or can join a group trip with other divers. Non-divers can accompany divers on the boat trip for a nominal fee, though this must be arranged in advance so the captain can plan for the extra space and refreshments.

There are several types of open-water dives common in the area. One of the most common is a reef dive, where divers swim or drift along the top of the reef. Off many beaches there is a steep wall within a few miles of shore, where the depth drops from about 80 to 100 feet to more than 1,000 feet, almost straight down, and on these dives either the divers swim along right at the edge of the drop-off, with the reef below them and the vast depths of the blue ocean just beyond, or they swim along the wall itself, with the reef to the side and the depths straight below. When wall diving this way, it is important for divers to watch their depth gauges closely, since it's deceptively easy to go deeper and deeper without even noticing. For recreational scuba diving, the maximum depth is usually considered to be 120 feet. Also worth noting, the deeper you go, the shorter amount of time you can stay, so most divers prefer to keep their maximum depth at around 80 feet, which gives them 30 to 40 minutes of underwater time.

Most dive boats carry sodas, water, and juice, and many stop for lunch between dives. Lunch can be taken on the boat, or the boat will pull up to the beach, where buffet meals are served. This is most common in Cozumel, though it's done in other areas as well.

Diving at night is a completely different experience than diving during the day and is a real thrill. All divers carry their own lights and backup lights and also wear glow sticks to make them visible, should all their lights fail. Octopuses, sharks, rays, squid, and other marine life are more prevalent at night, since this is the time they normally feed. The same dive site will look totally different at night, with different colors on the coral, different types of fish swimming around, and a different sense of depth for divers, since they can see only where they point their lights. On a clear night with a big moon, the divers can also see light from above and can sometimes see large fish or the dive boat silhouetted against the moonlight.

A UNIQUE SNORKELING OPPORTUNITY AT PLAYA MIA IN COZUMEL PLAYA MIA COZUMEL

SMALL BOATS CALLED PANGAS CAN BE CHARTERED FOR SHORT EXCURSIONS OR FULL-DAY ADVENTURES

CENOTES & FRESHWATER DIVES A surprise to many first-time Riviera Maya divers is the presence of many freshwater dive spots, just as close and accessible as the saltwater ones. Throughout the Yucatán Peninsula, there are caverns and spring-fed lagoons called *cenotes* that offer unique dive opportunities for both amateur and experienced divers. The word *cenote* comes from the Mayan word *dzonot*, which was used to describe the sinkholes that formed after the collapse of thin limestone earth revealed a cave underneath that then filled with freshwater from the water table (quite near the ground in the porous crust of the Riviera Maya). Once a major source of drinking water for the ancient Mayan villagers, these *cenotes* range from the size of a kiddie pool up to that of a large lagoon covering several acres of land. Some are on private ranches and have been recently opened to visitors. Others are commercially operated as recreational parks and have resident dive operations, on-site instructors, and tour guides.

The water in the *cenotes* is crystal clear and remains at a fairly constant temperature of around 72 degrees. Most *cenotes* are fairly shallow, making snorkeling and free-diving quite rewarding. Others have deeper holes, up to 50-feet deep, and are best explored with scuba gear. Since they are relatively small and the water does not circulate, it is important that all swimmers and divers rinse off any mosquito repellent or sunscreen before entering the water. The fish are colorful but fairly small, giving snorkelers and divers the feeling that they are diving inside an aquarium. The bottom is rocky and sometimes covered in algae, and the sides are craggy, making entry and

GEAR UP AT ONE OF THE SCUBA SHOPS AROUND TOWN AND PLAN AN OUTING

exit a bit tricky, especially in areas less frequented by visitors. The major sites, though, have wooden docks and ladders, and can be easily entered, even by divers in full gear. With their shallow depth, clear water, and easy accessibility, *cenotes* make for great dives for beginners. They are sometimes even used for training classes since there is no wave action and no current, and it's easy to keep track of where all the divers are.

Caves and caverns, on the other hand, offer a completely different scenario. Diving in these situations should be done only by experienced and certified cave divers, since they often require the use of specialized equipment, including redundant air systems, lighting systems, and navigation aids. Cave and cavern diving requires the diver to leave the open-water realm and enter restricted areas where there is no easy escape and no way to surface without retracing your path to the entry point. Without the proper precautions, this type of diving can be extremely dangerous, though it can also be rewarding for divers who know how to do it properly.

In these dives, divers carry extra air tanks and lights, because they do not have the luxury of surfacing at any time should something go wrong. They also run lines of rope from their entry point so that they can always retrace their paths without getting lost. Some caverns are quite narrow, requiring divers to actually remove their tanks from their backs and carry them in front of them so they can fit through. Others are wide enough to allow several divers through at a time and can even be enjoyed by relative newcomers to cave diving, as long as an expert guide is close at hand.

The Riviera Maya and the Yucatán are home to some of the world's best spots for this type of diving, and it's an amazing feeling to be surrounded by water as clear as air and witness the incredible cave formations, the underwater stalactites and stalagmites, and the fish that call this realm their home. Some of the dives involve entering the cave at ground level and swimming through a series of caverns prior to entering the more enclosed caves, which twist and turn their way for several hundred yards, sometimes opening up into wide rooms where divers can congregate and rest before continuing the adventure. With proper preparation, equipment, training, and guidance, cave diving doesn't have to be dangerous, and the experience will easily be one of the most singular you will ever have.

OUTFITTERS, INSTRUCTION & CERTIFICATION Each town has its own local dive shops, found around the town square, on the touristy streets, on the beach, or on-site at the larger hotels. Depending on the location, the shop may offer NAUI and PADI training and certification, boat dives, shore dives, drift dives, reef dives, wall dives, night dives, *cenote* dives, and cavern/cave dives, as well as name-brand equipment and gear for sale or rent. All reputable dive shops and tour operators require divers to have a current certification, commonly called a C-card, prior to renting equipment or going on any guided trip.

Instruction and certification are offered at most shops, and many of the larger hotels provide free scuba introductory classes at their on-site pools. In this confined and safe environment, people new to the sport can practice using a mask and fins, snorkeling, and even breathing underwater from the scuba tank through the regulator. This can be a great way to experience the thrill of scuba diving for the first time, and it just may convince you to take a class and do it in the ocean.

Most dive operators offer a "resort course," which includes a bit of instruction on scuba theory and techniques, some time to practice in the pool, and then an actual scuba dive in open water with a certified dive master right by your side. Though the diver will not receive certification with this type of training, it is the best way to go from having no experience to going on an actual dive in only half a day. For safety reasons, the dive master will keep the dive above a depth of 30 feet and will monitor the diver throughout the adventure.

Many dive shops in the area offer full certification classes and even private certification classes. Though normal dive courses are spread out over a few weeks, a private instructor can take the student through a legal certification program in just a matter of days, including classroom lessons, pool practice sessions, and the open-water checkout dive. Some student divers take the classroom and swimming pool portions of the class at home and then do their open-water certification dives while on vacation. If you plan on doing this, your home instructor will need to fill out a training referral form, and then your instructor in the Riviera Maya will complete the course with you and issue your C-card.

On group tours, the depth and bottom time will be recorded by the dive master, and there will be an interval after each dive for participants to note details in their log books. Dive operators use the recreational dive tables to plan the dives and determine the maximum depth, the required surface interval, and the available bottom time. Divers using their own dive computers may plan alternate dive profiles, as long as they communicate with the dive master and boat captain so everyone knows what to expect. The crew performs a head count at the start and end of each dive to ensure the safe return of everyone in the group.

While ascending from a dive of more than 30 feet in depth, it is customary to perform a safety stop at 15 feet for 3 minutes. This is a precaution to help eliminate any cases of decompression sickness. If anyone does experience symptoms of "the bends," the crew will take quick action to get the diver to a medical facility and even to a hyperbaric chamber, if necessary. There are several chambers in the Riviera Maya, usually within a 30-minute drive from shore. Most dive operators charge a $1 insurance fee for every dive, which ensures that divers will be covered if they need to enter the chamber. Divers should remember not to dive within 24 hours of flying on an airplane, since doctors say the risk of decompression sickness and other diving ailments increases if you do so.

For most dives, except for extensive cave and cavern diving, no special training or licenses are required beyond the basic open-water scuba diving certification. However you decide to dive, remember what you learned in dive training class: plan your dive, then dive your plan.

CANCÚN

Known across the world as a mecca for watersports, Cancún is at the far northern tip of the Great Mayan Reef and doesn't have as much coral growth as the areas further south. The water is as clear as a shot of tequila blanco, though, and some five hundred species have been documented here. Most of the dives—including **La Bandera**, **Punta Cancún** and **Punta Nizúc**—are fairly shallow and can be enjoyed by both snorkelers and scuba divers.

ISLA MUJERES

With an average underwater visibility of up to 100 feet and nearly fifty different dive sites within range of a 30-minute boat ride, Isla Mujeres, whose name translates to "island of women," is also the island of snorkelers and divers. Popular dive sites include **Camaronero**, a shrimp boat that sank in the late 1990s; the **Cave of the Sleeping Sharks**, where a brisk current allows sharks to temporarily halt their perpetual swimming and park themselves, in an apparent stupor; **Los Marinos**, a sunken Mexican Navy vessel that lies only 70 feet below the surface; and **MUSA** (www.musacancun.com), a stunning man-made site featuring striking submerged sculptures.

ISLA CONTOY

With white-sand beaches, shallow bays, and open-water drop-offs, this tiny island offers a lot of variety for snorkelers and divers. Contoy isn't sheltered by the mainland, so the water can be rougher than elsewhere along the Yucatán coast. **Ixlache**, a very shallow reef popular with snorkeling tours and beginners, and the virtually untouched **Las Calderas** are the primary places to dive.

COZUMEL

One of the most popular dive destinations anywhere, Cozumel has enough world-class dive sites that you could stay there a week, diving every day, and never go to the same spot twice. From shallow-water snorkeling spots to sheer walls that drop thousands of feet, Cozumel has superb options for every skill level. The most popular type of diving is drift diving, which can take some getting used to but brings a whole new dimension to the diving experience. Most dive sites are on the island's southwestern coast, facing the Riviera Maya mainland, where the reef runs parallel to the beach and the water is sheltered from the open ocean and thus relatively calm. This area is home to **Palancar Reef**, regularly ranked as one of the top five dive sites in the world.

Other popular dives include the **Santa Rosa Wall**, with an average depth of 90 to 100 feet, and the shallower **Tormentos** with a resident green moray eel, more than 6 feet long, known to sometimes eat fish right from the dive master's hand.

PLAYA DEL CARMEN & PLAYACAR

DIVERS ALERT NETWORK

Divers who want to be extra cautious should investigate the Divers Alert Network (DAN) (www .diversalertnetwork.com) before their visit. For a yearly fee, DAN provides diving safety information and offers air-evacuation insurance, should a diver need to be airlifted back home for treatment of a diving-related injury.

The unofficial capital of the Riviera Maya is also home to the greatest concentration of diving and dive-related activities and services. There are more than a dozen dive shops along Paseo del Carmen and in the water-sports centers of the larger hotels, particularly those in Playacar. Dive sites accessible by boat from Playa range from shallow reefs good for snorkeling to deep-water drop-offs best reserved for advanced divers. **The Playa del Carmen Hyperbaric Chamber and Clinic** (10th Avenue and 28th Street, www.sssnetwork.com), the leading facility in the treatment of diving accidents, including cases of "the bends," is open every day and is well known by all major dive operators.

One of the most popular dives in this area is **Las Barracudas**. This shallow-water reef is located just offshore from the Xcaret ecological park and is frequented by schools of large barracuda. Another site, **Chen Zubul**, is frequently visited by novice divers and is also popular for night dives. Nearby, **Moche Deep** is a deep-water reef with swifter currents, making it best for advanced divers only.

DIVE SHOPS **The Abyss** (Playa del Carmen and Tulum, www.abyssdiveshop.com) offers PADI and NAUI instruction, open-water dives, and *cenote* trips.

Open since 1983, **Cyan Ha Divers** (north of town, between Hotel Las Palapas and Mahékal Beach Resort, www.playadiving.com) has several boats, an on-site training pool, and PADI instruction. It specializes in small groups, *cenote* dives, and reef dives.

Scuba Playa Dive Shop (10th Street between 1st Avenue and Quinta, www .scubaplaya.com) offers a variety of open-water and *cenote* dives.

An old Playa standby, **Tank-Ha Dive Shop** (1st Avenue between 20th and 22nd Street, www.tankha.com) has grown over the years but can still be counted on for smaller dive groups and ecological awareness. It offers PADI and NAUI instruction, an on-site training pool, *cenote* dives, open-water dives, and reef dives.

Yucatek Divers (15th Avenue between 2nd and 4th Streets, www.yucatek-divers .com) offers one- and two-tank dives, night dives, cavern and cave dives, and scuba instruction.

PAAMUL

This relaxing beach is home to some of the best diving in the area. With little in the way of tourism development, the reefs are still in pristine condition and the sea life is healthy and prolific. The shallow bay also offers excellent snorkeling, even in just a few feet of water.

Good for all certified divers, the 45-foot-deep **Horst's Reef** offers some small swimthroughs. Large coral heads, sea sponges, and abundant marine life can be spotted at the intermediate **Paraíso Shallow**. The beautiful **Xel-Ha Reef**, offshore from the park, is open for exploration, provided that divers follow Xel-Ha's preservation rules.

PUERTO AVENTURAS

Boats depart from the Puerto Aventuras Marina several times per day, shuttling divers to the nearby reefs. Though it's always best to book ahead, dives can sometimes be planned at the last minute if a boat has extra space available. Local dives include the deep, 75-foot **Los Caniones**, known for its steep canyons, groove formations, and abundant fish; the easy-to-access **Brisa Caribe**, between the public marina and the Oasis beach; and the colorful **Mook-Che reef**, near Playa Xcalacoco.

DIVE SHOP The full-service **Dive Aventuras** (in the Omni Puerto Aventuras, www .diveaventuras.com) offers all levels of instruction in multiple languages, including a 45-minute tune-up course for certified divers who haven't been in the water for a while.

AKUMAL

Akumal is a shallow bay with calm water, slow currents, and coral beaches. There are many good spots to dive in the 20- to 40-foot range, making the area a good place for beginning and intermediate divers who want the thrill of an ocean dive but aren't quite ready for deep walls and cave systems.

More advanced divers will appreciate the deeper sites, such as **Gonzalo's Reef**, famous for frequent close encounters with a sea turtle, which reaches a depth of 85 feet in some spots.

Other favorites include **Dick's Reef**, named for the retired owner of the original Akumal Dive Shop; **Motorcycle Reef**, named for the sunken motorcycle lying 60 feet below; and the appropriately named **Shark Cave**.

DIVE SHOPS **Akumal Dive Adventures** (on the beach next to Del Sol Beachfront Hotel & Condos, www.akumaldiveadventures.com) offers snorkeling, cave dives, cavern dives, *cenote* trips, and dives in Akumal and other open-water sites.

Open since 1980, the American-owned **Akumal Dive Shop** (near the main gate to the Akumal development, www.akumaldiveshop.com) offers dives in and around the Akumal area, plus certification classes, "bubblemaker" classes for kids, and sailing and fishing trips.

Akumal Dive Center (located next to Lol Ha on Akumal Bay, www.akumaldivecenter .com) is the oldest dive center, leading tours of the world's second largest barrier reef since 1975, as well as *cenote* and night dives.

TULUM

Known for its Mayan ruins and relaxed atmosphere, the Tulum area also has some great snorkeling and diving sites, particularly **Tulum Reef**, within sight of the ruins.

DIVE SHOP Housed in a little *palapa*-covered hut on the beach in the hotel zone, **Mexidivers Tulum** (www.mexidivers.com) offering snorkeling, ocean diving, and *cenote* diving trips, plus fishing excursions and whale shark encounters.

La Calypso Dive Center (www.lacalypsodivecenter.com) doesn't offer a store, but does offer smaller exclusive excursions in the area. In addition to *cenote* and sea dives,

THE BEACH AT AKUMAL IS NEARLY ALWAYS CALM AND PERFECT FOR SNORKELING LOCOGRINGO.COM

they also offer half-day beginning dive courses and a 3-day advanced open-water dive course.

COSTA MAYA

The Costa Maya starts an hour south of Playa del Carmen and extends nearly to Mexico's border with Belize. The reef is especially healthy in this section because it sees fewer divers and cruise ships. The coral is healthier, the colors are brighter, and the fish are larger. It's also harder to reach, so expect longer boat trips.

Banco Chinchorro offers diving opportunities along its thriving and expansive coral reef. There are also dozens of viable, remote, and rarely visited dive sites at the protected biosphere reserve **Sian Ka'an**, a UNESCO World Heritage Site.

CENOTES

If you're looking for a vacation experience unique to the area, you should absolutely plan on visiting at least one *cenote* while you're in the Yucatán Peninsula. If you have transportation or plan on renting a car, you can follow Highway 307 south along the coast and make a day out of exploring *cenotes*. You can also take a taxi to the ones closer to Playa like Azul, Cristalino, or Kantun Chi, which are all about a 15- to 20-minute ride. The third option would be to hop on a shuttle bus or *colectivo* headed down Highway 307. From Playa del Carmen you can catch the *colectivo* on 2nd Street between 15th and 25th Avenues. Playa Express is one of the more popular companies, and you can get to Tulum and back on a *colectivo* without much hassle at all. You can also tell the driver the name of the *cenote* you're visiting to get off at the right stop. Remember to bring pesos for the bus. Most individual *cenotes* have an admission fee starting around $10, which will also be cash only.

CAMINO DE LOS CENOTES

Across from the main entrance to Puerto Morelos, a new, modern highway heads inland, beyond a tall archway etched with RUTA DE CENOTES at the top (at approximately km 321 of Highway 307). This road is a fairly straight shot for 25 miles, passing through the blue-collar town of Central Vallarta, past several *cenotes*, and on into Quintana Roo's interior. There are dozens of *cenotes* in the area, any one of which would make for a memorable day trip. *Cenotes* are relatively small and the water does not circulate, so it is important that all swimmers and divers rinse off any mosquito repellent or sunscreen before entering the water.

Popular stops include **Selvatica** (Ruta de Cenotes, km 19, www.selvatica.com.mx), the largest *cenote* in the area, which boasts a 160-foot-wide pool, perfect for cooling off and swimming. The park also includes a 300-acre preserve, zip-lining, canopy tours, aerial bridges, and ATV off-roading. Highlights of the adventure park's five different zip-line adventures include a human roller coaster, a Superman zip line, and an upside-down zip line. Shuttle service to nearby hotels is included.

At **Siete Bocas** (Ruta de Cenotes, km 13) there are seven different lagoons, a couple of them large enough for swimming and snorkeling in the clear, cool water. There is a rustic dirt road connecting the *cenote* to the main road, so you shouldn't have to share the stalactite formations or lazy afternoon swimming with big tour bus groups.

Cenote Verde Lucero (Ruta de Cenotes, km 16) has several different *cenote* openings, with underground caverns connecting them. There's not much to see underwater for snorkelers, but trained divers can traverse underground to the connected lagoons. The *cenote* is about a quarter-mile from the entrance and, like many such parks, this one offers a zip-line and cliff diving area for adventure seekers. Nearby parking makes for a minimal hike, and wooden steps down into the *cenote* facilitate accessibility.

Cenote La Noria has multiple options for accessing the below-ground *cenote*, including a somewhat steep dive from ground level, a short zip line midway down the staircase, or the most moderate—a full staircase option (which is still pretty thrilling). La Noria is a favorite of divers (it's nearly 60 feet deep) and photographers. A swing and floating platform are two of its unique features.

CENOTES BETWEEN PUERTO MORELOS & PUERTO AVENTURAS

Talk about renting a car for the day or see how far *colectivos* go. Less than a 30-minute drive from Playa del Carmen, a taxi still makes for a viable option for transport to and from this first set of *cenotes*.

BRING A BETTER SUNSCREEN

If you plan on visiting Xcaret, Xel-Ha, Garrafon Natural Reef Park, Chankanaab National Park, or any ocean near a coral reef, plan to bring a bottle of biodegradable sunscreen. Conventional sunscreens contain ingredients like PABA, octinoxate, oxybenzone, and butylparaben that have been proven to be one of the many human factors contributing to the destruction of the reefs and delicate ocean life.

Plan on making your purchase before your trip, as you'll spend exponentially more on sunscreen when you're in Mexico. Beware of brands falsely marketing "reef-safe" sunscreen while still containing harmful ingredients. The following brands can all be purchased on Amazon.com or at other major retailers:

- **Tropical Sands:** Available in a range of SPFs, this zinc-based sunscreen skips harmful ingredients and clearly lists "biodegradable" on the label. Recently renamed and rebranded from Mexitan.
- **Kiss My Face Organics:** Skin-friendly and environmentally friendly, another zinc-based option without harmful chemicals. Does not state "biodegradable" clearly on the label, but could be proven so by looking at the ingredients list.
- **Alba Botanica Hawaiian Sunscreen:** Biodegradable is listed twice on the front label, plus the brand contains green tea and aloe vera for healthy skin and no white residue.

Cenote Azul (Highway 307, km 266), half the size of a basketball court, is an open *cenote* with some more shallow areas perfect for smaller children. From the parking area, the lagoon is a short, picturesque walk through the lush jungle and has a rope swing and 10-foot-high cliff, perfect for jumping into the water. This is a popular *cenote*, so expect crowds on weekends or at midday.

Cenote Cristalino (Highway 307, km 269) is a standout in terms of amenities, including a well-stocked snack bar, bathrooms, lifejackets, and goggles available for rent. This is an open *cenote*, and the water is ideal for snorkeling. With easy entry points, a small cave, and a mostly shallow depth, this is a great *cenote* for kids and families to explore.

CENOTES BETWEEN PUERTO AVENTURAS AND TULUM

Cenote Jardín del Eden (Highway 307, 3 miles south of Puerto Aventuras), a *cenote* and cavern dive, is composed of two separate *cenotes* connected through an underground channel. Their wide caverns are easy to maneuver and swim around, helping to prevent feelings of claustrophobia. The main feature is an underground air dome called the Chapel, where divers can submerge and breathe natural air, even though they are under the water level. Above, the surrounding vegetation is lush, the snorkeling great, and large, barely submerged rocks make for natural lounge areas. Bathrooms and rentals are available.

A group of four *cenotes* and caverns, the **Taj Mahal** (Highway 307, 3.5 miles south of Puerto Aventuras, just past Xpu-Ha) is known for a cavern called the Beam of Light Room. This spot is less crowded than many others, making it a good place to linger over a picnic lunch. The connected **Sugarbowl** *cenote* has a large cavern open to the daylight, which creates mind-numbing rays of light under the water.

Dos Ojos (Two Eyes) is essentially two separate *cenotes* connected by a channel, and is the third largest underwater cave in the world. Basic dive certification is required to explore it, and there is natural light the whole way. The water is unimaginably clear, and if not for the air bubbles, it really would seem like outer space, especially given

KNOW BEFORE YOU GO

Even if you've done it a dozen times, discovering a crystal clear, sun-dappled *cenote* is always a magical experience. But to maximize the magic, there are a few things to consider before heading out on your day trip.

- If you're looking for a more private experience, note that most *cenotes* will be less crowded on weekdays and earlier in the morning.
- Be sure to bring your own towel, water shoes, biodegradable sunscreen, snorkel, mask, and cash.
- When spending more than a few hours or visiting multiple *cenotes*, plan on packing a few snacks or a light picnic. Most *cenotes* (especially the less touristy ones) will have little available for refreshments or food.
- Many *cenotes* offer fish food, but you can also bring a few pieces of leftover bread from breakfast. Even without luring them to you, expect to have tiny fish nibbling on your feet and legs if you sit still for any length of time. They can't actually harm or bite you, but it is an odd sensation if you've never experienced a fish nibble before.
- If you have smaller children or would like to enjoy some lazy snorkeling, many *cenotes* can provide life jackets, available for a small rental fee or as part of the *cenote* admission.
- Should you wish to dive into a *cenote*, be sure you've checked out the depth of the water or are choosing to jump from a designated spot.

the otherworldly scenery, which is unlike anything you would ever see on the land. For anyone with a snorkel, the numerous underwater stalagmite formations and dancing rays of light make for an amazing experience.

The next dive, the **Caverna de los Murcielagos** (the Bat Cave), has been known to bring divers to tears with its awesome beauty. The cave is as dramatic as it is exquisite, with a sublime combination of steep drop-offs, Disney-worthy stalactites, and elaborate features that have taken millions of years to develop. There are also hundreds of brightly colored tropical fish, elusive cave shrimp, and other critters. The depth is only 35 feet, making it especially safe for scuba newcomers and easily appreciated by snorkelers.

Popular with snorkelers and divers, **Gran Cenote** (2 miles inland from the main intersection in Tulum on the road to Cobá) features amazing underwater stalactites, stalagmites, and other limestone formations. You can swim a ring around the middle island sundeck area. It makes for a great stop-off after a trip to the beach or a long drive back to Playa from Cobá.

One of the region's better-known *cenotes*, **Aktún-Ha** or the Carwash (just south of Akumal, off Highway 307), is frequented by scuba-diving groups from the United States and beyond. The Carwash is only 50 feet deep, but the caverns are wide and long (nearly 2 miles long), making it very popular for certified cave divers. During the summer, the surface is covered with algae, but in the cooler months snorkeling is possible.

CENOTES SOUTH OF TULUM

Although small, **Cenote Angelita** (10.5 miles south of Tulum) is a favorite of divers as it's nearly 100 feet deep. Greeting divers halfway down is another natural phenomenon, a layer called the halocline where freshwater meets saltwater from the sea. This hazy layer creates the illusion of an underwater current, revealing crystal-clear water below and the ghostly branches of long dead trees.

CENOTE DOS OJOS IS ONE OF THE HANDFUL IN THE AREA THAT ALLOW FOR SCUBA DIVING CHIP RANKIN

WATER SPORTS & ACTIVITIES With **Dolphin Discovery** (www.dolphindiscovery .com), you can interact with live dolphins at one of five locations (Villa Pirata on Isla Mujeres, Avenue Juárez in downtown Cozumel, on the marina at Puerto Aventuras, at El Dorado Marina in Maroma, and at Hotel Sirenis in Akumal). Several 45-minute packages are available, from viewing sessions where participants pet the creatures and observe tricks to swimming sessions where guests are pulled through the water by a dolphin. For all programs, the minimum age is eight. Children ages eight to eleven must be accompanied by a paying adult. Pregnant women and people with physical and/or mental limitations are not permitted access.

Ikarus Kiteboarding (Quinta at 20th Street, Playa del Carmen, www.kiteboardmexico .com), which is PASA- and IKO-certified, offers lessons, equipment rentals, and sales of windsurfers, skateboards, and kiteboards. The shop also has bathing suits, backpacks, T-shirts, and beach games.

Although there are many opportunities for renting stand-up paddle boards or SUPs, **360 Surf School** (hotel zone, Cancún, www.360surfschoolcancun.com) supplies rentals, lessons, and guided SUP tours through the beautiful Nitchupte Lagoon. Certified instructors are also on hand to teach surfing and can provide group, semi-private, or private lessons. Kids ages 6-12 can also take surfing lessons on kid-sized boards.

A great option for snorkelers of all levels who want to wet their fins in the Caribbean, **The Snorkel Shop** (8th Street between 20th and 25th Avenue, Playa del Carmen, www .thesnorkelshop.com) offers a handful of themed tours depending on your interests

THERE'S NO BETTER ESCAPE THAN A FEW HOURS OF PADDLEBOARDING ON CALM WATERS ALOHA PADDLE CLUB

and abilities. Tours include transportation, meals, and a DVD with photos from your explorations.

With **Atlantis Submarines** (Carretera a Chankanaab, km 4, Cozumel, www.atlantissubmarines.travel), guests can bear witness to the amazing reefs of Cozumel, including Santa Rosa and Palancar, from the comfort of a chair. The air-conditioned sub goes 100 feet deep and passes many of the same sites that scuba divers visit.

In Cancún, **Aquaworld** (Boulevard Kukulcán, km 15.2, Cancún, www.aquaworld.com.mx) offers a wide range of water fun including snorkeling tours, scuba dives and certification, dolphin experiences, and comprehensive packages that offer a little bit of everything for maximum adventure.

If you're looking for something more self-guided and private, **Vida Aquatic Dive Center** (Mahekal Beach Resort at 38th Street, Playa del Carmen, www.vidaaquatica.com) rents everything you'll need, including snorkel gear, kayaks, and SUPs.

Located off the west coast of Isla Mujeres, **Museo Subacuático de Arte**, or MUSA, (Isla Mujeres, www.musamexico.org) is an artistic snorkeling site ranging from about 10 to 20 feet deep. Featuring sculptures of people and common objects by artist Jason deCaires Taylor, the project began in 2009 to draw visitors away from the fragile coral reefs while providing infrastructure for new coral growth. Already stunning, with more than 500 life-size sculptures of human figures, plans call for it to become the world's largest underwater sculpture gardens. Visits to the site are offered by local tour operators and include snorkeling groups, diving, and visits from a glass bottomed boat.

One of the top snorkeling spots in the area, **Yal-Ku Lagoon** (north end of Akumal Bay) has a mix of fresh and salt water, which provides a habitat for a wide variety of fish, including triggerfish, wrasse, parrot fish, needlefish, and sometimes sea turtles. The shoreline has several metal sculptures imported from Mexico City, as well as a few picnic tables and stairways leading to the water. The bottom and sides are more rocky than sandy, so walking can be treacherous, but a pair of water shoes and a careful eye make it worth the effort. Float along in the cool water, watch the colorful fish, and listen to the tropical birds singing from the trees.

HISTORY OF THE
PLAYA DEL CARMEN REGION

"In the beginning all was invisible. The sky was motionless. There was only water, the quiet ocean, the silence, the nights. Then there came the word."
—From the *Popol Vuh*, sacred Mayan scriptures

Playa del Carmen owes its growing popularity to the nearby resort town of Cancún, just 40 miles to the north, and Cozumel Island, just 12 miles to the east. The influence of these two towns has helped shape Playa since the days of the Mayans.

Playa del Carmen is named for Our Lady of Mount Carmel, the patron saint of Cancún. She was named for a town in Italy, which was the first place where a chapel was built in her honor, in 1263, before her ascension into heaven.

The first recorded visitors to the beaches of what is now Playa del Carmen came during the Early Classic Period (AD 300–600) of the Mayan civilization. Then called *Xaman-Ha*, or "waters of the north," Playa was a rest stop of sorts for travelers making their way from the great cities of the Mayan world to the island of Cozumel. These travelers readied their dugout canoes and prepared for the journey across the straits on the same shores that now house the restaurants, hotels, and nightspots of modern-day Playa del Carmen.

Cozumel—called *Ah Cuzamil Petén*, meaning "island of the swallows," by the Mayans—was a sacred site and home to Ix-Chel, the goddess of fertility and wife of Itzámna, the god of the sun. Young women across the Mayan empire, from present-day Yucatán, Honduras, Belize, and beyond, journeyed to Cozumel on a sacred pilgrimage to pay homage to Ix-Chel and pray for fertility and healthy childbirth.

In return for the dozens of shrines and temples that the Mayans constructed, Ix-Chel is said to have gifted the people with the graceful swallow, or *cuzamil*, which led the Mayans to give the island its name. Many of the temples for Ix-Chel have survived, including San Gervasio, which can still be visited today.

Meanwhile, on a sheltered sandbar known to the Mayans as *Kankun*, or "nest of snakes," the temples of El Rey were constructed as a ceremonial site and resting place for the society's nobles. The site is now adjacent to a golf course and across the highway from the Hilton Hotel, making it a popular destination for visitors to Cancún who want to see Mayan ruins but are not able to get to the more major sites in the region, such as Tulum, Cobá, or Chichén Itzá.

Cancún did not have many other sacred sites because it was so narrow and did not have good access to the mainland, though the ocean breezes and proximity to various shallow lagoons did make it a nice place to live for the natives who fished along its shores and harvested food from the mangroves.

During the post-Classic period (AD 1000–1500), the area around Playa del Carmen, Cancún, and Cozumel served as a major trade route and religious center, and the Mayan culture flourished and prospered. At its height, the walled city of Tulum contained splendors beyond belief, and the nearby town of Cobá, with a population at the time of nearly fifty thousand, was the spiritual center of the entire Mayan empire. Near the end of this period, the cities' populations dwindled as residents dispersed due to storms and wars, and to seek gentler climates.

Juan de Grijalva, a Spanish explorer, passed close by Playa del Carmen in 1518 when he discovered Cozumel while en route to Cuba, several hundred miles to the east. He didn't stay for long, but word of his find traveled fast, and his countryman Hernan Cortez returned the following year, bringing Catholicism and little appreciation for the Mayan way of life. Cortez and his men demolished Mayan temples and built a Catholic church. They also brought something else when they landed in Cozumel—smallpox. The disease spread quickly within the island's close-knit community, and the population was decimated, dropping from 40,000 to fewer than 200 within 50 years.

The first European settlement in the region was at Xel-Ha, just a few miles south of Playa del Carmen, which had been a Mayan outpost and is now an ecotourism theme park. Over the next 200 years, the Spanish traveled throughout the Playa del Carmen area and the Yucatán, spreading Catholicism and disease wherever they went. Many Mayans resisted the new religion, and small communities retained their traditional ways and sacred cultures. During the 1700s and 1800s, pirates set up shop on the nearly deserted shores of Cozumel, using it as a base for their marauding forays across the channel to Playa del Carmen and elsewhere around the region.

Meanwhile, trade continued in and around Playa del Carmen, given its location—midway between the port city of Veracruz to the north and Honduras to the south. Local commodities, including salt and honey, were bartered for goods imported from other regions, giving the area a taste of the diversity, commerce, and—yes—tourism that would eventually secure its fixed place within the Mexican economy.

John L. Stephens and Frederick Catherwood passed through the Riviera Maya in 1842 as part of their expedition to the Mayan ruins, documented in their excellent book, *Incidents of Travel in Yucatán*. In the book, Stephens writes about what they saw and the people they encountered, while Catherwood presents exacting drawings of the ruins. The book is incredibly precise and detailed, and it's still used by scholars, archaeologists, and Mayan enthusiasts today.

In 1848 the Mayans and various Spanish refugees began to resist the Spanish occupation more aggressively, leading to an uprising known as the War of the Castes. During the struggle, a large group of the oppressed set out from the Yucatán town of Valladolid and traveled across the peninsula to settle in Cozumel, leading to a regrowth of the island's population. Other native Mayans took cover in the ruins of Tulum, which made for a

MAYAN-INSPIRED SCULPTURES ADORN MANY RESORTS PHILIP GAMON

great fortress, given its walled perimeter. The town of San Miguel de Cozumel was officially established in 1840, and a couple decades later, United States President Abraham Lincoln pondered using the island as a place to send freed American slaves and even went so far as talking to the Mexican government about purchasing it.

Due to the remote location and its dense, inhospitable jungle environment, Playa del Carmen and the surrounding area kept a low profile for the rest of the 1800s. In 1902 the region was finally granted status as a Mexican territory and named after Mexican Gen. Andreas Quintana Roo. That same year, on November 17, the town of Villa del Carmen was officially founded near the site of what is now Playa del Carmen's Leona Vicario Park. Charles Lindbergh stopped in Cozumel in 1928 in the storied *Spirit of St. Louis* plane. The island was used as a base by the US Navy during World War II and was then abandoned again until the 1960s, when scuba adventurer and documentary film producer Jacques Cousteau visited the island with an underwater camera crew and began to show the world the beauties of the Great Mayan Reef, which runs between Cozumel and Playa del Carmen for hundreds of miles.

Tourism visionary Fernando Barbachano purchased much of the land that currently makes up Playacar in 1966. The sale included nearly a mile of barren beachfront, stretching south from where the ferry dock now sits. The price tag was a now-paltry $13,600 but represented a serious risk at the time. He subdivided the land and sold it in small parcels, the first of which in 1977 sold for $15,550, proving just how powerful his idea really was. The single most important factor in the development of the region came in 1967, when the Bank of Mexico and the country's tourism development commission

TULUM WAS THE MOST SACRED SITE IN THE REGION FOR THE ANCIENT MAYAN PEOPLE RIVIERA MAYA DESTINATION MARKETING OFFICE

GROWTH

If you think the Riviera Maya's explosive growth came as a surprise to the Mexican government, think again. The growth plan was forecast in the mid-1970s by then-governor of Quintana Roo Rojo Gomez. The following message was sent to President Luis Echeverria: "We have prepared an integral plan for the development of the coasts of Quintana Roo, whose beauty is unparalleled and which has many attractive sites. It has beautiful beaches, clear ocean water, wild jungles and hidden Mayan ruins, which have yet to be explored because of lack of access. We have located 100 kilometers of coastline whose features promise a great future for tourism in the area."

identified Cancún as the location for one of its mega-development projects (along with Ixtapa, Los Cabos, Loreto, and Huatulco). In the original government documents, the area was called "Kan Kun," which quickly morphed into the more Spanish "Can Cun," and then eventually shortened to just "Cancún."

Bridges were built, sewer lines were laid, and electrical poles sprang up. The first Cancún hotels, opened in the early 1970s, were the Palacio Maya, Playa Blanca, Cancún Caribe, Camino Real, and Club Med. In 1970 a wooden boat dock was built on the central beach in Playa del Carmen, and shortly thereafter, ferry service started to Cozumel. In 1974 Quintana Roo was granted Mexican statehood, and the Cancún International Airport opened for business—with a bamboo and palm air-traffic control tower and a single taxi waiting for arriving planes. Two years later, the city's Pok-Ta-Pok golf course opened with eighteen holes, many with views of the ocean and minor Mayan ruins. Over the next 10 years, Cancún grew from a coconut jungle visited only by traveling fishermen and a few loco gringos to a world-class tourist destination. The local population boomed as workers from across the country poured into Ciudad Cancún to find jobs and establish their families. The Playa del Carmen airstrip was laid in 1979, and the area's first hotel, the Balam Ha (where the Playacar Palace is now), opened the next year. Land along 5th Avenue was given away to employees of the Calica mining company.

Cozumel experienced a growth spurt of its own, as recreational scuba diving became more popular and affordable as increasingly divers came to witness for themselves what they had been able to see only on the Jacques Cousteau television show.

Despite a few bumps along the way, including lack of airline support, the devaluation of the peso, and a series of hurricanes, Cancún and Cozumel continued to grow and prosper. Somehow, though, Playa del Carmen lagged behind the city to its north and the island to its east. As development continued around it, Playa del Carmen was still known only as the ferry landing for boats traveling back and forth between Cozumel and the Quintana Roo mainland. A handful of fishermen lived in huts on the beach, and a few optimistic entrepreneurs sold tacos and handicrafts to the hurrying travelers, but tourists and locals moved quickly through town on their way to the more established locales.

In its hippie heyday, Playa del Carmen's visitors would while away the day along the beaches south of town. The small cove now occupied by the Gran Porto Real hotel was close enough to the town square to be convenient, but being just out of sight of the ferry dock made it the preferred place for those who preferred to sunbathe au naturel. At night, tourists returned to the beach for the freewheeling and ultra-casual nightlife under the stars, a refreshingly unpretentious antidote to the pulsating discotheques that were becoming popular in nearby Cancún. During a full moon, locals and tourists alike would congregate on the beach for a ceremonial "lunata" celebration—complete

WHERE DID MY BATHING SUIT GO?

If you continually misplace something on your trip, don't blame your traveling companion—it may be an *alux* (pronounced "aloosh") playing pranks.

Aluxes are, according to Mayan superstition, mischievous elfin or childlike creatures who live in the tropical jungle and play tricks on those who don't believe in them or give them proper respect. Some stories claim that the *aluxes* were originally clay or stone statues in Mayan religious temples that later came to life.

Many Mayans and other locals claim to have had run-ins with *aluxes*. They can cause the phone to ring at odd hours of the night, and when it's answered, no one is on the other end. They can move objects around the room and sometimes even steal bits of food. To curry the favor of the *aluxes*, many people build them little houses or shrines on their property. Once appeased, the *aluxes* become good luck charms, helping to ensure a good harvest, bring about good fortune, and protect the believers from other dangers.

Many hotels in the Riviera Maya, even some large and well-established ones, have homes for the *aluxes* on site, in hopes that appeasing them with a comfy dwelling will encourage them to be friendly, though they rarely talk about it. Ask your waiters and housekeepers, though, and chances are they'll know what you're talking about—and will probably have a story of their own to share.

---

with bonfires, cold Coronas, and skinny-dipping—a tradition that must have made the Mayan gods smile (especially Ix-Chel, the goddess of fertility).

But starting in the early 1980s, little by little, street by street, the tiny fishing village and ferry town began to grow. New shops, restaurants, and even a couple of new hotels opened their doors, luring the passing visitors to stay a while. The first hotels were built of bamboo and palm fronds, with slatted wood doors—not to keep out thieves, but to prevent the wild pigs from entering and looking for food.

Disaster struck in September 1988, when Hurricane Gilbert slammed into Cozumel and the Riviera Maya with 170 mph winds, blowing the roofs off hotels, pulling trees out by their roots, smashing windows, and flooding the streets. Inside the storm, the barometric pressure was 26.23 inches, the lowest sea-level pressure ever recorded in the Western Hemisphere. The hurricane caused more than $80 million in damage in Cozumel alone, and it changed the face of the region for years.

In the early 1990s, Playa del Carmen became a regular stop for the cruise lines, exposing Playa to a new breed of revelers. Soon after, the outdated Cozumel ferry boats were replaced with sleek and modern jet-powered watercraft, which made the trip from the island faster and easier on the stomach, bringing in even more visitors.

Guadalajara-based tourism giant Grupo Sidek purchased thousands of acres of land along the shoreline just south of the ferry landing, with designs to develop the area that had been dubbed "Playacar." First came the Continental Plaza in 1992 (now the Playacar Palace). Later that year, the Diamond Resort (now the Allegro Occidental) was inaugurated, marking the first opening of an all-inclusive resort in the Riviera Maya. A golf course opened in September 1994, and then hotel after hotel rose from the jungle, changing the face of the community forever.

On the other side of the ferry dock, development continued as well, but government-imposed density restrictions kept away large-scale hotel projects, and small, family-run inns dominated the landscape. From 1990 to 1997, the local population grew from 2,000 to 20,000, and roughly 100 new families were moving to town each month, establishing Playa del Carmen as Mexico's fastest-growing city, a title it held for most of the first decades of the twenty-first century.

The main road paralleling the beach, Quinta Avenida, or 5th Avenue, became the town's principal street and grew lined with restaurants, shops, hotels, and other businesses catering to the tourist trade. Favored by European backpackers and US and Canadian budget travelers, Playa del Carmen began to make a name for itself on the international travel scene. Known as the place where the hippie lifestyle was not only accepted but celebrated, "Playa," as the in-crowd called it, had arrived.

In 1999, the area's mayor, Miguel Ramón Martín Azueta, worked to popularize the term *Riviera Maya* for the land between Cancún and Tulum, which had previously been referred to only as the Cancún–Tulum Corridor.

By the late 1990s, Quinta had extended more than a mile north of the ferry dock, and much of it was closed to vehicular traffic, creating a pedestrian-friendly walkway that developed a unique character unknown in other parts of the world. In the early 2000s, Quinta stretched past Constituyentes Boulevard (between 18th and 20th Streets), and the area was dubbed "La Nueva Quinta," sometimes called "Little Italy," "Upper Playa," or simply "The New Playa." Italian-style cafés stood next to taco stands that stood next to gourmet steakhouses, creating a town with a truly eclectic and international flair. The beach north of Constituyentes also saw some changes. A second ferry dock was built, two large-scale resort hotels were constructed, and a couple of beach clubs sprang up, offering food and drink service, *palapa* and chair rentals, and towel service for the cruise passengers, day-trippers, and guests from hotels that weren't on the beach.

As the upscale all-inclusive hotels of Playacar introduced the town to more affluent travelers, the tone of the village continued to change. The thatched-roof bus station was rebuilt with electronic displays and molded plastic seats. Across the street, McDonald's opened up, then a couple of Starbucks, and up and down the coast, more and more resorts were carved from the jungle. Renovations began on Quinta as work

PLAYA WAS A TINY OUTPOST IN THE 1970S. THE CHURCH IN THE CENTER OF THIS PHOTO IS STILL THERE, AT THE NORTHWEST CORNER OF THE TOWN SQUARE CANCUN HISTORY CENTER

2012: THE ARRIVAL OF A NEW MAYAN ERA & PORTAL MAYA

The Mayan calendar ended at 11:11 AM on December 21, 2012 (the winter solstice), coinciding with an extremely close alignment of the path of the sun and the galactic equator (the Milky Way's midpoint). In the years leading up to the event, many said it would be the "end of the world," although the Mayans themselves had referred to the event as the dawn of a new "Golden Age."

In honor of the occasion, Mexican sculptor José Arturo Tavares was commissioned to create a new gateway to Playa that paid tribute to its Mayan ancestors and philosophies. Debuting on that fateful December date late in 2012, Tavares's Portal Maya became a new landmark in the heart of the square where the city began.

Today, the 50-foot-tall, 50-foot-wide bronze arch frames the Caribbean Sea, telling of the region's ancient and modern influences. It depicts a man carried on a spiral of wind joining hands with a woman atop a swirl of water. At either side, the bases of the arch feature relief sculptures of larger-than-life figures—ranging from ancient Mayans to noble fishermen to bikini-clad beachgoers.

As much a sign of Playa's own growth and evolution as it is a Mayan marker, Portal Maya acts as a magnet to those who encounter it. People move closer to take photos, inspect the sculptural details, watch the free evening Mexican and Mayan dance performances, and simply take in the view. So even as Playa del Carmen grows up and into a new era, it still manages to remain a place unlike any other.

COMMISSIONED TO MARK THE DAWN OF A NEW MAYAN ERA IN 2012, THE PORTAL MAYA ARCH WAS CREATED BY MEXICAN SCULPTOR JOSÉ ARTURO TAVARES CHIP RANKIN

QUINTA FEATURES A GROWING MIX OF INTERNATIONAL CHAINS AND LOCAL BUSINESSES CHIP RANKIN

crews buried the utility lines and paved the gravel road with cobblestones, giving the road a bit of colonial inspiration to go along with its nouveau chic attitude.

Hurricanes Emily and Wilma, both devastating storms with deceivingly demure names, tested the region's will in the summer and fall of 2005, when they sliced similar paths across Cozumel, Cancún, and the Riviera Maya. Emily raged with sustained winds of 135 mph, shearing off rooftops, leveling trees and signs, shattering windows, rearranging beaches, and sending sixty thousand tourists scrambling for shelter. Wilma completed the one-two punch by hammering the area 3 months later with 150 mph winds and a storm surge topping 11 feet in Cancún. Tourists were confined to shelters for days, and it took some nearly two weeks after the storm to finally get a flight back home. Hotels in Cancún were hit the hardest, though there was extensive flooding and wind damage all along the Riviera Maya. Some hotels closed for days, while others took weeks or even months to reopen.

The region bounced back, however, as communities worked together to rebuild and restore the splendor of the area. In

THE OLD AND THE NEW MINGLE PEACEFULLY IN COZUMEL

TURTLES, OFFSHORE SCUBA DIVES, AND A RELAXED FISHING VILLAGE VIBE ARE PART OF THE CHARACTER AND CHARM OF PUERTO MORELOS CHIP RANKIN

fact, the town's resilience through adversity seemed to prove its staying power, as the condo boom kicked into high gear in early 2007. One of Playa's original hotels, the Corto Maltes, turned to condos. The El Faro Hotel, site of the landmark lighthouse did the same. Up and down each block, workers could be seen converting hotels to condos and building new structures where there were none. The area north of Constituyentes saw an especially strong push, with new developments going up on nearly every block. Most complexes were small, with no more than twelve to fourteen units, but others were much larger, threatening to change the face of the town.

A massive beach renovation effort pumped in thousands of tons of sand from the ocean seafloor, building up the beachfront and widening it in many areas, which helped to reverse the effects of storm erosion and made the beaches wider and more beautiful than ever.

Playa del Carmen celebrated the end of the Mayan long calendar on December 21, 2012. Leading up to the event, many pointed to the date as an end-of-the-world proph-ecy. However, scholars of the Maya (and those who listened to them) knew the date represented a grand new era of rebirth. To mark the occasion was the debut of Portal Maya, a grandiose, 50-foot bronze arch commissioned from Mexican sculptor José

Costa Maya: The coastline south of the Riviera Maya (which officially ends at Tulum).

Federal: Used when referring to Highway 307, a federal highway.

Ha: Mayan for "water." You'll see it used everywhere.

Mole: A chocolate-based sauce made with dozens of herbs and spices, used in traditional Mexican cooking.

Muelle: Spanish for "dock," it's commonly used when referring to the ferry landing, which is also called the "embarcadero."

Nopales: Sliced cactus from the nopal tree, it's used locally in breakfast juice and can be served grilled or sautéed with any meal of the day.

Palapa: Thatched palm used to make roofing in the Riviera Maya. The tight weave keeps out rain and has to be replaced every couple of years. The word is also used generically to refer to any structure that has a thatched-palm roof.

Pan dulce: Literally "sweet bread," it's used to describe a variety of delicious, locally-made breakfast pastries. For a quick start to your day, order a *café con pan dulce*.

Parada: Spanish for "bus stop."

Playa: Meaning "beach" in Spanish, this is the short name used locally when referring to Playa del Carmen.

Playacar: A name created in 1992 to refer to the tourist development located just south of 1st Street and the ferry dock.

Propina: Spanish for "tip." Make sure you check your bill to see if the tip has already been added: *propina incluida*.

Quinta: Spanish for "fifth"—it's the name used for 5th Avenue, the main tourist strip in Playa del Carmen.

Riviera Maya: The name used to refer to the area from just south of Cancún to Tulum. The actual boundaries tend to change a bit, depending on whom you talk to. The phrase was coined in the early 1990s and is sometimes anglicized to "Mayan Riviera."

Tacos al pastor: Pork tacos cooked on a vertical spit, seared with licking flames and served with pineapple slices.

Tiempo compartido: Spanish for "time-share." If a deal is too good to be true, like a Jeep rental for $20 a day, chances are it's part of a *tiempo compartido* offer.

Arturo Tavares. Rising from the town square just behind the city's main beach, the curving structure ties the story of the Maya to the Playa del Carmen of today.

By 2017, the Riviera Maya had surpassed Cancún in the number of hotel rooms available and was celebrating its status as one of the top international tourist destinations in the world, with nearly ten million visitors each year to the state of Quintana Roo. Expatriates from more than forty-five countries around the globe now call Playa del Carmen home, and the town seems to thrive on the notoriety.

And through it all, Playa has stayed true to its roots, somehow preserving its magical charm and exceptional character. It is still a place where travelers from around the world come together to lounge on the beach, toast the day with a cold beer, sip a hot cappuccino, and celebrate life. And in a town where backpackers from crowded hostels, newlyweds from fancy all-inclusives, and European trendsetters from chic new condos all cozy up to the same bars, it's easy to understand why Playa so easily works its way into your heart.

The ruins of Xaman-Ha can still be seen in modern-day Playa del Carmen. The main temple is found along the beach just south of the Playacar Palace hotel and is now a popular spot for wedding ceremonies. Many other Mayan shrines dot the Playacar

HURRICANES OF THE RIVIERA MAYA

1951, Hurricane Charlie: Made landfall in the Riviera Maya with 125 mph winds.

1955, Hurricane Janet: Walloped the tiny towns of Xcalak and Chetumal.

1967, Hurricane Beulah: Came ashore as a Category 2 storm, causing widespread damage.

1980, Hurricane Allen: Weakened as it approached the region, sparing it from harm.

1988, Hurricane Gilbert: Smashed into Cozumel with 170 mph winds and a 15-foot storm surge, caused more than $80 million in damage on the island alone, stranded a 125-foot Cuban freighter (the *Portachernera*) on the beach in Cancún, and killed more than three hundred people after it crossed the Yucatán and hit northern Mexico.

1995, Hurricane Roxanne: Slammed into the Riviera Maya with 115 mph winds.

1998, Hurricane Mitch: This massive storm was expected to hit the area but curved away. An American tourist was killed in a boating accident near Cancún related to the rough water.

2003, Hurricane Claudette: Skirted the area with tropical-storm-speed winds before continuing on to Texas.

2004, Hurricane Ivan: Made a beeline for the Yucatán, causing heavy rains and high waves along the coast, before curving north and hitting Florida.

2005, Hurricane Emily: Struck Cozumel as a Category 4 storm, then crossed the Riviera Maya near Puerto Aventuras, causing widespread damage, some severe, though the area recovered after a quick cleanup.

2005, Hurricane Wilma: Just three months after Emily, Wilma became the most intense hurricane ever in the Atlantic Basin. The eye lingered over Cozumel and Cancún for nearly a day, causing severe damage to waterfront areas and flooding much of the region.

2007, Hurricane Dean: Made landfall in the middle of the night just north of Chetumal and Majahual, south of the Riviera Maya, as a Category 5 storm. Nearly 150,000 residents evacuated to shelters. Some small towns were cut off for days and about a third of the hotels in Tulum received at least moderate damage.

2008, Hurricane Dolly: Before it was a full-fledged Category 1 hurricane, the weak tropical storm crossed directly over Cancún with no noteworthy damage.

2010, Hurricane Alex: Still a tropical storm when it crossed the Yucatán Peninsula, Alex did only minor damage before entering the Gulf of Mexico, where it became a Category 2 storm and slammed into northeastern Mexico.

2011, Hurricane Rina: The fourth major hurricane of the 2011 season formed in the Caribbean Sea south of the Yucatán Peninsula. Though it barreled toward Cancún and the Riviera Maya, it suddenly weakened to a tropical storm before hitting the coast.

2012, Hurricane Ernesto: Ernesto hit the town of Mahahual with a fairly light touch, bringing lots of rain and knocking down some trees and power lines.

development, including its golf course. And though it may be hard to envision a time when the Mayans carved their canoes from local trees and plied the waters to Cozumel, today's visitors to Playa will undoubtedly feel a sense of the grand history, the sacred importance, and the incredible natural beauty that have lured visitors to its sandy shores for thousands of years.

As one longtime local resident puts it, "No one knows what makes Playa so special, but everyone seems to return."

INDEX